PLAID CYMRU

The Emergence of a Political Party

T0294226

For Siân,
the inspiration for this book and much more

PLAID CYMRU

The Emergence of a Political Party

Laura McAllister

Foreword by Gwynfor Evans

seren

Seren is the book imprint of
Poetry Wales Press Ltd
Nolton Street, Bridgend, Wales
www.seren-books.com

© Laura McAllister, 2001

The right of Laura McAllister to be identified as the Author
of this Work has been asserted in accordance with the
Copyright, Designs and Patents Act 1988.

ISBN 1-85411-310-0

A CIP record for this title is available from
the British Library

All rights reserved. No part of this publication
may be reproduced, stored in a retrieval system,
or transmitted at any time or by any means
electronic, mechanical, photocopying, recording
or otherwise without the prior permission
of the copyright holder.

*The publisher works with the financial assistance of the
Arts Council of Wales*

Printed in Times by
Bell & Bain Limited, Glasgow

CONTENTS

Acknowledgements

This book is the product of a long process. Its publication draws on my research in Welsh politics, and on Plaid Cymru in particular, over the last fifteen years. The idea for a book about Plaid Cymru in English came from Siân Edwards, former party Chair and someone who has been more central to its growth than she might modestly believe. Her enthusiasm and encouragement to turn that idea into reality has been priceless. Siân was the inspiration for this book and I hope she is not disappointed with the result.

I should set out my credentials for writing this book. I was a member of Plaid Cymru between 1979 and 1992, and stood in two general elections: in my home town of Bridgend in 1987 and in the neighbouring Ogmore constituency in 1992. I was also the party's vice-chair for political education between 1989-92. I resigned my membership of Plaid Cymru to concentrate on my academic and sporting interests, and have not been a member since.

My background in Plaid Cymru has allowed me an unprecedented, insider view of the party. It also brought immense practical advantages. I have benefited from ease of access to the resources needed to write this book accurately and analytically. Most important has been regular contact with the current and former party leaders and members. The book is heavily dependent on chats, discussions, correspondence, arguments – and, more occasionally, formal interviews – with many of these people.

I began to collect the core material during my PhD studies, and added to it incrementally since. Access was generously given by the *Pwyllgor Gwaith* to all of the Plaid Cymru archive, as well as to much contemporary information. Some of the material was accessed from the Plaid Cymru Collection in the Welsh Political Archive at the National Library of Wales, Aberystwyth. A larger proportion, however, came from human sources – correspondence, minutes of meetings, speeches and publications collected by some of the individuals listed below and from the party's offices in Cardiff and the regions.

Both Welsh and English language documentary sources were utilised. Some of the most significant material is only available in Welsh, but where versions exist in both languages, I have referred to the English language source to enable the interested non-Welsh speaking reader to follow up their reading. For reasons of consistency, I have used illustrations and quotations from English language sources in the main. However, translation has been used where the source material is available in Welsh only.

This written material was updated by a series of interviews during 2000-2001, which looked retrospectively at the reasons for the latest spurt in Plaid's growth as a political party, particularly during 1999. These proved invaluable in clarifying the book's principal themes. I am indebted to the large number of people who gave up their time to be interviewed, to complete questionnaires or to answer specific points during the course of my writing. In alphabetical order, they are Penni Bestic, Eluned Bush, Keith Bush, Cynog Dafis AM, Janet Davies AM, Jocelyn Davies AM, Karl Davies, Margaret Davies, Siân Edwards, Jill Evans MEP, Gwynfor Evans, Lila Haines, Elfyn Llwyd MP, Mari James, Elin Jones AM, Ieuan Wyn Jones AM, Helen Mary Jones AM, Gwerfyl Hughes Jones, Peter Keelan, Pedr Lewis, Ann Owen, John Osmond, Marc Phillips, Roseanne Reeves, Janet Ryder AM, Dafydd Elis Thomas AM, Dafydd Wigley AM, Emyr Wynn Williams, Dafydd Williams, Phil Williams AM, Carole Willis and Leanne Wood. The book has been hugely strengthened by their individual perspectives on Plaid Cymru.

Ensuring that the story can be understood and enjoyed by those not necessarily 'in the know' about Plaid and Welsh politics was an important consideration. In this, I have been helped enormously by Professor Helga Drummond, who helped me find a different (and, I hope, illuminating) way of communicating some of the central themes that characterise Plaid Cymru's development. Even more important was the constant support and motivation that Helga provided. I am indebted to her for the gems of wisdom and advice, as well as the depth of friendship, that she has shown. I must also thank my other colleagues at the Institute of Public Administration and Management at the University of Liverpool. Their quiet encouragement and assistance with other duties whilst this project has been at critical stages was instrumental in its completion.

Thanks, too, to those who have read and added their own thoughtful and incisive comments to chapter drafts: Penni Bestic, Professor Helga Drummond, Janet Davies AM, Jocelyn Davies AM, Karl Davies, Siân Edwards, Professor Fred Ridley and Dafydd Williams. Also to the team at Seren, especially Mick Felton, Cary Archard, Simon Hicks, Will Atkins and Karen Thomas, whose professionalism, planning and encouragement have been instrumental in the book's production.

My biggest debt is to those closest to me, to Helen who has suffered and supported most during the book's writing and without whom I would have been lost, to my mother and father, Ann and Keith, to Fiona, Nigel, Wil and Helen, and my closest friends, Sara Davies, Karen Jones and Michele Adams, all of whom have borne the brunt of the personal stresses and strains of writing. The emotional overspill from writing the book has been offset by the support of all of these people. I know I have been 'absent without leave' for most of the last eighteen months and can only thank them all for their enormous love, patience and understanding during that time.

Finally, I pay tribute to Cardiff City Football Club whose promotion season, 2000-01, coincided with the book's writing. Ninian Park offered welcome and defeat-free Saturday afternoon respite from the tribulations of writing. Roll on the Premiership!

Laura McAllister
Liverpool, June 2001

Glossary of Terms

This glossary is designed to help readers with the terms and references that appear most frequently in the book. Many are of them are Welsh language terms used by Plaid Cymru in its constitution, correspondence and publications.

Adran y Menywod
Plaid Cymru Women's Section, open to all women members of the party.

AM
Assembly Member. Elected representative in the National Assembly for Wales.

Cangen
Local branch of Plaid Cymru. A branch must have a minimum of ten members and pay an affiliation fee to the party centrally to be officially registered.

Cyngor Cenedlaethol
The National Council, the party's policy-making body which meets quarterly to frame policies, approve election manifestos and amend standing orders between annual conferences. It consists mainly of *rhanbarth* and *cangen* delegates.

Cynhadledd
Annual party conference, held alternately in north and south Wales in September. It decides policies and constitutional changes.

Etholaeth
Constituency committee of Plaid Cymru (as defined by Westminster Parliamentary constituencies).

Hydro
The Hydro Group was established at the 1982 annual conference to retain Plaid Cymru's traditional focus on Welsh self-government and to resist the use of the term 'socialism' in the party's aims.

MEP
Member of the European Parliament. Plaid Cymru elected its first MEPs in the June 1999 elections.

Mudiad Ieuenctid
Plaid Cymru Youth Movement, open to all members of the party aged twenty-five or under.

National Assembly for Wales (NAfW)
Established in May 1999 in Cardiff Bay, Wales's first national, elected government in modern times. It has sixty members and exercises secondary legislative powers in the areas of health, education, agriculture, economic development and transport. It has no tax-varying powers and is considerably weaker than the Scottish Parliament set up at the same time.

National Left
Pressure group set up in 1980 to press for a more focused, socialist perspective to Plaid's nationalism. It allowed members of other parties to join, as well as those with no party affiliation.

NOPTU
National Association of Plaid Cymru Trade Unionists.

Plaid Cymru, Plaid Genedlaethol Cymru, Plaid, Y Blaid, Plaid Cymru The Party of Wales
All forms of the party's name used between 1925-1999. It shortened its name from Plaid Genedlaethol Cymru to Plaid Cymru in 1945, and became Plaid Cymru The Party of Wales in 1998.

Pwyllgor Gwaith Genedlaethol
National Executive Committee. The principal executive body which manages the party and its finances, as well as guiding policy formulation and strategy. It has approximately twenty-five members, meets monthly and is chaired by the national party chair.

Radical Wales
Quarterly magazine, set up in 1983 [partly funded by Plaid Cymru,] to "broadly reflect the Blaid's underlying philosophy, with its fundamental commitment to decentralised socialism in an independent Wales". The magazine folded in 1991 when Plaid Cymru withdrew its funding. It was resurrected in 2000, by a new editorial board and financed by subscription. It brought out three issues between 2000 and 2001.

Rhanbarth
District committee of Plaid Cymru on which each *cangen* is represented.

Talaith
County committee of Plaid Cymru (disbanded in 1994 when new local unitary authorities were introduced).

The Welsh Nationalist, Welsh Nation
Plaid Cymru's English language newspaper, established in 1932. Its title

was changed to *Welsh Nation* in January 1949.

Y Ddraig Goch
Party's Welsh language newspaper (The Red Dragon), established in 1926.

Ysgol Haf
Plaid Cymru Summer School. A forum for debate on policy and strategy and a crucial part of the party's annual calendar until the 1960s. It was revived between 1990 and 1995, although it has never recovered its early significant status in shaping party debates.

Foreword

It is with great pleasure that I greet the publication of this important new book on Plaid Cymru. I have followed Laura's research for some time now and I am delighted to see it reach fruition in the form of this long-awaited analysis of Plaid Cymru's remarkable political growth since 1945.

The fundamental lesson we can learn from Plaid Cymru's modern history is that an independent Welsh party alone secures substantial constitutional reform for Wales. The remarkable survival and growth of Plaid has brought about changes which would have been impossible if it had not existed. The inter-war decades did not see a single political measure which strengthened Welsh national life.

Plaid was still a tiny party at the end of the War. When I was elected to Carmarthenshire County Council in 1949, I was the only elected member representing Plaid Cymru on a county council anywhere in Wales. As the party grew in the post-war period, a series of reforms were secured. The by-election successes in Wales and Scotland in the 1960s led to the establishment of a Royal Commission which, in 1973, advocated the creation of an assembly for Wales. Labour moved reluctantly and passed an Act in 1979 which would establish an assembly only if a majority of Welsh voters supported it in a referendum. The catastrophic 'No' vote in the referendum was the consequence of the Labour Party's opposition to Welsh devolution.

We then suffered eighteen years of Conservative rule, a party which had little to lose in Wales and little regard for its people who had rarely given it their support. Plaid Cymru's performance in the 1979 General Election was disappointing. This again proved the importance of independent political action for, concluding that Welsh nationalist growth was at an end, the Conservative Government decided to renege on its promise to establish an independent Welsh language television channel. The strength of public opposition forced the Government to change its mind.

By the time of New Labour's election victory in 1997, Plaid Cymru had grown dramatically. It was becoming the second largest party in

Wales in the number of local and parliamentary seats held. Labour felt compelled to move again. Another referendum was held on the creation of an assembly and this time, it was narrowly approved. In the elections to the new National Assembly in May 1999, Plaid Cymru achieved its best results ever and became the official opposition in Cardiff Bay.

Plaid Cymru's growth has been the catalyst for Wales to secure more control over its own affairs. Although there is still a long way to go, it is fair to say that this is the most significant achievement of Plaid Cymru The Party of Wales.

This is an ideal time for the publication of a serious and thorough analysis of the remarkable development of Plaid Cymru as a political force. I am delighted to see this critical evaluation of the party's modern history, a book which points out the peaks and the troughs in the its growth, the weaknesses as well as the strengths of those who have led and influenced the party. I have no doubt that it will enhance our understanding of Plaid Cymru's substantial influence on modern Welsh politics.

Dr. Gwynfor Evans,
Honorary President of Plaid Cymru,
Pencarreg, Carmarthenshire, July 2001

INTRODUCTION

This book tells the story of Plaid Cymru's emergence as a political party. Remarkably, during the period 1945 to 1999, Plaid Cymru developed from a tiny organisation with no elected politicians to an important player in Welsh politics. This book explains some of the principal dynamics underpinning the party's dramatic growth in size, support and influence.

Plaid Cymru's post-war development is poorly documented, let alone analysed. Yet it is a critical era in its history, representing the modern phase of the party's growth when it moved from the fringes to the centre stage of Welsh and, to a lesser extent, British politics. In 1945, Plaid Cymru was a small party with no local councillors, let alone Members of Parliament; in 1999, it was the largest opposition in the National Assembly for Wales, had four MPs and two MEPs, and controlled three of Wales's local councils.

This book is not a straightforward history. It analyses some of the central people, debates and events that have shaped its growth, and evaluates their importance in the pace and pattern of Plaid's development since 1945. It is essentially the story of the maturing of a political party. Its first twenty years, from 1925 to 1945, are considered briefly, as background to the party's later development. This outline of the early years does not undervalue their importance in shaping the party's history. However, the choice of 1945 as a starting point is quite deliberate. At the end of the Second World War, Plaid Cymru began to modernise in earnest. From this time, there was a consensus that it must begin to transform itself into a serious political party if the objective of a government for Wales was to be achieved.

Plaid Cymru is the only constitutional nationalist party in Wales. There have been other nationalist groups and organisations seeking different measures of autonomy for Wales, but Plaid alone has survived over time. It is also the one to pursue methods normally associated with a political party to advance its goal of self-government.

Central to this story are the distinctiveness of Plaid Cymru's politics and, especially, the nature of its nationalism. The dynamics shaping the gradual metamorphosis of Plaid Cymru are the main focus of this book. Plaid's development has not been a straightforward, staged growth from movement or pressure group to political party; rather, it has been an uneven and, at times, erratic process. Part One of the book assesses Plaid Cymru's changing status, first as a broad, political-cultural movement with an unconvincing and, at times, almost incidental electoral interest, then as a more focused pressure or campaigning group on broadly-defined Welsh issues, and finally as an organisation which met most of the accepted characteristics of a political party. Whilst Plaid Cymru in 1999 is, to all intents and purposes, a conventional political party, the debate about Plaid Cymru's status and role is by no means resolved. Part One is intended to appeal to the reader who wants hard, factual information about Plaid Cymru during this period, while the thematic perspectives of Part Two shed further light on this narrative and will interest the reader who already knows something about Plaid Cymru.

The *Mappa Mundi*, the medieval map of the world displayed in Hereford Cathedral, is a fascinating example of historical interpretation. It is a perspective on the world at a particular moment. Medieval map-makers were both creators and depicters; they used existing information to represent the world and its people, whilst also adapting this information to a Christian perspective. Often described as an *estoire,* or story, the *Mappa Mundi* is coloured by internal judgements, cultural perceptions and a large dose of subjectivity. It contains as many omissions, errors and misunderstandings as accurate representations of world geography, topography and culture. The vivid and demonstrative map sketched on vellum, is consequently part accurate, part inaccurate. That is the *Mappa Mundi*'s essential value, as well as its appeal.[1]

The scale of the task facing the mapmakers was awesome – how to represent the world, its countries and its cultures on a single animal skin some 64 inches by 54 inches in size. There are modest parallels to be drawn between this account of the modern development of Plaid Cymru and the task facing the *Mappa Mundi* creators.

This book is written with a deliberately selective approach to the subject. Plaid's development is viewed from a number of different perspectives, which allow variants on the story. Of course, there are many different perspectives that might have been selected. Those used here offer, I believe, particularly significant insights into Plaid's identity, as well as the nature and pace of its development, and are deliberately wide in scope. They offer a number of different areas to be developed within the broad headings used in part two of the book.

The first chapter sets out the context, rationale and objectives of the book, as well as providing a review of the party's early years and a selective critique of existing interpretations of Plaid Cymru and of Welsh nationalism.

Chapter two explores the party's intellectual heritage, locating it within different models or understandings of nationalism and nationalist parties. In addition to laying a theoretical foundation for the evaluation of Plaid's development, it also tries to clarify the type of nationalism Plaid espouses and identifies some of the ideas and influences that have shaped its politics.

Chapter three presents a chronological overview of Plaid's development between 1945 and 1999. It offers a critical narrative of the contribution to party development of the party presidents. Individuals are important in a small party like Plaid Cymru and the party's leaders, as well as its ordinary members, feature prominently.

Part Two presents different angles on the story. Chapter four explores Plaid's growth through the perspective of its involvement in elections and campaigns. The backdrop to this approach is the debate (that arose both within the party and from external sources) surrounding Plaid's status as a broad-based pressure group or as a more conventional, electorally-focused political party.

Chapter five looks at Plaid from a constitutional perspective, exploring a sequence of important landmarks in European, British and Welsh constitutional history and examining Plaid Cymru's role in, and response to, these events. It includes the debates on devolution, Europe and the House of Lords and assesses the party's position on each of them, for example its deliberations on the merits of devolution as a step towards greater Welsh autonomy. It also explores Plaid's response to the election of the Labour government in 1997 and its devolution proposals, as well as Plaid's role in the subsequent referendum. The party's performance in the first elections to the National Assembly for Wales in May 1999 are also considered.

Chapter six is concerned with ideology, specifically the internal debate surrounding the nature of Plaid's nationalism. It focuses on Plaid's efforts to define its nationalism through a commitment to a form of socialism, and its links with the Wales Green Party in the late 1980s and 1990s.

Chapter seven offers a unique and groundbreaking perspective on the post-war development of Plaid through the eyes of women.[2] This is a crucial and hitherto missing slant on the story, exploring the role of individual women and the party's Women's Section. This chapter also surveys the input of feminism and ideas of equal representation for women to Plaid's political programme.

The final chapter, in Part Three, recounts the main dynamics that underpin Plaid's post-war growth. It also offers some projections for the likely future of the party.

Notes

1. Alington, G., *The Hereford Mappa Mundi, A Medieval Map of the World,* (Gracewing, 1996).
2. There has been little written on women in Plaid or in Welsh nationalism, other than Davies, C.A., "Women, Nationalism and Feminism" in Aaron, J. & Rees, T. (eds), *Our Sisters' Land, The Changing Identities of Women in Wales,* (University of Wales Press, 1994); McAllister, L., 'Gender, Nation and Party: An Uneasy Alliance for Welsh nationalism', *Women's History Review,* Vol. No. 1, pp. 51-64, 2001; and Edwards, J. & McAllister, L., 'One Step Forward, Two Steps Back: The Position of Women in the Two Main Political Parties in Wales', *Parliamentary Affairs,* special issue, (forthcoming).

ONE

1. Telling the Story of Plaid Cymru

What Kind of Party is Plaid Cymru?

As I consider the story of post-war Plaid Cymru, it is worth putting down some markers. Exactly what kind of party is the body variously called Plaid Genedlaethol Cymru, Plaid Cymru, the Welsh Nationalist Party and latterly, Plaid Cymru The Party of Wales?

My starting point is that Plaid Cymru is a nationalist party. That simple statement is, in itself, a little controversial: the words of former party president, Dafydd Elis Thomas – "I will never let anyone get away with calling me a 'nationalist', and I will never call myself that, if I ever did" – come immediately to mind. Nevertheless, the fact is that Plaid Cymru is a nationalist party. The real question is what is the nature of its nationalism?

> Plaid Cymru believes that Wales is a nation which has the right to live
> a full national life. That is why Plaid Cymru is a nationalist party.[1]

This story of Plaid Cymru assumes no two nationalist parties are the same. The conditions, character and status of the nation determine that each nationalist party assumes a different hue. That is to say, the specific political and historical context for each nationalist party shapes its character to such a degree that it is impossible to move beyond broad categorisations of such parties.

Plaid Cymru's Political Inheritance

Nationalism in Wales inevitably predates the establishment of a separate nationalist party. Before 1925, the main parties in Wales, the Liberals and the Labour Party, represented some of the key principles of Welsh nationalism. There had been other organisations like Cymru Fydd (Future Wales) which operated in two phases between 1886 and 1890, and 1894 and 1896. Its aim was "to secure a national legislature for Wales, dealing exclusively with Welsh affairs i.e. Home Rule for Wales".[2] However, no political party existed whose sole *raison d'être* was a government for Wales. Why then was there felt to be a need for a separate nationalist party in 1925?

Plaid Cymru's early years were inauspicious. The party spent the first twenty years of its life finding its feet on the slippery stage of Welsh politics. Jostling for space in a fairly hostile political arena took up most of the party's early energies, especially in the context of the Liberal Party, which, historically, had close associations with the demand for more political autonomy for Wales. The 1868 General Election had seen the return of twenty-three Liberal MPs from Wales. Against a backdrop of nonconformist pressure, temperance and the eviction of tenant farmers by Tory landlords and demands for land reform, the Liberal Party had successfully became the party of Welsh radicalism, much of which rested on a sense of a distinctive Welsh identity. Despite the challenge posed by the Labour Party after the war, the Liberal Party still commanded considerable support from the Welsh people.

The Labour Party (initially as the Labour Representation Committee) was formed twenty-five years before Plaid Cymru. In the General Election of autumn 1900, Keir Hardie was elected for Merthyr Boroughs as Wales's first Labour MP. Hardie represented a distinctive form of nationalism, claiming that "the Labour Party alone was truly nationalist for it alone wanted the land of Wales to belong to the people of Wales".[3] By the time of the two general elections of 1922 and 1923, the Labour Party returned first eighteen, and then twenty, of Wales's thirty-six MPs, signalling the end of Liberal hegemony and beginning an epoch, lasting for the rest of the twentieth century, in which Labour returned the largest number of MPs (and from 1945 an absolute majority) from Welsh constituencies. Labour was seen to offer a more decisive social and economic assessment of Wales's problems that challenged the traditionally more religious and cultural appeal of Liberalism. So, by the time Plaid Cymru was established, Labour was taking over as the dominant player in Welsh politics.

The Early Years

> It was no small matter to establish... the party. It demanded a substantial sacrifice on the part of a small number of young Welshmen who are not politicians by vocation or by nature...[4]

Saunders Lewis's remark underlines the extent to which the founders of Plaid Genedlaethol Cymru were ill-prepared to lead a conventional political party. His comment hinted at some of the subsequent problems the party faced.

Plaid Genedlaethol Cymru was established at a meeting on the Wednesday of National Eisteddfod week in August 1925 at the Maesgwyn Temperance Hall, Pwllheli on the Lleyn peninsula in north-west Wales.[5] The founders were a rather amorphous group of six members of two separate nationalist groupings, Byddin Ymreolwyr Cymru (The Welsh Home Rule Army) and Mudiad Cymreig (The Welsh Movement). The outcome of the meeting was an agreement to merge the two groups to form Plaid Genedlaethol Cymru. In fact, that was the sole decision of the meeting; little more emerged from it. It set the tone for, during its early years, Plaid Genedlaethol Cymru was a complex aggregate of individuals representing different organisations that were united, in theory at least, by the common goal of establishing a Welsh government. As Saunders Lewis said: "Plaid Cymru is the only political party that exists solely for the Welsh people".[6] The diversity of its members was the direct legacy of there having been no single political voice for Welsh nationalism. Historically, its interests had been served by a plethora of groups and organisations, some political, some cultural, some religious and some combining elements of all three. This was Plaid Cymru's principal dilemma. The range of nationalist-inclined organisations meant there was no singular or distinctive platform upon which to start building an independent political party that could challenge Labour.

As many cultural as political impulses inspired the foundation of Plaid Genedlaethol Cymru. Indeed, it was scarcely a political party by normal definitions. It was set up as much as an agency to protect Welsh culture, broadly defined, as a party to fight elections and to elaborate policies. This cultural emphasis conditioned the early character and appeal of Plaid's nationalism.

The identity of the new party was clearly moulded by its first leaders, most notably Saunders Lewis (party president between 1926 and 1939). The influence of key personalities is an important dynamic that reappears in the development of Plaid Cymru. Lewis is the key to answering the question: why an independent Welsh nationalist party in 1925? Essentially, it was Lewis's personal conviction that nationalism was a separate, distinct political philosophy, not merely a qualification or appendage of another ideology, that gave impetus to the foundation of an independent party. Lewis believed that political nationalism needed to be moulded within a single party committed to Wales. In a speech to the Welsh School of Social Service in 1923, he argued that nationalism was a doctrine of conservation and preservation (echoing Edmund Burke) and could not be represented by either the individualism of the Liberal Party or the socialism of the Labour Party. His speech injected a new intellectual and practical impetus to the drive to establish a separate party.

Ideas and Outlook

The party's initial aims were deliberately loosely defined to attract members from all of the other existing parties: "Adopting a definite policy would tie us down before we start work".[7] They were closely entwined with the protection of the Welsh language, inheriting the 'Welsh Wales' ambitions of Mudiad Cymreig and Saunders Lewis's preoccupation with resurrecting Wales's language and civilisation: "Language is the fruit of society, is essential to civilisation".[8]

Rooted in the concerns of the two converging groups, the political objectives and strategy of the new party were not set out at its inaugural gathering. The principal aim of Plaid Genedlaethol Cymru was to create a free and self-governing Wales that would preserve and consolidate the components of Welsh identity, especially the language. Determining precisely how this might be achieved through political means remained uncertain: the goal was the protection of Welsh culture, not constitutional change, which was seen as a means to that end. As Saunders Lewis put it, if it were possible to safeguard the language and culture of Wales "without any radical change in the relation of England and Wales, then I for my part will be content." The balance between means and ends was to shift as the party grew.

There was little clear or unanimous strategy amongst the founders as to how self-government might be won, because some of its leaders were completely new to politics, and also because many were motivated primarily by the perceived threat to Wales's cultural heritage. Although they were aware of what was at stake, they were unable to formulate the appropriate political tactics to tackle the issues. This original lack of clarity would characterise many of the later debates surrounding the party's proper status in Welsh politics. The circumstances in which the new party was formed and the early context in which it operated set the tone for many of the tensions that Plaid Cymru faced subsequently. The new organisation was forced to appease all its key members (many of whom had a very different approach to politics *per se*, as well as to the declared objectives of the new party), whilst trying simultaneously to appeal more broadly to Welsh voters. Again, this became a constant challenge for the party. These inauspicious beginnings meant considerable ambivalence about the best form the new party should take. In particular, there was scepticism of the appropriateness of conventional political party tactics. This scepticism arose simultaneously from its own membership and from its political rivals. Lloyd George remarked that the new party had "sprung up in a day and a night like Jonah's gourd and will disappear quickly". He was right on the first account, but wrong on the second.

Nevertheless, for its first five years, Plaid Cymru struggled to produce a clear ideological identity or a practical organisational base. Some elements within the Plaid leadership recognised early that an exclusive appeal for the protection of the language would not be enough to succeed electorally. From 1930, more specific political objectives were formulated. Saunders Lewis declared "Our movement is a political movement. Our party is a political party. In politics, the foremost thing is to define aims, lest we dissipate our strength fighting for vague things".[9] Yet, the defining of aims did not extend to a clear elaboration of the party's political ideology. This proved another enduring characteristic of Plaid Cymru. It had unambiguous cultural and administrative objectives – to obtain sufficient political independence to guarantee the cultural survival of Welsh identity. However, the priority and expediency of economic issues usually form the motor for lasting political allegiances. The party failed to prioritise and publicise its economic perspective, despite Saunders Lewis and D.J. Davies relating Wales's economic problems to the flaws of a centralised political administration. The tentative moves towards elaborating and broadening Plaid's policy portfolio did not allow it to shake off its early identity as a language movement or a cultural pressure group.

Building a Political Party

One section of Hywel Davies's definitive account of Plaid's early years is entitled 'Creating a Movement'. Whether a movement or a pressure group, there can be little argument that, before 1945, Plaid could hardly be termed a party according to conventional definitions. Despite this, the seeds of a political party were clearly sown at Pwllheli in 1925. Its members were unable to be members of another party, for instance. They discussed whether elections were the priority for the new party. It was initially ambivalent about intervention in the electoral arena. This was manifested in a commitment to boycott Parliament should Plaid candidates be elected. Members were also barred from voting for the candidates of other parties in elections where Plaid was not standing. It maintained an enthusiasm for local elections, viewing them as a more legitimate platform for its electoral campaigning (although it still managed to put up only a handful of candidates in the early years).

Plaid fought its first seat, Caernarfonshire, in the General Election of May 1929, with the Reverend Lewis Valentine, the party's first President (1925-1926), as its candidate. Debate continued as to the appropriateness of fighting elections, and it is unlikely that all in the party ranks "were united during the campaign", as Davies suggests.[10]) There was, of course, inevitable excitement at contesting its first election. Members held high hopes that a good result for Plaid would "make it impossible for the English Government to control Wales", Plaid fought the election on a platform of refusing to have anything to do with Westminster. The purpose was to show the Welsh people's rejection of English domination. Plaid vowed not to take up its seat if Valentine were to win. He polled 609 votes, 1.6% of the total 38,043 votes cast. After 1930, the Sinn Fèin-style 'Wales Alone' strategy advocated by Lewis and party secretary, H.R. Jones was portrayed by some as a major obstacle to the party's electoral progress.

The Caernarfonshire result reignited the debate within Plaid on strategy. The key split was between those who wished to continue the boycott stance and those who preferred to see the party pursue more conventional political tactics, including fighting elections and taking office if successful. The prioritising of elections represented a key dilemma for the new organisation and one which continued to ask real questions of the party's nascent political strategy. Plaid's incursions into the electoral arena during its first twenty years were sporadic and *ad hoc* in approach, contesting the occasional seat at general elections and by-elections. It was only during the post-war period that Plaid began to fight elections in a more serious and organised manner.

In 1930, Plaid duly abandoned its policy of boycotting Parliament and embarked on a period of policy consolidation. Drafted in 1934, Lewis's *Ten Points of Policy* document was the foundation for Plaid's early policy stance, although it represented a largely personal viewpoint on some of the key economic and social questions. Lewis argued for a social and quasi-economic philosophy, *perchentyaeth*, which translated literally means 'ownership of house-ism'. Policy developments came from a general feeling that Plaid had to behave more as an 'orthodox' political party if it was to progress. Hywel Davies is right in seeing this as "a new beginning for the party",[11] but the real question is to what extent this shift sparked the next stages in Plaid Cymru's passage towards becoming a conventional political party?

In addition to an uncertainty of the value of electoral contests, the terminology used to describe the party's constitutional objectives was inconsistent. 'Freedom', rather than 'independence', was Lewis's preference: he was pragmatic about the extent of political authority needed to safeguard Wales and its cultural traditions.

The early 1930s saw new constitutional objective, gaining 'dominion status' for Wales. This meant Plaid sought for Wales the same political recognition as enjoyed by Canada and New Zealand. Wales was to "be an equal, free and self-governing member of the British Commonwealth of Nations".[12] Plaid also confirmed its goal of a 'co-operative democracy' which was to become a prominent feature in the party's later policy statements. While these commitments offered Plaid the opportunity to distinguish itself from the dominant ideas of state socialism and capitalism, they were insufficiently developed to convince the Welsh electorate to vote for Plaid.

This period also saw the party abandon its Welsh-only language policy. J.E. Jones, who took over as party secretary in 1930, pressed for English to be given equal status within the party's administration and in its plans for Wales's future. Its first English-language paper, *The Welsh Nationalist*, was launched in 1932. These were significant and radical developments in the maturing of the party, signalling a recognition of the need to broaden Plaid's base by reaching out beyond its 'natural' support in order to grow.

Such policy shifts were hastened by the work of D.J. and Noëlle Davies, whose backgrounds were quite different from many of Plaid's other early leaders. Indeed, D.J. had been a member of the Labour Party. With his wife, Davies led the push for the 'dominion status' policy. It became Plaid's constitutional objective in February 1931. Noëlle drew on her Irish heritage and understanding of the Irish economy to develop political solutions for Wales. She wanted to ensure that sufficient policy-making authority was gained by Wales to deal with its pressing economic problems. The Davieses' was a pragmatism quite different to that of Lewis. They were driven by the economic case for a Welsh government. For them, this was the fundamental rationale for Welsh nationalism and they undertook a rigorous economic analysis of Wales's problems, drafting policy statements which assumed a programme of reconstruction once dominion status had been gained, based predominantly on decentralist socialist policies and including the large-scale nationalisation of key industries. The Davieses injected a new and much needed economic realism into the early Plaid Cymru which was fundamental to its later growth.

The Burning of the Bombing School

Events also shaped the party's identity. In 1935, the Air Ministry proposed a training base at Penyberth on the Lleyn Peninsula for the Royal Air Force to practice specialist bombing techniques. The proposal represented a crossroads for Plaid Genedlaethol Cymru. The symbolism of the plans for a bombing school could hardly have been greater: a military establishment aimed at destruction in one of the cultural and linguistic heartlands of Wales was, Gwynfor Evans argued,"A threat to Lleyn ... thus a threat to the entire Welsh nation". It also meant the party was forced to clarify its position on direct action, and to decide whether non-electoral campaigning should feature alongside, or receive a higher priority than the more conventional strategy of contesting elections. It asked crucial questions of the leadership and membership as to what kind of organisation Plaid Genedlaethol Cymru was to be.

After secret planning, three of the party's leading members, Saunders Lewis, D.J. Williams and Lewis Valentine, set fire to the timber frame workmen's huts on the site of the school. Having committed the arson, the three men immediately reported to the local police station and confessed their actions. The historian, Gwyn Alf Williams later called it "a moment of martyrdom".[13]

Certainly it was a symbolic action, designed to highlight Wales's powerlessness. The subsequent imprisonment of the three Plaid leaders in January 1937 heightened the profile of the party dramatically. It was of particular significance to the maturing of Plaid Cymru. Witnessing the passionate scenes at the release of the prisoners might lead one to assume that the objective of increased profile and popularity was fulfilled. In addition, the RAF eventually found the Lleyn site unsuitable due to the inclement local weather conditions and abandoned its plans. Yet, while the arson and trial inspired the patriotic fervour of the Welsh people at a key juncture in the party's history, it is less certain that this was translated into support for Plaid Genedlaethol Cymru or gave a new political impetus to its activities (it fielded few candidates in the local elections of November 1936, for example). Equally, the outcome was neither a new commitment to direct action nor an eschewing of such action in favour of a conventional electoral strategy. Ultimately, it was a dramatic act of symbolism that underlined that Plaid Genedlaethol Cymru would have a clear role in Welsh politics, even if it was to be an unconventional one.

The Impact of War

The outbreak of the Second World War in 1939 put a brake on many of the party's political activities. The pacifist inclinations of some of its leaders were quickly apparent. The Plaid leadership took a neutral line on the conflict and was strongly opposed to conscription. It also actively encouraged conscientious objection to individual involvement in the war. Charges of disloyalty and fascism were regularly levelled at Plaid during the war; a reflection of both the political climate and the stance of the party leadership.

Saunders Lewis resigned the party presidency a month before war broke out but directed the party for its duration, both intellectually and politically. On the latter front he contested the University of Wales seat in the 1943 by-election, a constituency particularly suited to Plaid. Although he was beaten by the Liberal candidate, W.J. Gruffydd, Lewis gained a creditable 22.5% of the vote. Gruffydd had been deputy vice-president of Plaid for a brief period and there were claims he had been selected by the Liberals to deliberately split the nationalist vote.

The first twenty years of Plaid's existence saw the origin of many of the critical debates surrounding the party's role, status, priorities and strategies. As many key questions remained unresolved they continued to characterise subsequent debate within the party. The Plaid Cymru that emerged into the era of post-war politics remained a rather unconventional creature, seeking to bridge, often uneasily, the demands of the disparate communities in Wales and within its own membership. Despite having grown in size and scope during the war period, it remained poorly funded and minimally staffed, mostly operating on a skeleton structure of highly committed volunteers. Yet it could also boast a number of talented intellectuals who began to establish the foundations of a political party, through the painstaking elaboration of constitutional and economic policies in particular. In the longer term, they helped guide the party to its later successes. On this basis, it was fair for J.E. Jones, party general secretary from 1930 to 1962, to claim that the party had grown stronger during the war. In some ways, it had. But the war years were an artificial political context and the biting reality of the new post-war era soon hit Plaid hard.

1945: A New Start for Plaid Cymru

The period 1925 to 1945 is important to us now because it is in the origins of the infant party that many of the dilemmas, tensions and, indeed, opportunities that Plaid Cymru was to later face can be found. The period 1945 to 1959 might be described as the modern party's youth, when it moved hesitantly from infancy, and increasingly acquired more of the hallmarks and responsibilities of the adult party.

Some have argued that the title of Welsh Nationalist Party for the organisation set up in 1925 "proved to be a misnomer that pre-dated the appearance of a nationalist political party by at least twenty years". I take this argument a stage further and suggest that this is a generous interpretation of the conventions of a political party and might be better set back by another twenty-five years.

I have taken the end of the war as the starting point of Plaid Cymru's development for two reasons. First, Plaid can scarcely be described as a political party in its first twenty years. Secondly, 1945 marks the point at which it is possible to identify some of the dynamics that shaped the maturing of Plaid Cymru into an important force in Welsh politics.

The party contested seven constituencies in the 1945 General Election, as many as it had in total during the first twenty years of its existence. Also, somewhat conveniently, this was the time when the party began to refer to itself as 'Plaid Cymru', rather than 'Plaid Genedlaethol Cymru'. Its leaders recognised that there had to be a marriage of electoral and campaigning activities for it to be recognised and acknowledged as a political party, its post-war objective. The party also transferred its headquarters from Caernarfon to Cardiff. The 1945 election, although unsuccessful for Plaid, marked the beginning of a long and arduous transformation from movement and pressure group to political party.

What Has Been Said So Far

Relatively little has been published in English on Welsh nationalism, and even less on Plaid Cymru specifically. Much of what has been written has tended to lean towards atheoretical, anecdotal and often nostalgic accounts of Plaid and its history. Many of these books and pamphlets have been written by party insiders and must therefore be regarded as propaganda as much as objective analysis. Other accounts of its modern development have approached Plaid as part of the British party politics scene. They have viewed Plaid as a kindly aunt might a pleasant, but mis-

guided, young nephew: the party has been described in a largely patron-
ising tone, and viewed as a distinctive feature in Welsh politics, whilst
showing a basic ignorance of the complexity of the party and its distinctive political role.[14] As such they fail to illuminate the real factors that
have determined Plaid Cymru's growth since 1945.

Although, there are no accounts of post-war Plaid Cymru that adopt a
developmental perspective, the body of literature on nationalism and on
Welsh politics in general[15] is by no means irrelevant to an understanding
of the party. However, general explanations of nationalism only tell half
the story as nationalist parties like Plaid Cymru have unique characteristics due to their specific contexts.

Writing on Plaid itself divides into two categories, historical and
sociological. The historical approach also has two forms: the specific,
dealing with a defined period, and the general which attempts to tell the
party's whole history. In the former category, Hywel Davies's analysis of
the first twenty years of Plaid Cymru's history is easily the definitive
historical narrative.[16] Among the latter category, many accounts come
from within the party itself. Former party president Gwynfor Evans has
contributed many volumes on Wales, its history and its nationalist party[17]
There are also accounts from former chair, Phil Williams[18] and party general secretary, Dafydd Williams, the latter offering a straightforward
overview of the party's history.[19] If not quite polemics, these are largely
positive portraits which skate over some of the shortcomings of its leaders and weaknesses of party strategy. However, they still offer the reader
some documentary illustration of the way in which Plaid Cymru has
developed. Like Evans, Phil Williams attempts to locate the growth of a
party representing Welsh nationalism within the wider context of Welsh
and British politics.

Historian John Davies has published widely on Plaid's history, including on the party's seventy-fifth anniversary, a lecture tracing some of the
landmarks in the party's development.[20] All of these writings offer valuable 'insider' perspectives on the party's growth.

In the area of historical-ethnic studies of Welsh nationalism, Aull
Davies[21] pays particular attention to the role of nonconformity in shaping
the early Plaid Cymru. She also relates the growth of Welsh nationalism
to general interpretations of Celtic nationalism like that of Hechter.[22] This
literature on the history of Plaid Cymru is restricted by its scope more
than its objectivity; it suffers from the absence of a broader theoretical
and comparative context for its arguments. Butt Philip's[23] detailed look at

Welsh nationalism between 1945 and 1970 is a useful overview of the principal themes that have characterised Plaid Cymru's development. However, at thirty years old it lacks contemporaneity and anyway offers a narrative more than a political evaluation.

There is little robust conceptual analysis of the political or ideological outlook of Plaid Cymru. Although there are overlaps with the histories of nationalism and of the party described above, sociological approaches have offered a different perspective on the way Plaid Cymru has developed. There have been sociological deconstructions of Welsh nationalism specifically,[24] but also studies relating Plaid Cymru's growth to wider social change.[25] Many of these combine historical and sociological approaches through an explanation of the dynamism of Welsh nationalism linked with key historical events in Welsh and British history. There are important positives to most of these writings, but there are also key limitations in breadth and depth. Again, there is little analysis identifying the social and political dynamics that have shaped Plaid's growth since 1945. There have also been attempts to categorise Plaid Cymru as a way of explaining its growth; for example, exploring the character of its membership, motivation, or support.[26]

Political history is often told through recounting the words and deeds of leaders. Although such accounts have their value, they are also limited. Such an approach obscures much that is relevant and interesting about a story like Plaid's. The role of ordinary members in the debates on Plaid's vision and strategies is every bit as important as that of the party presidents. Pressure from English speakers, for example, forced the party to assess the nature of its appeal, and the contributions of the Plaid Cymru Women's Section forced the party to address the issue of equality (not just gender equality) more seriously.

This book offers a different account of the pattern and influences on Plaid Cymru's growth to most of those previously published. It explores the people and events that have shaped Plaid Cymru, but does not concentrate solely on the usual suspects, though the following chapters do review the role of the party's leaders. This format, I believe, best explains the pattern and pace of Plaid Cymru's development in the second half of the twentieth century.

Notes

1. *Plaid Cymru Aims*, party pamphlet, (no date).
2. For further information on Cymru Fydd see Williams, E.W., *The Politics of Welsh Home Rule 1886-1929, A Sociological Analysis*, University of Wales, unpublished PhD thesis, 1986; George, W., *Cymru Fydd: Hanes y Mudiad Cenedlaethol Cyntaf*, (Gwasg y Brython, 1945).
3. Quoted in Morgan, K.O., *Wales in British Politics, 1868-1922* (University of Wales Press, 1963).
4. Lewis, S., *Y Ddraig Goch*, April 1927.
5. For a full account of the establishment and early years of the party, see Davies, D. Hywel, *Plaid Cymru 1925-1945, A Call to Nationhood* (University of Wales Press, 1983).
6. Lewis, S., letter to H.R. Jones, undated (Plaid Cymru archive, National Library of Wales).
7. Lewis, S., *Y Faner*, 6 Sept. 1923.
8. *ibid*
9. Lewis, S., *Principles of Nationalism* (Plaid Cymru, rpt 1975).
10. Davies, D.H., *op.cit*.
11. *ibid*
12. Jones, J.E., Plaid Genedlaethol Cymru Amcanion (Swyddfa'r Blaid Genedlaethol, n.d.)
13. Williams, G.A., *When Was Wales? A History of the Welsh*, (Penguin, 1985).
14. See Pilkington, C., *Issues in British Politics*, (Macmillan, 1998); Budge, I, *et al*, *The New British Politics*, (Longman, 2001); Jones, B., *et al*, *Politics UK*, (Longman, fourth edition, 2001), Fisher, J., British Political parties (Prentice Hall, 1996).
15. See Smith, A., *Nationalism in the Twentieth Century*, (Martin Robertson, 1976); Greenfeld, L., *Nationalism: Five Roads to Modernity*, (Harvard University Press, 1992); Jones, G.E., *Modern Wales A Concise History c. 1485-1979* (Cambridge University Press, 1984); Thompson A., & Dunkerley, *Wales Today?* (University of Wales Press, 1999), Fevre, R., & Thompson, A., (eds) *Nation, Identity and Social Theory: Perspectives from Wales* (University of Wales Press, 1999).
16. Davies, D.H., *op. cit*. This impressive monograph explores the early years of Plaid Cymru between 1925 and 1945. It is an important historical contribution, which documents only the early years of Plaid Cymru, from its establishment in 1925 to the end of the Second World War. It traces the formation of a political party out of a broad cultural and social movement. Davies's conclusion was that, by 1945, Plaid had moved some of the way towards party status without adopting all of the characteristics associated with such a body. The reality, for Davies, was that by 1944 "the Welsh nationalist party was a social and educational movement which created a dedicated core of cultural nationalists rather than a political group campaigning vigorously to gain popular support for the objective of Welsh self-government".
17. Evans, G., *Land of my Fathers, 2000 Years of Welsh History*, (Y Lolfa, 1992); Evans, G., *Fighting for Wales* (Y Lolfa, 1991); Evans, G., *Wales can Win* (Christopher Davies, 1973); Evans, G., *Rhagom i Ryddid*, (Bangor, 1964). The former president of Plaid offers his own perspective on Welsh history and the need for a party like Plaid Cymru. Evans is the supreme historian, constantly locating the necessity for a separate party "fighting for Wales" within broader political and historical events. In many respects, Evans takes the teleological approach looking back to the earliest influences on nationalism and also forward to its ideal outcome, a "free, self-governing Wales". If one cuts through the party spin, Evans's work still gives us a flavour of the motivations for forming Plaid Cymru in 1925 and some of

the dynamics which have driven the party's progress within the Welsh political arena subsequently.

18. Williams, P., *Voice from the Valleys*, (Y Lolfa, 1981).

19. Williams, D., *The Story of Plaid Cymru*, (Plaid Cymru, 1990).

20. See Davies, J., unpublished lecture on Plaid Cymru's seventy fifth anniversary, 2000; Davies, J., *A History of Wales*, (Penguin, 1993); Davies, J., (ed.), *Cymru'n Deffro, Hanes y Blaid Genedlaethol, 1925-75* (Y Lolfa, 1981), Davies, J., *Plaid Cymru oddi ar 1960 / Plaid Cymru Since 1960*, Welsh Political Archive Lecture 1996 (National Library of Wales, 1997).

21. Aull Davies, C., *Welsh Nationalism in the Twentieth Century, The Ethnic Opinion and the Modern State*, (Praeger, 1989). Aull Davies's most valuable contribution comes in the application of a history of Wales to the modern context, examining how the development of a state infrastructure from the 1960s onwards, including the way in which the growth of new Welsh institutions, like the Wales TUC and the Welsh Development Agency, augmented a new political identity. Davies used this assumption to explain Plaid's emphasis that the exploitation of Wales was that of a national unit or community, rather than an economic class. Her central thesis links the speed of growth in Welsh nationalism to the emergence of a state bureaucracy and its increasing impact in social affairs. This can be usefully applied to discussions on the contemporary position of Wales within an evolving European Union.

22. Hechter, M., *Internal Colonialism: The Celtic Fringe in British National Development, 1536-1966*, (Routledge and Kegan Paul, 1975).

23. Butt Philip, A., *The Welsh Question, Nationalism in Welsh Politics 1945-1970*, (University of Wales Press, 1975).

24. Adamson, D., *Class, Ideology and the Nation, A Theory of Welsh Nationalism*, (University of Wales Press, 1991); Aull Davies, C., *op. cit.*; McAllister, L., *Community in Ideology: The Political Philosophy of Plaid Cymru*, University of Wales, unpublished PhD thesis, 1995.

25. Adamson, D., *Modes of Production, Social Class Structure and the Development of Welsh Nationalism*, University of Wales, unpublished PhD thesis, 1988; Williams, E.W., *The Politics of Welsh Home Rule 1886-1929, A Sociological Analysis*, University of Wales, unpublished PhD thesis, 1986. Adamson looked at theories that explain the growth of ethnic nationalism. He focused in particular on three writers, Kedourie, Gellner, and Smith, accompanying this appraisal with an outline of Marxist theory on the nation and on ideology. His conclusion was that there could be no universal theory of nationalism. Rather, it was appropriate to treat the study of nationalism as a wide framework that represented a method of enquiry. Nationalism was class-neutral. However, it was given its specific character in particular contexts by its association with a definite class grouping. Adamson has also discussed the emergence of a new "class fraction". A fraction was a variant on a class, rather than a new, independent group in its own right. Adamson talked of this new grouping as the "new working class". It has emerged in Wales as a result of significant changes in the economic and productive base of that country. The "new working class" has a shifting ideological terrain as a result of its mongrel origins, and has found an electoral home in Plaid Cymru in Wales, but in the former Alliance parties in England. He used Gramsci and his theories of "hegemonia" and the "national-popular" to explain the central relation of political faction and party to social class, concluding that the history of parties synchronised with specific stages in the historical development of particular social classes. The first part of Adamson's thesis is convincing. There clearly is a new, emergent class structure taking shape in Wales during the 1980s and 1990s. The second part of his argument, however, is undeveloped. Williams, meanwhile, explored Wales in the period between 1886 and 1929. The early part of this period showed the extent to which Wales was integrated into the

British social formation. The Liberals, despite their status as the party representing most of Wales, could boast few uniquely Welsh characteristics. Starting in 1886, which signalled the genesis of the new home rule movement that was to dominate Welsh politics in ensuing years, Williams traces the rise and decline of both important phases of the home rule movement. More interesting, however, is the author's account of why the broad movement floundered. Williams identified the emergence of a new relationship – that between capital and labour – as central to this debate. The way in which parties in Wales located themselves within this new relationship was particularly significant.

26. Rawkins, P., 'An Approach to the Political Sociology of the Welsh Nationalist Movement', *Political Studies*, Vol. XXVII, No. 3, 1979; Corrado, R., 'Nationalism and Communalism in Wales', *Ethnicity*, No. 2, 1979; Granik, S., PhD research, London School of Economics (2000, ongoing); Denney, D., 'The Social Construction of Nationalism: Racism and Conflict in Wales', *Contemporary Wales*, Vol. 4, 1991; Combs, T., *The Party of Wales, Plaid Cymru: Populist Nationalism in Contemporary British Politics* (University of Connecticut, 1978); Trent, J., 'The Politics of Nationalist Movements: A Reconsideration', *Canadian Review of Studies in Nationalism*, 2,1, 1974.

Rawkins explored the character of Plaid's members, dividing them under the following headings: (i) fortress nationalists; (ii) party loyalists; (iii) militant cultural nationalists; (iv) modernists. Members of the latter category, the modernists, were seen to control election strategy and party policy. While Rawkins's typology is interesting, it has a number of flaws, most prominent being that many of the party's members, particularly those in leadership positions, could fit into any or all of Rawkins' categories, as they often contained characteristics of each group. This article is based on Rawkins's doctoral thesis which used a structural analysis of twentieth-century social and economic development in Wales to discuss the role of the contemporary Plaid Cymru. His typology of nationalist membership led him to conclude that the identity of the modern Plaid Cymru member was not solely dependent on language, but instead drew upon a number of "socio-psychological" threads. Rawkins's conclusion was that uneven economic development was a major spur to nationalist activity, since economic imbalance heightened cultural and thus, national awareness. There has been little modern reappraisal of Rawkins's theories of nationalist membership in Wales. This might cast an interesting new light on the character of Plaid's contemporary membership.

Amongst the many theories stressing the ethnic factor in understanding nationalism, Corrado offered a distinctive Welsh perspective. He attempted to show the lasting role of ethnicity in the formation of identity. There have been premature declarations of the redundancy of ethnicity since the advent of capitalism. Corrado argued that ethnic group remained a key determinant of social and economic behaviour, even in modern societies, and that this fact was best illustrated by the continued appearance of nationalist movements. Corrado considered Wales and Welsh nationalism as part of this attempt to illustrate the continuing role of ethnicity.

Granik's doctoral research is based on a major survey of Plaid's membership conducted in April 2000. Its objective was to find out what motivates activism amongst the members. The research explores the characterising features of Plaid's membership such as demographic profile, rates of participation and experiences of party membership. Amongst its conclusions were high acknowledgements of membership satisfaction, and of effective socialisation within the party. Granik's findings hint at the depth of unity and cohesiveness shown by Plaid's members, a theme that features prominently in this book.

Denney developed an "ideal-typical", three-fold classification of Welsh nationalist motivation on the following basis: (i) racial separatism; (ii) socio-lingualism; (iii) cultural pluralism. Denney argued that Welsh nationalism rested on a belief in genetic Welsh characteristics shared by the whole of the population. This, in turn, meant the relation of Welsh nationalism to an understanding of race, although he conceded in an admission heavy with understatement, that "the case for a clear link between racism and Welsh nationalism has yet to be made". This is a somewhat superficial analysis which fails to observe the defining characteristics of nationalism in Wales.

Combs argued that nationalism required a modifier such as populism to furnish it with a clear ideological identity. His appraisal of the philosophical roots to Plaid Cymru led him to conclude that it is "a unique type of socialist party". However, the appeal of Plaid's socialism is moral, not material, since it is closely bound up with nationality on the one hand, and Christianity on the other. Here, Combs reinforced K.O. Morgan's idea that nonconformity, and not industrialisation, formed the basis to Plaid's early ideological commitment.

Trent offered an interesting treatment of the role of community in nationalist discourse, describing elite attempts to portray deprivation as a community grievance, as opposed to an industrial or class-based inequality.

2. Plaid Cymru's Intellectual Heritage
The Ideas that Shaped the Party

Tracing the emergence of a political party involves not only a historical account of events and the role of important personalities, but also an understanding of the ideas, philosophies and theories that influenced its development. This chapter seeks a path through the maze that is Plaid Cymru's intellectual influences. The party has not been homogeneous or uniform in either its membership or its support. It is the proverbial broad church, and the ideas that have shaped its distinctive brand of nationalism are correspondingly diverse.

It is worth marking a clear trail through the maze of influences. Two prominent themes emerge in this chapter. The first is the location of Plaid Cymru within the various models of nationalism, which helps establish the parameters of Plaid's distinctive brand of nationalism. The second is an examination of some of the specific concepts and ideas that have influenced Plaid Cymru. Included here are individual writers and thinkers, as well as broad concepts or schools of ideas which have impacted directly and indirectly on the party's changing intellectual outlook. They include the concepts of community, religious nonconformity, decentralisation and the 'small is beautiful' schools, utopianism, anarcho-syndicalism and guild socialism, and three thinkers who have particularly influenced Plaid Cymru: Saunders Lewis, D.J. Davies and Raymond Williams.

Nationalism: A Mongrel Ideology?

> Welsh nationalism is but a specific expression of a universally occurring political doctrine.[1]

The term 'ideology' is used here to refer to those ideas, or groups of ideas, which set out a view of how society and individuals should be organised. Some have argued that nationalism is not a serious and conventional political ideology at all. It is a question which has long coloured debate on, and within, nationalist parties like Plaid Cymru.

As a "doctrine invented in Europe at the beginning of the nineteenth century"[2], nationalism's demise has long been predicted, by Weber, Marx and Durkheim amongst others who viewed it as a temporary response to a particular political and historical context. However, nationalism remains a powerful political influence at the start of the twenty-first century.

Since there are as many nationalisms as countries in the world, it is not surprising that nationalism has been widely interpreted since its first use by Barruel during the French Revolution of 1789. The French Revolution was the advent, not of nationalism itself, but rather of its modern manifestation. There are post-feudal origins to nationalism, but the Revolution gave rise to a new form, that may be termed 'nation-statism'. Nineteenth-century Europe saw the gradual gestation of this modern interpretation of nationalism. This, in turn, defined the new ideology as the quest for coterminous national and political boundaries. It effectively sought the political apparatus of the state for a historically defined national community. As we shall see, this understanding of nationalism was to pose some serious difficulties for the new party established in Wales in 1925.

Defining Nationalism

Plaid Cymru is committed to a democratic form of nationalism. This is not racially or ethnically defined, and has been pursued by the party through constitutional, non-violent political and electoral means. Although Plaid has occasionally used direct action to advance its case, as in the burning of the Bombing School at Penyberth in 1936, it has generally avoided acts of violence. Plaid is, first and foremost, a committed participant in conventional democratic politics. It is a mainstream nationalist party with predominantly electoral strategies for gaining power and for influencing the political agenda.

As such, Plaid's nationalism falls into the category of so-called 'minority' or 'sub-state' nationalisms. Parties like Plaid Cymru originate and grow on the basis of a shared national history and culture, and a desire to decide their own political futures. Guibernau, in her excellent discussion of *Nations Without States*, suggests that such nationalisms are stimulated by "nations without states as cultural communities sharing a common past, attached to a clearly demarcated territory, and wishing to decide upon their political future which lack a state of their own. These communities are included within one or more states which they tend to regard as alien, and assert the right to self-determination, sometimes understood as further autonomy within the state, though, in other cases it involves the right to secession".[3] This is a good starting point for an investigation of Plaid Cymru's distinctive nationalism.

A host of explanations or models of nationalism exist. The following classifications help locate Plaid Cymru's distinctive brand. Common foundations for 'sub-state' nationalist beliefs include the theory that individuals are determined by their collective identity (that is by the groups to which they belong); that such groups are quasi-organic (they occur naturally, and the ends of the group cannot be separated from those of the individual involved); that the ends that individuals pursue are collective, and often national, ones and that the nation's interests are sacrosanct.[4]

These beliefs establish a model of nationalism based on the politics of individual harmony within the national community. It is essentially a conservative position, seeing the nation as a natural or organic construction, and the individual as a stage in the process of nation building. The stages are teleological, in that the natural end for the individual is to be found, via collective associations like the family and the community, within the nation.

However, there is a further understanding of the relationship between individual and nation which sees nationalism as an interest in itself (similar to class). The nation offers a sense of identity and is a means in itself, rather than an end, as some nationalisms might imply. These are recurring themes in Plaid Cymru's politics and feature in the ideas of two former presidents, Saunders Lewis and Gwynfor Evans, especially.

Within the range of theories explaining the growth of modern nationalism, four categories help distinguish Plaid Cymru's brand: modernisation theories; conservative (or historical) theories; popular and civic theories; and political and cultural theories.

Many explanations of the growth of nationalism link it with the process of modernisation. They argue that the social and economic dislocation that arises from the processes of modernisation almost invariably mobilises a distinct cultural group to seek autonomy within, or apart from, existing state boundaries. Both the Marxist (Nairn) and non-Marxist (Hechter) perspectives of nationalism can be accommodated under this heading.

Within modernisation theories, Hechter's idea of uneven development is crucial to understanding the development of Welsh nationalism within the United Kingdom. As a state grows, economic development does not occur consistently throughout its territory. Thus, states Hechter, those who have benefited less can be mobilised through popular protest, often calling for national or regional autonomy. Such theories originate from a notion of tension between centre and periphery, with the latter developing nationalist movements as a result of alienation from the centre.[5] Gellner argues that nationalist movements emerge as part of an inevitable overspill from the unsettling processes of modernisation.[6]

Plaid has itself used this language to present Wales as an 'internal colony' within the United Kingdom: "Wales's incorporation within the British State as an internal colony has gained us nothing".[7] Without national status or political recognition, it argued, Wales would continue to be exploited as a colony. Its natural resources, mineral wealth for example, would be manipulated in the interests of England, the dominant centre. This was to become a crucial argument in Plaid's political weaponry.

Unlike the reliance on material ends contained in modernisation theories, conservative and historical theories instead emphasise the fundamental historic characteristics of the nation. Nationalism is interpreted as essentially 'civic-territorial', based upon recognition of a shared land and a common civic culture. Kedourie divorced nationalism from its social and economic context, and argued instead that its origins lay in the philosophy of Kant, Fichte, and the intellectual tradition associated with the Enlightenment, which understood the nation as the natural unit for social organisation.[8] This is rather limited in its application to Welsh nationalism, for it takes little account of the context of Plaid Cymru's development. Its relevance lies in underlining the links between the role of ideas and individuals in the formation of nationalist movements and for instigating change in their political strategies. Applied to Plaid Cymru, this asserts the importance of the ideas of its leaders ahead of the wider social and historical dynamics that have shaped the party's development.

Popular and civic explanations offer an interesting caveat to understanding Plaid Cymru's nationalism. Popular nationalism has been best elaborated through the writings of Antonio Gramsci, who addressed the national question specifically within his understanding of hegemony.[9] Gramsci was a Sardinian nationalist, at least in the early stages of his political development. Departing from traditional Marxism, he emphasised the role of the institutions of civil society, those private organisations like the family and the church, in opinion forming. It is in these institutions that we see the struggles for hegemony and the development of one of Gramsci's most potent political ideas, that of the 'national-popular'. He posits that not every economic struggle can be reduced to a straightforward class explanation. Instead, struggles such as women's liberation and, more importantly for this book, those associated with national liberation, are considered to be related to the overall class struggle, but not reducible to it. Gramsci's understanding of nationalism is a valuable aid to understanding the Welsh variety. The merging of a class and national basis to political struggle in the Gramscian idea of the 'national-popular' helps explain some of Plaid's motivations. The ideas of Gramsci have also been used directly by opinion formers within Plaid Cymru, like Dafydd Elis Thomas, Gwyn Alf Williams and Emyr Wynn Williams, to explain the logic of the party's own strategies.

Those who explain nationalism as a civic concept argue from a rather different position. They emphasise the existence of a set of minimum values and beliefs which bind together members of the same national community. Nationalist parties then highlight these as the basis for their popular rationalisation. Plaid Cymru has regularly engaged in this kind of appeal: "The continuity of the Welsh pattern of values and qualities from pre-Christian times to our own day is a striking testimony to the tough stability and strength of the national community".[10]

Greenfeld argues that nationalism is a general, non-specific ideology that need not be particularist. What is interesting about this is the way that the nation, portrayed as a unique, particularist and sovereign concept, is distinguished from nationalism (a broad political ideology which is generic).[11] This has limited relevance to Wales, especially if Welsh nationalism is seen as a broader movement than just Plaid Cymru.

McNeill also uses a civic orientation to explaining nationalism, pointing to the historic isolation of an educated intelligentsia from political life. This intelligentsia was steeped in a form of civic patriotism that helped fuel nationalism as both theory and practical movement from the eighteenth century.[12] This has more resonance for the story of Plaid Cymru that follows.

Our final category contrasts cultural and political explanations of nationalism. The former focuses on the cultural distinctiveness of the nation and its essential organicism. The political nationalist is fundamentally rationalist, while the cultural nationalist is more romantic and traditionalist, pointing to the common past shared by communities within a nation.[13]

Smith identifies the core attributes of an ethnic community as being a proper name, a myth of common ancestry, shared histories, a common culture, association with a specific territory or 'homeland', and a sense of solidarity. Thus, the appeal of nationalist parties campaigning for political recognition for their ethnic communities is often based on three ideals: "collective self-determination of the people, the expression of national character and individuality, and finally the vertical division of the world into unique nations".[14] This has led to Smith's idea of nationalism as 'civic-territorial' where members of a nation share a common civic culture that bonds them in a variety of ways. There are quite different characters to nationalism though, as specific conditions shape its character and manifestation. Smith's is essentially a political approach to explaining nationalism, with economic and cultural forces in the background. Cultural bonds, especially language, serve to homogenise the territory and, in turn, unite potential nationalist support.

The Influence of Community

The word 'community' appears with telling regularity in discussions of Plaid Cymru's nationalism. However, there is little consistency within the party in its understanding or application. Definition of what Plaid means by 'community' is difficult therefore. Yet it is also crucial to an assessment of its place in the ideas of the party. Perhaps the best way of building an operational definition is to look at some of community's principal characteristics.

Place or territory is often seen to be a key component of community. Community has been defined as "a physical concentration of individuals in one place".[15] Miller described nationalism as coming from "people who form a national community in a particular territory [who] have a good claim to political self-determination".[16] Scherer explained how inhabitants created fundamental and enduring attachments to their own locality, establishing a community.[17] Community was thus a by-product of personal contact and interaction. Whilst it coincided with place, territory alone could not determine the boundaries of community. Redfield attributed to community preconditions of smallness, claiming that size promotes homogeneity and self-sufficiency, in turn the foundations of a secure social organisation.[18]

Size features regularly as an index for community, with the strength of its internal relationships linked to its size. Thus, a strong community is based on the ease of frequent face-to-face relationships. Discussion on the optimum size for a community is related to the conceptualisation of the nation as the 'imagined community', in which only a small proportion of members can know each other, yet are united through their perceived membership of the nation.[19] Anderson talked of modern nations as 'imagined communities', imagined because "the members of even the smallest nation will never know most of their fellow-members, meet them, or even hear of them...", communities, "because, regardless of the actual inequality and exploitation that may prevail in each, the nation is always conceived as a deep, horizontal comradeship". This is in direct contrast to the organic view of nations as natural communities.

There are many manifestations of community. We talk regularly of the business community, the rural community, the student community and the gay community. Unless we are clear as to its application, there is a danger of community meaning everything and nothing. In contemporary residential neighbourhoods, people co-exist with others who have completely different outlooks, cultures and backgrounds. If they are bound together as a 'community' it is because of their shared dependence on local services, their shared sense of threat from, for example, re-development plans, or their shared desire to improve local amenities and conditions. This kind of community identity is comprehensible to most people.

Earlier I identified the French Revolution as the beginning of modern nationalism. Community's relationship with the nation was only properly established at a time when the nation represented popular sovereignty. Since then, terms such as nation, region, and locality have been used to describe the collective political locations appropriate for the individual. From 1789 on, the nation referred to a political community based upon principles of participation, equality and democracy. This has subsequently developed into a symbiotic relationship in which the nation has become synonymous with the idea of the modern, democratic political community. This is the backdrop to the permanent popularity of the term community for Plaid Cymru.

Minar and Greer declared "Community is both empirically descriptive of a social structure and normatively toned. It refers both to the unit of society as it is and to the aspects of the unit that are valued if they exist, desired in their absence".[20] Community is pivotal in distinguishing Plaid's nationalism.[21] Its value comes first, from its origins within the early development of political ideas and the subsequent emergence of ideologies and second, from its application within most social science disciplines. Thus, community has a stake in the past, the present and the future. Perhaps its greatest and lasting attraction lies in its visionary appeal, meaning it has attracted idealists from every corner of the ideological map. Community also features within many of the other ideas that have influenced Plaid Cymru.

Community has two specific main uses: first, it describes a particular type of social arrangement (this can be termed the empirical function); second, it internalises statements about how an organisation should operate (its normative, or evaluative, function). In its political application, there is a synthesis between the normative and empirical dimensions to community. This relationship is critical in reinforcing the importance of community to Plaid Cymru. Within Plaid, community has been painted as an alternative to domination by a centralised authority: "... it is by the wise development of the sense of community, of self-identification with a group and with a place, rather than by enslavement to a world power that mankind is to be saved".[22] This social psychological factor is of paramount importance. Nationalism usually engenders a fierce loyalty to community and to its manifestation in the nation; a sentiment which is less powerful in some other ideologies. The emotional appeal of the national community is massive, and imbues nationalism with its distinctive ideological character; commitment to belonging to a national community is often used to explain the ideological location of nationalism. That is, the lack of ideological solidity and clarity that is often a feature of nationalism is the outcome of its vague emotional appeal.

Religious Nonconformity

Hywel Davies pointed to the historic link between Welsh nationalism and nonconformity, it "had long been linked with religious nonconformity, but it had still to develop as a real political force".[23] The relationship between religion and politics is usually difficult to decipher. The relationship between Plaid Cymru and nonconformity is certainly not straightforward. Yet, exploring the connection is important because it helps isolate another important ingredient in the party's intellectual heritage.

It has been said that, during the twentieth century, "religion lost its saliency as a factor in the personal and intellectual development of Labour leaders".[24] This was not the case for Plaid's leaders. From Saunders Lewis to Gwynfor Evans, and even Dafydd Elis Thomas, religion has strongly influenced their political vision for Wales.

Of all the key social phenomena at the time of Plaid Cymru's birth, the most important was religious nonconformity and the recent movement to disestablish the Church of England in Wales. The nonconformist legacy looms large in the history of Plaid Cymru and can be shown to have influenced many aspects of the party's outlook. The key to appreciating its influence is to understand that "in Wales the Nonconformist chapels were always more than purely religious institutions".[25] Nonconformity also provided a social and political centre. Whilst the precise character of nonconformity is hard to decipher, there are a number of central themes that reinforce its relevance as a social, as well as a religious, phenomenon in Welsh history.

Nonconformist denominations proliferated in Wales in the period after 1737 until, by the middle years of the nineteenth century, three-quarters of the Welsh population had abandoned the established Church of England in favour of various dissenting denominations. Levels of non-conformist allegiance were far higher in Wales than they were elsewhere in the United Kingdom, indicated in the Religious Census of 1851, which provided information about the church and chapel provision made by each religious group. At the start of the twentieth century, 25% of the Welsh population was nonconformist, compared to 5% of the United Kingdom's. The established church, meanwhile, could claim only 10% of the Welsh as adherents. Thus, the extent of nonconformist influence in Wales was immense. Gladstone was reputed to have proclaimed that "the nonconformists of Wales are the people of Wales".

The political peak of nonconformity came during the early years of the twentieth century, when it enjoyed both a direct and an indirect influence on Welsh politics. Those issues central to nonconformist thinking, like disestablishment, land reform, and temperance were becoming political matters (having started as broadly social ones). Nonconformist preachers were engaged in most areas of Welsh political and social life, exercising particular influence in education, economics and morality. The chapels also performed a wider welfare function which, in turn, assisted the integration of religion with broader social life. The Welsh language remained a constant and important binding agent that helped insulate nonconformism as a distinctive Welsh phenomenon. Nonconformists had long regarded Wales as a national unit or community, and its vocabulary reflected this. There was a clear sense in which nonconformity helped render national the particular regional identities of Wales. Nonconformity is thus a vital piece in the Welsh nationalist jigsaw, for its pronouncements and preoccupations reinforced the idea of Wales as both a national, and a natural, political community.

Once again, the stimulus for this perception of Wales came from the social elite which formed the integral leadership of nonconformity. Disestablishment, in particular, became the most contentious contemporary issue in Welsh politics, and was portrayed as a debate on the very terms of national identity. Matters of local and national grievance were successfully transformed into political issues by an ever-conscious, predominantly nonconformist, political elite. This elite was composed largely of the Welsh lower middle-class, which was politically educated and personally ambitious. As such it resembled the elite referred to in cultural explanations of nationalism. We are also reminded of Guibernau's claim that an intellectual elite is required "to select, transform and create the new culture which in most cases will have deep roots to the community's folk culture".[26]

The overlap between nonconformity and Liberalism in the first instance, and then nonconformity and Welsh nationalism, suggests a political transfer from one to the other. Yet this does not tell the whole story. Since nonconformism was not exclusively religious, its leaders were naturally suspicious of 'rival' organisations in Wales, such as industrial unionism, which it viewed as an atheist attack on its natural territory. Unionism was criticised first, as an English import and second, on the basis that religious faith alone could ensure individual material and spiritual salvation. It was thus a way of rejecting a straightforward class analysis of politics and society and as such was a direct overlap with the ideas of the early Plaid Cymru. This class versus community analysis became a recurring tension in the later development of Plaid Cymru.

The legacy of religious nonconformity lies in its supplying geographic, linguistic and economic bonds between the disparate communities of Wales, as well as its distinctive economic classes. In this way, it superimposed a national framework on Wales at a time when the local and the regional prevailed. It was also a dynamic which adapted, and was adapted by, other movements. Thus an important aspect of nonconformity was its binding together wider societal forces and values. Through its capacity to adjust, nonconformism was able to maintain its proactive character and to sustain its lasting importance within Welsh politics.

The powerful linking of class deprivation with the oppression of the Welsh nation and promotion of self-denial through the temperance movement by nonconformism meant the Welsh population began to develop a distinctive consciousness. Though it influenced the Labour Party in Wales, it was within Plaid Cymru that the various components of national identity and political grievance were best articulated.

Nonconformism provided Welsh nationalism, in a general sense, with a ready-made context for its ideas. Plaid's first leaders, Saunders Lewis and Ambrose Bebb, both came from nonconformist backgrounds (although Bebb did not follow Lewis and Catherine Daniel, wife of vice-president J.E. Daniel, who converted to Roman Catholicism). Unsurprising given its dominance, most of the party's early members were nonconformists. The converting Saunders Lewis found himself leading a strongly nonconformist party, an issue which caused some discomfort to both sides: "I am convinced that the party must have a Protestant or an anti-Catholic agnostic as a leader..."[27] Although, by the time Plaid Cymru was established in 1925, nonconformity was in decline – disestablishment had been achieved in 1919 and trade unions were beginning to assume many of the social responsibilities of the chapels – this was not the end of its influence on Plaid Cymru. The decreasing importance of the Liberal Party opened up political space for an independent nationalist party. Many of the values and themes of nonconformity were then taken up to form the new political identity for Plaid Genedlaethol Cymru.

The unopposed election of Gwynfor Evans as party president in 1945 signalled a new start for Plaid Cymru. Evans was a nonconformist and a pacifist, and led the party in a quite different manner to Saunders Lewis, drawing on and adapting many of the principles of nonconformism. Another reason for seeing 1945 as the start of the party's modernisation.

Small is beautiful?

"Wales is an ideal size for efficient government. Britain is far too large", stated an undated pamphlet titled *Plaid Cymru Aims*. There is a heavy emphasis on the small-scale in the political thinking of Plaid Cymru, which originates from two core beliefs: first, the legitimacy of decentralisation and second, a strong anti-state bias in the party's outlook. Politically they come from Plaid's desire to distinguish itself from the Labour Party, which was seen to represent centralised, state-authorised power. Its decentralist inclinations were most prominent under Gwynfor Evans's leadership. Evans regarded the question of size as crucial to 'proper' government: "Size is more often than not bound up with centralisation, which in turn tends to lead to totalitarianism and the erosion of decision-making by individual persons and by communities".[28]

The appropriate scale for political, social and economic organisation has been an important feature of Plaid's policies for Wales. Some of the inspiration for this came from the work of Leopold Kohr who, in *The Breakdown of Nations*, made a direct connection between the organisation of society on a large-scale, and social and economic problems. Kohr's arguments centred on the difficulties of managing large units and the inherent problems with politics and economics conducted on a vast scale, contrasted with the economic benefits of small-scale organisation. Plaid Cymru seized upon Kohr's visionary ideas as validating its own long-standing commitment to decentralisation. Interestingly, Kohr moved to Wales from Puerto Rico and later joined Plaid Cymru.

Plaid's Phil Williams took up this thinking in the 1970s: "Whenever it is practical for a decision to be made locally or centrally, we believe it must always be made locally, by the people affected".[29] Significantly, Plaid showed a commitment to the principle of 'subsidiarity' long before the European Union advanced it as a way of ensuring a better balance between the voices of local communities and the administrative heart of Europe in Brussels. Plaid had consistently linked the organisation of Wales into small communities as a precondition for its political destiny. As well as Gwynfor Evans, who saw the small-scale, local community as the most appropriate unit for political organisation – "Wales... is as near as one can get to an ideal size for the purpose of good government,"[30] – other important thinkers in Plaid, like former Gwynedd Council chief executive, Ioan Bowen Rees, developed these ideas into a proposed scheme of 'government by community', whereby politics was organised on the basis of local units which could ensure the identity of the community.[31]

During the 1960s, Schumacher's 'small is beautiful' school gained international acceptance and added further legitimacy to Plaid's ideas for small-scale, local organisation. "It makes no difference as far as ordinary people are concerned whether they work for a capitalist or the State. Both are far removed from the individual and both are his master" stated the party's youth magazine, *Y Wawr* in 1961.[32] The second dimension to Plaid's decentralist thrust springs from the anti-state bias of the party: "At the heart of politics are freedom and community, values which are central to a humane society. It follows that the state must be subordinated to these social ends".[33] This idea reappears regularly in Plaid's political development, especially in the party's debates on ideology. There have been periods where the party talked openly of the need for a Welsh state but for most of its history it has tried to present different local units for the future organisation of a self-governing Wales. The notion of small-scale organisation later became a defining mechanism for distinguishing Plaid Cymru's particular interpretation of socialism, based on the diversity of community, not the uniformity of the centralised state.

Utopianism, Anarcho-syndicalism and Guild Socialism

At first sight, these ideas might appear strange in a discussion of Plaid Cymru's ideological influences. However, utopianism, anarcho-syndicalism and guild socialism have all informed its intellectual outlook. Not only were writings about these subjects read by party leaders, many of the ideas associated with them were adjusted and applied to the Welsh context, through the party's philosophies and policies. The influence of some of these schools is more indirect than direct, but we will see also prominent features in Plaid's political programme drawn directly from these schools of thought.

Utopianism remains a trend in political thought, rather than a tightly argued and cohesive doctrine. Drawing heavily on Enlightenment ideas, modern utopian thinkers produced an alternative order to society, which held human potentiality at its centre. The individual was fulfilled primarily through a collective social life, they argued. On this basis, the three components of utopianism – association, community and co-operation – would bring about the utopian state of harmony.

But where lies the connection between utopian ideas and Welsh nationalism? Analysis of the early Plaid Cymru reveals that it displayed a millenarian quality in its political outlook and direction. This is maintained in the modern party's aim of a self-governing Wales in terms similar to the organisational representations of utopian objectives in Charles Fourier's 'phalanx' and Robert Owen's 'experimental community'. All were presented as advances on the political, economic and social status quo. The idea of a political and administrative system which accords with the natural social and collective inclinations of its members is the objective of nationalists and utopianists alike. As party president, Gwynfor Evans argued that in "a community of autonomous persons, the more fully will people live". As we shall see, Plaid's policies were rather rudimentary and idealistic in the party's early stages: Welsh self-government was presented as the utopian solution to every policy dilemma. Utopianism and Plaid's brand of nationalism also share a political vocabulary. The terminology of co-operation and solidarity, of self-government and personal fulfilment feature prominently in both.

Plaid Cymru's intellectual heritage contains some less predictable influences, anarcho-syndicalism being one, though here it is a case of indirect influence rather than direct impact on the party's outlook. The appeal of anarchism has given it a place within the ideologies of socialism, liberalism and some forms of modern nationalism, albeit with differing intensities and with differing degrees of acknowledgement to the original source. Welsh nationalism shares many of the principles that inspired anarchism, and more specifically, anarcho-syndicalism.

Anarchism internalises a rejection of authority, an organic approach to politics and the positive promotion of freedom as the natural human condition. It is crystallised in the anarchist slogan: 'co-operation, not coercion'. Although each of these themes is apparent within Plaid Cymru's political vision, it is anarchism's preoccupation with organic development that most overlaps with Plaid's politics. For most anarchist writers, society is a natural composition of parts called individuals and communities. The social process is a natural one, in which community is the arena within which human relations can be fulfilled. Contract, mutualism and exchange are all best conducted within community.

As a merger of anarchism and syndicalism, anarcho-syndicalism found most favour with the industrial working-classes. Despite the philosophical doubts of some within the broader anarchist movement, anarcho-syndicalism was an important variant, blending as it did the industrial and economic with the political and organisational. As a movement, anarcho-syndicalism had a limited life span and was already a recent memory by 1925. It did, however, develop some of the themes of anarchism that gave its ideas their modern and lasting relevance.

There has been a direct input of anarcho-syndicalist ideas into the political heritage of Wales. *The Miners' Next Step*, published in the Rhondda in 1912 was a revolt against the collectivist ethos of the executive of the South Wales Miners' Federation. It typified the successful merger of anarchism and syndicalism in the industrial valleys and paralleled contemporary movements in France and the USA. The specific relevance of anarcho-syndicalism as a doctrine of industrial autonomy and democracy to the nationalist ideas of Plaid Cymru can be considered in three different areas. First, the aims of the two ideologies overlap, in their focusing on federalism and decentralisation and the associated vocabulary of each. Secondly, both anarcho-syndicalism and nationalism absorb the wider educational, social and cultural aspects of politics, moving beyond a strictly economic focus. The anarcho-syndicalist vision of a society built upon syndicates emphasises these aspects, whilst Plaid Cymru's objective of a self-governing Wales is similarly presented as a model in which individuals are properly fulfilled. The third connection lies in their avoidance of the themes of class and the vocabulary of class politics. Anarcho-syndicalism, like anarchism and Plaid Cymru's nationalism, substituted community for class in its arguments for alternative social and political arrangements (although anarcho-syndicalism looked for wider co-operative relationships than the national community). Nevertheless, it is this idea of community – both in terms of relationships between people within a particular location, and in the sense of a distinctive kind of social organisation – that parallels Plaid Cymru's portrayal of community as the arena for the fulfilment of self-government.

Based upon the writings of A.J. Penty and A.R. Orage particularly, guild socialism developed an alternative appraisal of political organisation based upon a formal structure of groups. Penty and Orage tried to recreate the medieval notion of 'crafts guilds', taking many of their ideas from a theoretical heritage that included William Morris and John Ruskin. But they were interested in more than romantic restoration. They saw the emergence of guilds, which were to develop from existing trade unions, as a way of avoiding the traditional and alienating division of labour induced by the Industrial Revolution. G.D.H. Cole elaborated many of these ideas during the First World War, making guild socialism "an intermediary position for those who wished to accept the State and get on with their business within its confines and in terms of its responsibilities".[34] The notion of a guild (defined as "an association of people for mutual aid or the pursuit of a common goal") overlapped with community. Again, there is a shared vocabulary between guild socialism and Welsh nationalism, concerning representation, accountability and decentralised democracy. Cole emphasised the subjective content of community; that is, community was realised through the collective and conscious identity of its members. The purpose of community was to provide a 'centre of feeling' for people with much in common, offering 'a real and operative unity' for its members.[35]

Many of Plaid's ideas for the political and industrial organisation of Wales duplicate the central themes of guild socialism. The commitment to industrial and political pluralism enshrined in guild socialism rested upon a system of industrial guilds. By their constitution and role, guilds offered a challenge to the unitary and centralised state. The projection of Wales as a 'community of communities' is an enduring concept in the political discourse of nationalism, and one that echoes the composite of the guild system. In the 1950s and 1960s particularly, Plaid advocated co-operatively-owned factories and farms, drawing on the guild theme, as well as the co-operative ideas of D.J. and Noelle Davies.

Gwynfor Evans also claimed a direct input from guild socialism to his own political outlook. Plaid Cymru has long seen the individual as the source of all natural authority and has gone on to recommend national self-government as the most appropriate political structure for individual and community fulfilment.

Three Key Thinkers

In this final section, I turn to some of the individuals whose ideas and writings have influenced the development of Plaid Cymru's politics. The extent of their direct input on the party varies (two were important leaders in the early years, the third joined the party but was associated for much of his life with the Labour Party). All, however, contributed to the maturing of Plaid's political vision and strategies.

There is no doubting the influence of Saunders Lewis on the party's early development; he became its second president, between 1926 and 1939. However, Lewis's influence extends beyond this period and his ideas continued to shape the party's political outlook for a large part of its subsequent history. Lewis's role in the maturing of Plaid Cymru features throughout this story. I concentrate here on the practical impact of his own ideas on the development of the party's politics.

What distinguished Lewis as a politician was his motivation by spiritual, rather than material, values. He argued that Welsh nationalism should appeal to a spiritual dimension in addition to the cultural and political. Lewis believed in the organic society, and the organicism which characterised his ideas was drawn directly from European influences. The tenets of Aristotle and Aquinas run throughout Lewis's writings on Wales and especially in his commitment to 'freedom' rather than 'independence'. For him, it was from the individual, through the family, to the formation of a community that the origins of the nation as the ultimate aggregate of communities could be traced. The nation was thus presented as the ultimate realisation of this organic process.

I referred earlier to the importance of religion to Lewis's politics. He was a Roman Catholic leader of a largely nonconformist party yet, his distinctive ideas left an indelible print on both the organisation and philosophy of Plaid Cymru. His views were strongly shaped by traditionalist French Catholicism in which the writings of Maurice Barrès and Charles Maurras figure prominently. Their ideas concurred with Lewis's longstanding conviction that Wales was a nation firmly located in the European tradition, and defined within the context of medieval Christianity. The prominence of concepts like freedom and leadership by a responsible elite drew heavily from Catholicism (they also remind us of some of the theories of nationalism considered earlier). Lewis's *Principles of Nationalism* (based on a lecture to the 1926 party Summer School) located Wales within a medieval European civilisation where the Welsh nation was naturally and organically at ease. It was Lewis's development of the all-embracing notion of civilisation that enabled him to bypass much of the conventional terminology normally associated with nationalism.

Lewis's focus on the nation as an aggregate of communities helped him rationalise his fundamental opposition to the state. The state, he proposed, was an unnatural construction imposed through the Protestant Reformation upon the natural organisation of society, whereas the nation represented the outcome of a natural, organic socialisation process. The hallmarks of the European dimension were the principles of decentralisation and pluralism. This contrasted favourably with the reality of centralised, authoritarian state-rule. Moreover, the British state was seen as the antithesis of the small-scale, decentralised national community to which Lewis and the early Plaid Cymru aspired.

Lewis's appraisal of contemporary Wales rested on three important convictions: first, that the nation was the natural political unit arising from an amalgamation of local communities; second, that Wales was part of a long-established European civilisation; and third, that the true values of Wales and its people were historic, Christian ones and could only be reincarnated under the auspices of Christianity. This was supported by a conviction that "the government of Wales must be Welsh in spirit and language", "Wales must be planned in a Welsh way, and her whole life made Welsh". It was Lewis's historic BBC radio address in 1961, 'The Fate of the Language', that led to the creation of the Welsh Language Society, *Cymdeithas yr Iaith Gymraeg*, in 1963. Without a guarantee of the status of the Welsh language, Lewis regarded self-government for Wales as worthless.

Yet, Lewis was not trying to make Plaid Cymru a cultural pressure group. He was convinced it should become a proper political party with coherent policies and strategies. His *Ten Points of Policy*, drafted in 1934, was designed as a personal manifesto which could act as the basis for policy discussion in the larger party.[36] It rejected both capitalism and imperialism and advocated a distinctive form of co-operative democracy. Lewis envisaged agriculture as the foundation for a self-governing Wales: "Agriculture should be the chief industry of Wales and the basis of its civilisation". He drew on the methods of pluralism and distributivism to offer an alternative model – *perchentyaeth* – of how society should operate: "Ownership should be distributed so widely among the families of the nation that neither state nor individual nor a collection of individuals can oppress the people economically". Despite the wholesale modernisation of Plaid and its dramatic progress since the days of Lewis's leadership, many of his ideas, on community and the Welsh language for instance, continue to inform the party's ideological and constitutional arguments.

D.J. Davies is rightly credited with adding some detail to the politics of the early Plaid Cymru. In fact, he and his wife, Noëlle, did a lot more than that. They offered a crucial and timely challenge to the young Plaid to begin to act as a political party, and as such supported Lewis's vision of Plaid as a party not a pressure group.Their emphasis was different, however. The Davieses injected a strongly pragmatic and economic dimension to Plaid's policies, stressing that the economic case for self-government was the crucial one to be communicated to the Welsh public. Their previous membership of the Labour Party, as well as their associations with the folk movements in Denmark and the related ideas of co-operatism, helped shape Plaid's early commitment to co-operative social democracy.

D.J. Davies was from Carmel in Carmarthenshire, although his father had worked in the Rhondda coal fields until the industry's decline forced the family to move west. He met Noëlle Ffrench in 1924 whilst they were studying at the International People's College at Elsinore in Denmark where the ideas of cultural nationalism, merged with liberal social and economic policies, were dominant. On their return to Wales and to study at Aberystwyth University, D.J. Davies met many of the founders of the newly formed party, Plaid Genedlaethol Cymru. He joined Plaid in 1927, "apparently perceiving it as an organisation whose programme had yet to be determined".[37] Together, Davies and his wife quickly became involved in the development of Plaid, their experience of Scandinavian social democracy a balance to Lewis's influences from the French radical right.

The Davieses were instrumental in shaping the early constitutional and economic strategies of the party: the commitments to dominion status and to economic strategies based on guild socialism were two of their clearest legacies. They acted as a two person research department, producing some seminal pamphlets and books that helped inject a much needed realism and precision to the rather vague economic policies of the early Plaid Cymru.[38]

D.J. and Noëlle Davies also appreciated the importance of appealing to the English-speaking majority in Wales, instead of seeing the Welsh language as the only legitimate vehicle for converting people to the nationalist cause. A result of this belief was the launch of the party's English-language paper, *The Welsh Nation*, in January 1932. They also recognised the historic integrity of Monmouthshire and Wales, and argued for a decentralised, locally-based form of social and economic democracy which respected and built upon the different traditions of Wales's communities.

Essentially, the Davieses injected a distinctive type of socialist analysis into Plaid Cymru during the first thirty years of its existence based on their respect for history and tradition, allied with radical elements: "I think the combination of the two adjectives [conservative and radical] quite fairly sums up our own Party's conclusions regarding economic policy".[39] They also acted as a counterbalance against the more cultural brand of nationalism advocated by Saunders Lewis and some of his contemporaries. This was timely in view of the economic crises facing Wales. It was also much needed in an organisation which, until then, had interpreted politics largely from a cultural perspective. Moreover, the particular brand of co-operative, decentralist socialism promoted by the Davieses merged neatly with Plaid Cymru's existing commitment to the small-scale economic unit, and its anti-state focus.

The Davieses were not only instrumental in conditioning the policy outlook for Plaid during its infancy; the legacy of their socialist and co-operative stance can be seen in some of the debates on policy that feature later in this book. The Davieses' rejection of the anti-state bias to socialism in favour of decentralised, small-scale industrial and economic order are apparent in the party's vision as late as the 1990s. Their most permanent legacy may well be the number of new and different party recruits that their political ideas encouraged. Gwynfor Evans insisted that it was the development of the economic rationale for Plaid's nationalism within Davies's *The Economics of Welsh Self-Government* that convinced him, as a sceptical undergraduate, to join the party (Davies responded to the compliment, saying "in which case it would be a very important landmark indeed!").

Although he joined the party quite late in his life, the writings and ideas of Raymond Williams (1921-1988) played a crucial part in the political and ideological outlook of Plaid Cymru. In particular, his ideas gave coherence to the party's understanding of community and small-scale organisation discussed earlier.

Unlike that of Lewis and the Davieses, Williams's influence came relatively late in the party's maturing, from the 1970s onwards. Plaid had, by then, begun to operate within the structures of conventional politics, developing the more extensive social and economic policies required by electoral competition. His ideas were absorbed directly by many influential figures within Plaid ranks, who saw his interpretation of Welsh identity as crucial to the broadening of Plaid Cymru's appeal. Here, for the first time, was a distinguished Welsh academic who published solely in English, but whose work contained an overwhelmingly Welsh perspective.

Williams's writings thus offered Plaid some symbolic value. He was a thinker who, for much of his career, had been closely associated with the Labour Party and British New Left politics. Yet, late in his life, he decided to join Plaid Cymru, seeing the party as the rightful inheritor of the Welsh radical tradition.

Williams was the son of a railway signalman from the small agricultural village of Pandy, near the border between Wales and England. He "drew certain fundamental values from his own background and early experience that enabled him to share a deep sympathy with anti-colonial struggle and peasant resistance".[40] Wales, or at least the Welsh community with which he was most familiar, formed the backdrop for the development of his ideas. It was within the framework of this border country, where a pattern of social relationships was firmly established and adhered to, that Williams developed his vision for political change. The characteristics of Pandy offered a microcosm of the issues of identity that Williams sought to resolve within wider society. Williams talked of "a specific local identity" being "much stronger" for him than a national one. In many ways, this prominence came from the border location of Pandy. It encouraged "a curious sense in which we could speak of both Welsh and English as foreigners, as 'not us'." Williams confessed, "it's true that much of my political belief is a continuation of a very early formation", admitting that "I saw Welshness after Welshness and neither was quite mine nor that of my own people". These different interpretations of identity helped Plaid look again at the various forms of Welshness that existed.

Williams's own outlook altered a number of times, often reflecting changes in his own circumstances. For instance, on leaving Pandy to study at Cambridge University, Williams became involved with the Communist Party, preferring its revolutionary ideas to the revisionism of the Labour Party for which he had previously, if somewhat sceptically, worked: "I would work for Labour in the elections because there was no other choice. But I always had a very reserved attitude to the Labour Party". Some of his intellectual shifts might be attributed to the trauma of arriving at a place so conspicuously alien as Cambridge. Referring to Williams's own understanding of his political position, one commentator has suggested that Williams was late to recognise the significance of 'Welshness' to his political thinking: "Suddenly Wales was every-where".[41] Moreover, within these shifts in self-location, Williams's links with Marxism were unclear. Bennett et al. claimed there was a significant shift around 1977, but pointed out quite rightly that Williams's new iden-tity as a Marxist originated as much from the decline in economic reductionism within Marxism as it did from any significant sea-change in Williams's own mind. This viewpoint is supported by the fact that he was quick to attribute the problems of modern society to the disruptive impact of capitalism and its agents.

Although he belonged to many intellectual constituencies (often simultaneously), Williams has been presented as the first socialist to recognise and treat Wales as a modern European nation. He later recon-ciled his own experiences with the characteristics of Welsh society. It was from then on that his ideas influenced Plaid most directly. He saw Wales as representing "a whole community, integrated and cultured, to hold up as worthy example against the more rootless life of the university, factory, city". Wales embodied many of the social relationships that Williams regarded as the basis for a new political order, and was the inspiration for much of Williams's writing. He later confessed that: "The way I used the term community actually rested on my memories of Wales", and re-con-firmed this location for Wales at the centre of a new politics, in the context of Europe. Discussing the EEC referendum in 1975, Williams argued for "frontier-crossing internationalism". He was convinced that in the future "we shall indeed be thinking about and working in Europe, but about and in a different Europe from any the orthodox campaigns now see or propose". Again, during the referendum, Williams related his pro-European vote to his Welshness: "It seems that I shall be one of the very few socialists as distinct from social-democrats voting 'Yes' in the refer-endum... any 'national' solution is politically inconceivable. Culturally, I find more sense in a Welsh European identity than in the dominating English versions of sovereignty and tradition". Even later, Williams explained his own self-location as a 'Welsh-European' in response to a question about his feelings for Wales: "Suddenly England, bourgeois England, wasn't my point of reference any more. I was a Welsh European, and both levels felt different".

Williams's most important intellectual legacy for Plaid Cymru comes from his treatment of Wales as a community, in every sense of the word. This recognition gave renewed confidence to Plaid Cymru in the formulation of its political programme and the special role of community within this. Williams, by virtue of his own background, felt Wales epitomised many of community's components: "...if you trace the word 'community' through my work, you would find, on the one hand, that you are opposing a notion of community to a notion of competitive individualism, and then you are finding that the idea of community is being appropriated by precisely the people who say that we have a national community which sets boundaries to the way people think and feel and, moreover, which imposes certain responsibilities".

Williams widened political recognition for Plaid's particular brand of nationalism. Europe and world events became the new backdrop for Welsh politics. The foundations for the European enthusiasm which was to characterise Plaid Cymru from the beginning of the 1980s were laid, and were manifested in the 'Wales in Europe' policy. Neither of these two levels of identity – Welsh or European – had been adequately explored or rationalised before. Williams's imaginative contribution to the debate crucially influenced the reformulation of a European strategy which was to become central to Plaid.

Williams's writings imparted ideas that could then be translated into a specifically Welsh context by the modern leaders of Plaid Cymru. It is telling that Williams is frequently identified as a crucial part of Plaid's intellectual inheritance by many of its modern leaders, from Gwynfor Evans to Dafydd Elis Thomas. Williams's application of the terminology of community to Wales paralleled Evans's own thinking, based possibly on shared influences from guild socialism, utopianism, and syndicalism. Both Evans and Dafydd Elis Thomas were attracted to Williams's emphasis on the small-scale and on community as the appropriate location for a new radical politics. It also validated Thomas's belief that Europe offered a suitable backdrop to Plaid's political strategies. Thomas absorbed many of the New Left's ideas and was to later draw heavily on Williams's writings to argue the case for a leftward shift by Plaid Cymru and to reformulate the idea of Wales in Europe.

This chapter has traced some of the ideas and individuals that have shaped Plaid Cymru's politics. They have had differing impacts on the party, direct and indirect, and have proved to be continuing or to have influenced at specific points in its history. I began by outlining some of the explanations of the existence of nationalism in its various forms. The difficulties in finding a precise home for Plaid Cymru amongst these models underlines the complexity and specificity of nationalist parties within their own distinctive contexts. The only common denominator that exists between nationalist parties is a belief in the integrity of the national territory, however it is defined.

Despite a diverse intellectual heritage, it has been possible to isolate some themes that have shaped the most significant debates in Plaid Cymru's ideological development. The ideas of community, Europe, decentralisation, anti-statism, and co-operatism all feature prominently. Together, they form the cocktail of Plaid Cymru's political inheritance.

Notes

1. Adamson, D.L., *Class, Ideology and the Nation, A Theory of Welsh Nationalism,* (University of Wales Press, 1991).
2. Kedourie, E., *Nationalism* (Hutchinson, 1960).
3. Guibernau, M., *Nations without States: Political Communities in a Global Age,* (Polity Press, 1999).
4. Kellas, J.G., *The Politics of Nationalism and Ethnicity* (Macmillan, 1991).
5. Hechter, M., *Internal Colonialism: the Celtic Fringe in British National Development, 1536-1966,* (Routledge & Kegan Paul, 1975).
6. Gellner, E., *Nations and Nationalism,* (Blackwells, 1983).
7. Plaid Cymru, 1983 General Election Manifesto.
8. Kedourie, *op. cit.*
9. Gramsci, A., *Selections from the Prison Notebooks,* edited and translated by Quintin Hoare and Geoffrey Nowell Smith, (Lawrence and Wishart, 1971).
10. Evans, G., *Wales Can Win,* (Christopher Davies, 1973).
11. Greenfeld, L., *Nationalism: Five Roads to Modernity* (Harvard University Press, 1992).
12. MacIver, R.M., *Community* (Macmillan, 1917).
13. Hutchinson, J., *The Dynamics of Cultural Nationalism* (Allen & Unwin, 1987).
14. Smith, A.D., *Theories of Nationalism* (Duckworth, 1971).
15. Minar, D.W. & Greer, S., *The Concept of Community – Readings With Interpretations* (Butterworth, 1969).
16. Miller, D., *On Nationality,* (Clarendon Press, 1995).
17. Scherer, J., *Contemporary Community* (Tavistock Publications, 1972).
18. Redfield, R., *The Little Community and Peasant Society and Culture* (University of Chicago Press, 1960).
19. Anderson, B., *Imagined Communities, Reflections on the Origin and Spread of Nationalism* (Verso, 1991).
20. Minar & Greer, *op. cit.*

21. See McAllister, L., *Community in Ideology: The Political Philosophy of Plaid Cymru,* unpublished University of Wales PhD thesis., 1995

22. Stephens, M., 'On Certain Objections to Nationalism', in *Y Wawr*, Plaid Cymru Youth Magazine, No 11, Summer 1961.

23. Davies, D.H., *The Welsh Nationalist Party 1925-1945, A Call to Nationhood,* (University of Wales Press, 1983).

24. Lewis, R., in Tanner, D., Williams, C., & Hopkin, D., (eds.), *The Labour Party in Wales,1900-2000* (University of Wales Press, 2000).

25. *ibid.*

26. Guibernau, *op. cit.*

27. Lewis, S., in a letter to J.E. Jones, 7 April 1938, (Plaid Cymru Collection, National Library of Wales).

28. Evans, G., *Wales Can Win,* (Christopher Davies, 1973).

29. Williams, P., *Voice from the Valleys,* (Y Lolfa, 1981).

30. Evans, G., *A National Future for Wales,* (John Penry Press, 1975).

31. Rees, I.B., *Government by Community,* (Charles Knight, 1971).

32. Editorial in *Y Wawr*, Plaid Cymru Youth Magazine, No. 11, Summer, 1961.

33. Evans, G., (1973), *op. cit.*

34. Barker, R., *Political Ideas in Modern Britain,* (Methuen, 1979).

35. Cole, G.D.H., *The Social Theory*, quoted in Hirst, P.Q., *The Pluralist Theory of the State, Selected Writings of G.D.H. Cole, J.N.Figgis and H.J. Laski,* (Routledge, 1989).

36. Lewis, S., *Ten Points of Policy, Deg Pwynt Polisi, Canlyn Arthur* (Gwasg Aberystwyth, 1938).

37. Williams, E.W., 'D.J. Davies – A Working Class Intellectual within Plaid Genedlaethol Cymru, 1927-32', *Llafur,* Vol. 4, No. 4, 1987.

38. See Davies, D.J., *The Economics of Welsh Self-Government* (1931), and Davies, D.J. & Noëlle, *Can Wales Afford Self-Government?* (Welsh Nationalist Party, 1939).

39. Davies, D.J., "The Development of Plaid Cymru's Economic Policy", *Triban,* Vol. 1, No. 1, Autumn 1956.

40. Blackburn, R., introduction to Gable, R., (ed), *Resources of Hope,* (Verso, 1989).

41. Ward, J.P., *Raymond Williams,* (University of Wales Press, Writers of Wales series, 1981).

3. Growing Pains:
Stages in Plaid Cymru's Maturing

This chapter focuses on Plaid Cymru at certain key points in its post-war history. Through an overview of its three presidents between 1945 and 1999, I assess the contribution of each to the maturing of Plaid Cymru as a political party, and provide a critical commentary on the period. I also identify the distinctive characteristics of Plaid Cymru in 1945 and in 1999 and gauge the scale and permanence of the political progress made by the party during that period.

A Tale of Two Parties

In 1999, Plaid Cymru had seventeen Assembly Members, four MPs, two MEPs and controlled three of Wales's twenty-two local authorities. At the new National Assembly for Wales, it was the main opposition party, first to the minority Labour government and later to the Labour-Liberal Democrat coalition. As well as having representation at every elected level for the first time in its seventy-four year history, Plaid also employed a larger staff than ever before (approximately sixty paid workers), operated on a much sounder financial footing and had a far more streamlined, modern organisation.

In many ways, the Plaid Cymru of 1999 is so fundamentally different to that of 1945 that direct comparisons pose problems. However, given

Table 1: Plaid Cymru in 1945 and 1999: two very different parties[1]		
	1945	**1999**
Membership	6,000	16,000
Turnover	£2,904	£500,000
Income from St David's Day Fund	£2,181	£19,652
No. of Branches	150	220
Paid Staff	3	60
MPs	0	4
Local Councillors	0	206

these differences of substance and status, analysing events between these dates helps us chart the scale of transformation that Plaid Cymru has undergone.

From Child to Adult

The Child is father of the Man. – Wordsworth.

1945 has been described as Plaid Cymru's coming of age, which suggests its transformation into a political party. The year is significant since prior to this, the description 'political party' sat uncomfortably on Plaid. It was a national movement, a pressure group, still loose and amorphous in structure and outlook, and owning only a few of the conventional characteristics of a political party. Plaid Cymru had been a social, cultural and educational movement for the first two decades of its existence. The end of the Second World War began a new era. The party had a new president and there was widespread consensus that it must broaden its appeal.

However, such a verdict on Plaid Cymru in 1945 is premature. Plaid was clearly not a fully-fledged political party in 1945 nor, indeed, was it until several decades later. It was the adolescent party that still faced some considerable maturing. Yet, in every child, features of the adult are seen. This reinforces the value of this survey of the key stages in the party's history.

The selection of a firm date for Plaid's 'conversion' into a political party is misleading for two reasons; first, because the date itself may be judged premature, and secondly, because the identification of a single date is inappropriate for what is essentially a dynamic, and multi-dimensional, process. The history of Plaid Cymru sees it shifting between the twin, but not mutually exclusive, roles of political party and pressure group, merging an electoral focus with an enthusiasm for campaigns.

Although, it began to adopt some of the structures of a political party in 1945, the immediate post-war years *started* the process of change rather than completed it. Such a process is inevitably a gradual and ongoing one and, in the case of an organisation as distinctive as Plaid Cymru, a process which may never be fully completed.

Influences on the Maturing Process: The Party Presidents

The best way to eat an elephant is in small bites, as the saying goes. In Plaid's case, these bites are the periods of office of each of Plaid's three

Table 2: The Presidents of Plaid Cymru 1925-2000	
Lewis Valentine	1925-1926
Saunders Lewis	1926-1939
J.E. Daniel	1939-1943
Abi Williams	1943-1945
Gwynfor Evans	1945-1981
Dafydd Wigley	1981-1984
Dafydd Elis Thomas	1984-1991
Dafydd Wigley	1991-2000

presidents between 1945 and 1999: Gwynfor Evans, Dafydd Wigley (who served twice) and Dafydd Elis Thomas.

Gwynfor Evans, 1945-1981

> Its feat has been to get rooted and grow.

Gwynfor Evans[2] was born in Barry on the south Wales coast. He was elected president of Plaid Cymru in 1945, at the age of thirty-one, having served as Abi Williams's vice president for two years. He described those years as a "valuable breaking-in period" when he learnt much about the president's duties. Evans was to lead the party for a remarkable thirty-six years. After thirty years in post, he tried to retire but was persuaded to stay on for another six years. Upon his eventual retirement in 1981, the party created a new post, that of Honorary President, which Evans has held ever since. He has continued his involvement with the party in Carmarthenshire where he lives, acting as secretary of his local branch.

Evans's period of office spanned some of the definitive shifts in the party's development – in its internal modernisation, its external reputation and its political direction. His presidency also encompassed important changes in Welsh political history. This period saw the start of institutional decentralisation from London to Wales. From Churchill's Minister for Welsh Affairs to the recognition of Cardiff as Welsh capital in 1955, from Atlee's Welsh Council of 1959 and the 1964 creation of a Welsh Secretary of State in the Cabinet, through to the plans for a devolved assembly in 1979, the government of Wales and the question of devolution were high on the political agenda. Shifts in Welsh politics meant changes for Plaid Cymru. This is an important theme in the story of the party – the way in which Plaid has reacted and reinvented itself in relation to political developments.

Gwynfor Evans's nationalism is a largely straightforward extension and extrapolation of patriotism (defined as love and pride for the nation to which one feels a sense of belonging). He described himself as "a Welsh radical", claiming to have "fallen in love with Wales at the age of sixteen and with the land of Wales especially" which was deepened by journeys and holidays throughout the country. He learnt Welsh as a teenager and described his passionate attraction to the language after being introduced to it through Welsh literature and history.

He was educated at the Universities of Oxford and Wales (Aberystwyth), and joined Plaid Cymru as an Aberystwyth student in June 1934. Evans describes his membership of Plaid as representing "a kind of religious conversion". It could equally be called a lasting love affair. He gives his reason for joining as a belief that "the nationalists had an economic case", formed after reading D.J. Davies's *The Economics of Welsh Self-Government*. Evans identifies Davies and his economic rationale for nationalism as "runner-up" to Saunders Lewis as the main influence for himself and the early Plaid Cymru. Interestingly, many of the other powerful influences on Evans were non-Welsh: G.D.H. Cole and Tawney, for example.

Evans claimed to have no "blinding vision" as party president. Although his immediate predecessor was Abi Williams, Evans's real intellectual inheritance came from Saunders Lewis who led the party for fourteen years from 1926 to 1939. It is the parallels with and departures from Lewis's leadership that reveal the deeper nature of Evans's politics.

His politics were fairly conspicuously to the left of Lewis's. He was a pacifist and religious nonconformist in contrast to the Catholic and ex-serviceman Lewis. Evans was secretary of the Welsh Pacifist Movement during the Second World War and this pacifism coloured his views on the organisation and style of political nationalism in the immediate aftermath of the war.

Evans's politics were driven by a faith in the organicism of society. This became the core of his political vision. An organic approach to politics implies that society functions in the same way as does a living creature. It suggests that the significance of the components of society comes from their contribution to the system as a whole. Thus, the notions of interdependence and functional dependency are instrumental for an organic interpretation of politics. For Evans, the nation was "a basic organic form of society".

Like Lewis, the human being was Evans's starting-point. He preferred the term, 'the individual person', to 'the individual', for each person could achieve the bounds of humanity only through bonding with others, first to form a family, then a community, and finally to assume the ultimate status as a member of a nation. For Evans, this was a natural, organic process that could be hindered only by deliberate sabotage.

The family was a vital element in this process. He regarded the family as the authentic and original natural community: "the structure of society depends more upon this than any other entity within it". This idea of nationhood as representing the best and ultimate form of civilisation enabled Evans to connect the life of the nation with that of the individual. In this way, "Wales must live her own life as a nation so that each member of the community can be himself or herself as fully as possible". Evans saw individual fulfilment as conditional upon the establishment of full nationhood.

A Community of Communities

> Community has a venerable place among Welsh values and the concept is central to nationalist ideology.

Community is another key theme in Evans's politics. The term appears with telling frequency in his writing. In a letter to the *Western Mail* in October 1994, Evans related moves to grant parliamentary self-government to Northern Ireland to Wales's position, employing the vocabulary of community prominently. He used the term to refer to small-scale, collective social relations. Evans was attracted to small-scale organisation and to the ideas of Kohr and Schumacher especially. He saw small as being conducive to close and meaningful social interaction, which itself was a prelude to community. In this way, Wales's physical size was an advantage, since "small nations have a sense of belonging together that huge populations know only when threatened from the outside and this can make possible a greater measure of co-operation and responsibility". So for Evans, decentralisation of power was a prerequisite for democratic nationalism, for "It is in small communities that the individual person counts for most, participating more in community life and having a greater power of fashioning his environment". This was the essential logic of Evans's vision of community politics and is reflected latterly in Plaid Cymru's decision to make local government success a priority.

The nation is the ultimate political manifestation of community. It represents the natural, organic progression from the local community to a higher status. At the same time, the state is the antithesis to community. As an artificial edifice, it could be constructed, destroyed and reconstructed. The nation, however, was: "a unique historical community, the fruit of long historic growth". The nation cannot be renewed: "no resurrection follows the death of a nation". An anti-state focus to Plaid's policies is another of Evans's legacies.

So, for Evans, community symbolised the desirable conditions of nationhood. It was also a metaphorical term which served as a cohesive or binding agent to link the small and disparate geographical areas of Wales. Once again, Evans consciously followed Saunders Lewis in considering Wales 'a community of communities'. It was a useful term, simultaneously implying difference and likeness. That is, it allowed for the different geographical and cultural character of Wales's disparate and distinctive communities to be acknowledged, without undermining the nation as the principal unifying force. In keeping with the organic theme of his writings, to Evans the nation was the sum of its component communities. Without the interaction of communities, a nation cannot exist: "A nation is a community which grows through the interaction of a people, their language and other traditions, and institutions and their land". The term 'community of communities' has since become a frequent one in nationalist analyses of Wales, although it is rarely properly elaborated.

The nation was not the final point in Evans's organic odyssey however. He recognised to the need for international co-operation since such relationships represented an opportunity to for Wales to "join the world". This internationalism was to be based upon a relationship of equals. He chastised "naive cosmopolitanism" which gave the nation-state a false credibility in the international arena by assuming it was the only legitimate political unit. For Evans, imperialism was the antithesis of nationalism for it represented "the extension of the powers of the state over the territory, place and resources of another land". Imperialism's most heinous crime was to elevate the artificial (the state) above the natural unit (the nation).

Freedom was another core idea in Evans's politics. He echoed Saunders Lewis's assertion that freedom, not independence, was the goal for Wales's nationalist party. Lewis had viewed independence as part of the armoury of imperialism: "The age of empires is fast passing, and afterwards there will be no meaning or value in independence". Both Evans and Lewis sought a local dimension to freedom instead. They believed that local involvement enhanced freedom through the expansion of the individual's sense of belonging. This is a further connection of the local with the national, a constant theme in Evans's politics.

History was also important for Evans. The nation was the ultimate, organic community because of its established roots "deep in the past". The natural unit was that which could be traced back in time and which revealed continuing customs and traditions. Thus, "the continuity of the Welsh pattern of values and qualities from pre-Christian times to our own day is a striking testimony to the tough stability and strength of national community". Evans saw the nation as shaped by its shared history. That history was, in turn, determined by the persistence of a national language, Welsh, and a more broadly defined national culture. In seeing the language as the key to the survival of Wales Evans was following his predecessor as president. Language was the most prominent badge of belonging; it represented "the heart of the community": Its importance came from the function of language, not just as a means of daily communication, but also as "the cement which holds together all the generations in the nation's edifice". If community was a unifying force for the nation, then language was the factor which made the nation cohere. The nation's role was to communicate values from generation to generation, a function which Evans saw as "done through the vehicle of the national language".

Evans was also motivated by a belief in the supremacy of the spiritual over the material. He attacked the growing materialism of society, "getting on in the world – getting a good job was the thing that mattered". Evans regretted this increasing emphasis on material values as a yardstick to progress because it meant the human being was little more than an economic unit. In keeping with his organic approach, Evans regarded the individual as a composite of different characteristics, whose ultimate identity and fulfilment were dependent on their wider social position. Materialism was concerned with the human only as an economic entity, which is misleading since "man is neither economic man nor political man, however important economics and politics may be to him. He is a member of many groupings, all of which contribute to the enriching of his personality". The obsession with economic gain at the expense of spiritual progress was inherently damaging since: "man's complex personality is spun into the warp and woof of society, and he cannot be torn out of the society in which he was nurtured without causing him grave injury". For Evans, "Those who rely on the economic arguments, in opposing Welsh freedom, are confusing means with ends", "for man is an essentially social creature, whose humanity and dignity require a place in a fitting cultural environment, at least as much as they require proper economic provision". His faith in Christian values led him to revere the spiritual above the material. Non-material values like co-operation and freedom were the 'natural' principles upon which Welsh society should rest, for they were rooted in Wales's Christian past. His own background is instrumental here: "Christianity did not contribute towards making me a nationalist, but it deepened my nationalism". Thus Evans's conviction that "Welsh nationalism accords with Christianity" conditioned his politics.

It is certainly difficult to locate a thinker as eclectic (and as disarmingly optimistic) as Gwynfor Evans. He absorbed many different influences and was conscious of having inherited various political traditions. Despite this diversity, his starting-points were fundamental commitments to Wales, to pacifism, and to individual and personal liberty. These values were interdependent and moulded Evans's nationalism. Perhaps the most interesting feature of Evans's politics is its combination of conservative and radical elements. A respect for the past, for what is deemed natural and traditional, is merged with a rebellious desire for change and improvement.

Based on what we know of Evans's ideas and influences on him, what was his contribution to the political and electoral development of Plaid Cymru during his presidency? Like Saunders Lewis, Evans regarded electoral contests as a means by which concessions might be gained from the governing party. It should be remembered that in 1945, when Evans took office, there was little serious chance of Plaid Cymru actually winning seats – in general elections at least.

Evans believed that two strategies were followed during his leadership: one was to campaign for Wales in the broadest sense; the other was to gain footholds of power and influence at various levels. He felt these strategies sat comfortably together, and there was little opposition to them from the party membership. This is revealing, for this dual approach appears to bridge the theoretical gap between the roles of pressure group and political party. It is all the more significant if the party leader was aware of this strategy and, indeed, saw its success as one of his main achievements.

Evans has consistently argued that many of the devolved and important recognitions of Wales as a national entity were achieved through Plaid Cymru pressure. Without Plaid Cymru, he claims, "there would have been no Welsh Office, no Secretary of State or the host of national institutions that have developed since the war". He points to concessions like the siting of the new steelworks at Llanwern, near Newport, and the Royal Mint at Llantrisant. He also identifies Plaid's role in introducing legislation to end the treatment of Welsh as a foreign language in the legal system, which had denied citizens the right to give evidence in what might be their first language. These are all examples of Plaid functioning as a pressure group.

There is some truth in these claims, although they are difficult to prove conclusively. Evans claims that it was not until the by-elections of the 1960s that Plaid Cymru began to adapt its pressure group focus which, until then, had conditioned the bulk of its political strategies. The period of Evans's leadership was consequently one of transformation for Plaid Cymru "from an isolated pressure group into an organised political movement with a momentum of its own".[3] However, this is not the whole story, for the tensions underpinning this dual status continued.

In terms of quantifiable progress, a superficial examination of the beginning and end of Evans's presidency suggests that the party made only limited electoral advances during this time. From the start of his term of office in 1945 until its end in 1981, the party's electoral fortunes would appear to have improved only marginally. In the General Election of July 1945, Plaid fought seven constituencies. Its vote across the constituencies averaged 9.1%, with Dr. Gwenan Jones gaining an impressive quarter of the total vote in the University of Wales seat and Gwynfor Evans himself, a creditable (but disappointing in his eyes) 10.3% in Meirionnydd. Even so, it is worth remembering that Saunders Lewis had polled almost 30% of the vote in the University of Wales seat some fourteen years earlier.

In 1981, although the party had two MPs (Dafydd Wigley for Caernarfon and Dafydd Elis Thomas for Meirionnydd Nant Conwy, both elected in the February 1974 General Election), Plaid would appear to have been no closer to achieving its goal of self-government. The referendum on devolution two years earlier had seen a resounding vote against government proposals for a limited form of devolution in Wales.

To say little had changed is misleading, however. Events in between tells us the real picture of the progress made under Evans's presidency.

Plaid's electoral breakthrough came in July 1966 when it gained its first MP. Evans himself won the Carmarthen by-election. The scale of his success in the west Wales seat, with a record swing against the incumbent government was momentous. The reverberations in Welsh politics were lasting. The victory was a watershed for Plaid. It signalled a transformation of its self-image, and also of the way it was perceived by the other parties. Of course, a breakthrough such as this brought with it new pressures. Evans described his immediate concerns upon his election to Parliament: "I was desperately afraid of letting people down". Unprecedented attention was focused on him as Plaid Cymru's first MP.

In some ways, Evans's leadership was unstrategic, in the conventional sense at least. He adapted the party to external events, in the same way that a yachtsperson changes tacks and sails as the wind shifts. Yet, this is not necessarily a criticism; indeed, as we shall see, this approach was repeated by at least one of his successors as party president. However, such a policy has inherent dangers: the dilution of the party's image as a political organisation, for instance, and its diversion into campaigns which might not meet its development needs. Perhaps the best way of describing Evans's political strategy is pragmatic, using events as an operating context for development and refinement.

Later I will look at three significant campaigns – in 1955, to save the north Wales village of Tryweryn from being deliberately flooded to provide water for Merseyside; the campaign for a Parliament for Wales between 1950 and 1956; and in 1981, the fight for S4C, in which Evans himself took centre stage, vowing to fast to death, Ghandi-style, unless the government fulfilled its promise to establish a Welsh language television service. It is interesting that two of the most significant events, the 1966 by-election and the campaign for a Welsh fourth channel saw Evans in the principal role. He was representing both aspects of Plaid Cymru: the electoral and the campaigning.

The party structure inherited by Evans in 1945 was flimsy to say the least. Plaid's finances were parlous and its work was sustained by the enormous contribution of its volunteers. Evans recalls a crisis in 1937, when the party's £350 debt was sufficiently serious to warrant an emergency executive meeting to consider whether the party could actually survive. It was on a political and organisational knife-edge when Evans took over. Although at the end of his leadership, Plaid Cymru had consolidated its internal organisation as well as its finances, it would be wrong to suggest that the party was ever completely securely based. The foundation for the financial revival was the launch and rapid growth of the annual St. David's Day appeal which allowed the expansion of Plaid's campaigning efforts.

The relationship between financial and electoral success is a clear one. Plaid's finances were boosted by its gradually expanding its electoral appeal. Decent performances in the by-elections of the 1960s helped establish the party on a far sounder financial footing as donations increased, allowing the employment of around twenty people in its main office in Cardiff.

In organisational terms, Evans identified the creation of the position of party Chair as one of the most significant innovations during his leadership. Prior to this, the Party President chaired every meeting of the party (including conferences, executives and national councils). The creation of a party Chair relieved the president's workload. Evans felt it enabled him to devote more attention to overall strategy. It also saw the introduction of new, talented individuals who Evans identified as key influences on the party's development, such as Phil Williams, Gwynn Matthews, and later, Siân Edwards and Marc Phillips.

Evans was responsible for a gradual widening and deepening of policy formulation. The party broadened the scope of its policies whilst also elaborating their detail. There could no longer be legitimate criticism of Plaid for having no analysis of the Welsh economic situation and, generally, there was a more rigorous air to policy development. In 1969, some of Plaid's younger members at that time, including Phil Williams and Dafydd Wigley, formed a research group that produced *An Economic Plan For Wales*.[4] The plan was an in-depth study of the state of the Welsh economy and set out objectives for constructing a new national economic strategy. It was significant for, amid national strategies and calls for government action, Plaid was also able to emphasise the central need for political self-government. In this way, Plaid Cymru began to relate its overarching political objective to economic conditions. The *Economic Plan* also reinforced the redirection of Plaid away from the cultural and towards the economic. It was a major contribution to the ideological change that the party underwent in subsequent years.

The very length of Evans's thirty-six year period as president means that a large part of the party's post-war growth happened under his leadership. Yet it is not just the duration of Evans's term of office that distinguishes his presidency. His tenure spanned a number of hugely important changes within the party (and also within Welsh politics more broadly), many of which were instigated or encouraged by Evans himself. He saw his priority as converting Plaid from his rather rudimentary inheritance in 1945 to something more closely resembling a political party. To achieve this aim, Evans pursued a tireless round of public meetings across Wales (he claimed his choice for a family home in Llangadog came from it being a central location from which to travel the country) during which he presented Plaid Cymru as a constant reminder to England that Wales existed. This, he said, was a basic preliminary to "re-igniting the Welsh consciousness".

If these were his objectives as president, Evans can be judged an unqualified success. Yet there remain some questions over his ability in strategic matters. Emyr Williams has argued that Evans's period of leadership marked the reinforcement of a very clearly conservative ideological character for Plaid. He described 'Gwynforism' as a form of "fundamental nationalism", a highly ideological position that could be equated with a "Welsh version of English Toryism". Williams regarded this position as untenable, or at least restricted to sustaining support from the small percentage of the Welsh public which traditionally backed Plaid.[5]

At heart, Evans was an evangelist, refusing to be swayed from his conviction that one day Wales would gain control of its own affairs. Evans was the preacher president, spanning both the early era when this was the norm for the leader of a political party, to a later epoch when leaders were the more pragmatic strategists we see today. It is an achievement in itself that Evans was able to bridge the two roles, most of the time successfully.

Dafydd Wigley, 1981-84

> I suppose I'm a pragmatist. I'm interested in making politics work, as opposed to the doctrinal level.

Dafydd Wigley[6] served as president of Plaid Cymru for two separate periods, between 1981 to 1984, and from 1991 to 2000.[7] He was first elected in a contest with Dafydd Elis Thomas which was portrayed within and outside the party as a left-right battle. This is an oversimplification that distorts a proper understanding of Wigley's own politics and his larger role in the maturing of Plaid Cymru.

Dafydd Wigley was born in Derby in 1943. His family moved back to Wales when he was a small child and his formative childhood years were spent on a farm in Bontnewydd, near Caernarfon, a village where he still lives. Wigley was brought up as a Welsh-speaker by his university-educated parents. He worked for Ford, for Mars as Chief Cost Accountant and became Head of Finance at Hoover in Merthyr Tydfil.

In some aspects his career differs from those of other Plaid leaders. Wigley was a business executive, not a teacher, preacher or lawyer. He was to draw on this background, using his own self-image as dynamic and a 'doer' rather than a talker, to become a quite different leader of the party. However, although in this respect he offered a break with the past of Evans's presidency, his term of office was also a continuation of many of the qualities – broad appeal and a simple passion for Wales – of Evans himself. To bridge the old and the new in a relatively seamless manner was Wigley's greatest feat.

Wigley's first term as president was bound to be difficult. He succeeded a leader who had become a party institution after thirty-six years as president: "one didn't remember anyone but Gwynfor as president". Moreover, Wigley was elected to the leadership in the wake of the devolution referendum vote in 1979 which had been a massive blow to Plaid. The party was struggling to come to terms with the electorate's rejection of even the mildest form of devolution: "The morale of Wales as a nation, and Plaid Cymru as a party, was at rock-bottom".

The damage of the referendum defeat was marked and lasting. Later, Wigley's own successor to the presidency, Dafydd Elis Thomas, suggested that the "legacy of 1979" remained a defining feature for him some six years afterwards. Wigley saw his first term as president as coinciding with "an uncomfortable time" when "there was a kind of nihilism surrounding the party". This reawakened some of the more "fundamentalist", "theological" positions that had threatened the party's development at other critical points in its history. As he said, "If things go wrong, people look for extremities, not the middle way".

The context for his leadership was scarcely ideal. Whilst Wigley's first term as leader, in the wake of the 1979 vote, was always unlikely to bring Plaid the fast fix of electoral success it coveted, it did lay further foundations for extending Plaid's appeal, most importantly beyond its traditional heartlands. Interestingly, some thirty-six years after Evans took office with a similar goal, Wigley's self-defined task as president was "to re-engender pride in the nation". In doing this, he built on some of the foundations laid by Evans himself. Continuity is thus a feature and an aim of the leadership of Plaid under both Evans and Wigley.

Wigley was certainly no great ideologue, in the sense of possessing a grand intellectual and political rationale. He described himself as "a pragmatic radical", claiming "I never pretended to be a political philosopher... I leave that to Dafydd El". Of the three party presidents considered here, it is certainly hardest to tease out Wigley's intellectual influences. That is not to suggest, however, that no larger philosophy conditioned his politics. However, pragmatism was the driving force for many of Wigley's leadership decisions: "I was influenced by what I saw in communities". His political consciousness was informed by practical experience – his own and those of others in the party. Thus the experiences of slate quarry workers and farmers in his own Arfon teenage years played a defining role, as did, later, disability politics and the experiences of rural and urban poverty.

His politics were also informed by broader ideas such as the European idea of Wales within a confederation of self-governing nations. He also proved unafraid to stand apart from popular opinion. Wigley's position on the EEC Referendum in 1975 is a case in point. Whilst Plaid campaigned against UK membership, Wigley argued in favour.[8] He identified himself as primarily an egalitarian and a republican, as well as a supporter of the main principles of socialism. Like Evans, Wigley also drew on the 'small is beautiful' philosophies of Kohr and Schumacher, to argue for decentralisation of power and governmental functions, although he was quick to point out that, as a management accountant, he felt unable to use the concept "in its entirety".

Although not deliberate, it may well be that Wigley's shunning of doctrine and ideology assisted the development of the image he sought for the party. Throughout his first term as president, Wigley was able to represent the image Plaid Cymru had always strived to convey, to the electorate and to its own members. He presented himself as a compassionate, honest, articulate, all-Wales leader, with popular appeal across the different linguistic, socio-economic, geographic and cultural divides. The advantages of this for Plaid, which was perceived as a minority party, were enormous. The image was cultivated and enhanced by Wigley's public and media appearances. By the time of the first National Assembly elections, he was widely seen as one of the most popular politicians in any party, consistently receiving the highest levels of support of all four party leaders in Wales in opinion polls. There is a sense in which the lack of a powerful ideological basis to Wigley's politics may have contributed to his appeal.

Wigley saw his role as president "to hold Plaid Cymru together and to try to rebuild the party as relevant at a very difficult time". Measured against this aim, he was a relative success. Of course, the expectations of the wider party were greater. Not only did it need to recover from the disappointment of 1979, it had also to prove its lasting role in Welsh politics in the wake of the rejection of the mildest form of devolution.

It is true that Wigley's first term as president hardly glittered with tangible electoral or political success, but perhaps the party could only hope for a period of consolidation rather than breakthrough. Much of the party's energies were spent on internal matters, none more important than efforts to revive a bruised and battered membership in the aftermath of 1979. Despite a brave attempt at relocating the party's campaigning efforts by the internal Commission of Inquiry which reported in 1981, the strategy for developing a more robust and extended appeal had to wait until egos had been massaged and spirits rekindled. The pace of Plaid Cymru's development as a political party during Wigley's first term as president was understandably slow.

In one way, it is inappropriate to offer a judgement on the legacy of Wigley's first term as president as it was curtailed by tragic personal reasons.[9] He conceded that the experience of this enormous emotional trauma made it impossible for him to devote the necessary attention to leading the party at the time. Plaid's involvement in the coal dispute in 1984-85 brought this home to him: "I was very aware of the need to campaign much harder in the miners' strike. I was conscious of being unable to give the necessary time to the strike efforts".

At the very least, Wigley's first stint as president laid the foundations for later Plaid successes: his greatest achievement was in providing groundwork for subsequent advances. He succeeded in dragging the party out of collective depression and demoralised morass following the devolution referendum. The job may not have been anywhere near completion on his handing over to Dafydd Elis Thomas in 1984, but Wigley can, none the less, be credited with lifting some of the mists of depression and instilling a degree of confidence and belief amongst its membership that Plaid Cymru retained an important role in Welsh politics. His recognition that expansion beyond the party's heartlands was a requirement of future success, forced the party to think seriously about how it might broaden its appeal.

Fundamental to this and to his later achievements was Wigley's undisputed ability to bridge many of the different communities in Wales: linguistic, geographical and socio-economic. Over his two periods as president, his personal appeal broadened and, with it, that of Plaid

Cymru. Of all the party's post-war leaders, Wigley was the most straight-forwardly unifying.

Dafydd Elis Thomas, 1984-91

I've got the best record in the party of being right ten years too soon!

Dafydd Elis Thomas[10] was elected president of Plaid Cymru in 1984 in a straight contest with Dafydd Iwan, another Gwynedd-based politician. However, the two candidate's personal images and ideas for the party's future could hardly have differed more. Iwan was a former chair of *Cymdeithas yr Iaith Gymraeg* (the Welsh Language Society) and was seen to represent the 'traditionalist' wing of the party. Thomas was portrayed as a left-winger with radical ideas for broadening the party's base. This meant the presidential election was again seen as a left-right battle and Thomas's subsequent victory seen to reflect the ascendancy of the left in Plaid Cymru. This is a simplistic interpretation of the two politicians which reveals less about them than about the splits within Plaid at this time.

Although in purely electoral terms it is difficult to disagree with Thomas's own assessment that "there was no success" for Plaid during his presidency, he was at its head during one of the more interesting periods in it's modern history. Thomas was driven by a desire to reinvent Plaid. He was responsible for encouraging and stimulating many key strategic debates. Put simply, he wanted to make the party rethink its role in Welsh, British and European politics. The party's focus was certainly not fully redirected under Thomas, but he did push it towards a new identity and a different role in Welsh politics.

Thomas regarded the party as unready for his brand of leadership, though I suggest instead that his attempts to change Plaid were never likely to be accepted wholesale. They were controversial precisely because they were different. The extent of Thomas's influence on the maturing of the party can be measured by the way the party mirrored some of Thomas's own identity shifts. In 1984, Plaid Cymru was a party caught between identities; its electoral base in north west Wales was relatively secure and founded on a rather straightforward correlation between the traditional components of Welsh identity (cultural, linguistic and political) and Plaid as the party most likely to represent them. However, to achieve its wider objectives, Plaid needed not only to broaden its appeal beyond this identification with things traditionally

Welsh, but also to secure electoral footholds in the Labour-voting south. This was a challenge that Thomas took up with relish: "I was primarily concerned with broadening the base of the party... I was motivated by the idea of Plaid not being a *nationalist* party but a *national* one" (my italics).

In political terms, Thomas is something of a chameleon, changing priority, focus and identity across different periods of his political career: "I am always positioning myself in relation to some trend that I believe to be happening in society or intellectual thinking... perhaps I do that a bit publicly!" From Marxist ideologue on the picket line to Peer in the House of Lords, there is no doubting Thomas's capacity for sizeable and significant shifts in political perspective and priorities. That is not necessarily to attack his politics; it can equally be portrayed as an indication of his ability to understand different political contexts and to mould strategies accordingly. That is certainly how Thomas himself has rationalised his political career.

The influences on Thomas's own politics are hardly archetypically Welsh, nor are there that many overlaps with his two immediate predecessors as president, Wigley and Evans. Thomas's intellectual inspirations came more from sources outside Wales than they did from indigenous ones. During his presidency, Thomas's reputation within the wider British Left was greatly enhanced. He embraced this with enthusiasm, and for part of his leadership was arguably more popular outside Plaid Cymru than with his own party members.

His predilection for the whole gamut of New Left politics and the construction of a new profile for himself helped shift Plaid Cymru from the margins of the British political scene to a far more central and respected position. Against the backdrop of a strident Thatcher government and a stumbling Labour opposition, Thomas was able to offer Plaid Cymru as a refreshing, overtly socialist alternative to the Welsh electorate: "I had certain ideas about politics in Wales... within the context of the New Left". That is not to say this shift translated neatly into electoral support for Plaid, though it did ease the path for the relocation of the party in relation to Labour in particular.

Within Plaid Cymru, Thomas was instrumental in solidifying the left of centre perception of the party's image and substance. And he was an enthusiastic supporter of further substantive changes in this direction. He spoke of the need to tighten up the policy profile of the party to ensure that it was offering the electorate a realistic and rigorous operational portfolio of commitments. He also supported moves before and during his presidency to acknowledge and confirm Plaid Cymru as a socialist party with a commitment to 'decentralist socialist' objectives on its member-ship card and in its constitution. Later, as Presiding Officer of the National Assembly for Wales, Thomas reiterated the importance of these debates during the 1980s: "I think it's an important argument in Plaid Cymru and it hasn't finished yet".

Thomas helped form the 'National Left' group in Plaid Cymru, as well as playing a prominent part in the debate on full and equal representation for women. He contributed regularly to a new quarterly magazine, *Radical Wales*, launched in 1983, which was financed and edited by Plaid Cymru. *Radical Wales* reflected the wider mood, exploring Welsh issues from a simultaneous socialist and nationalist perspective (the magazine was relaunched without Plaid Cymru support in 2000 in the new context of post-devolution Wales). It was in a *Radical Wales* review of Hywel Davies's monograph on the first twenty years of Plaid Cymru's history that Thomas made his now famous declaration: "I will never let anyone get away with calling me a 'nationalist' and I will never call myself that, if I ever did". Thomas defended his remark nearly twenty years later, "I always stuck by that... I could never turn around and say I'm a nationalist – ever, because the word is so badly misused...it's a word you can't recover".

This conviction that misuse of the term nationalist had rendered it almost unusable in any positive sense meant that Thomas focused on alternative definitions of Plaid Cymru's politics. He was desperate to rid the party of many of the ideas of 'statist' nationalism, the ideological form which is preconditioned by the need for a state apparatus. He "was interested in the reinvigoration of Wales as a European nation, not a nation-state". This is an instance of overlap with his presidential prede-cessors. The debate is far from over. Thomas remains a strong supporter of advancing the constitutional debate within Plaid. He argued that fixed or finite statements of Plaid's constitutional position were ill-advised, since a constitutional blueprint which was not contextual and thus time-related was just not feasible. What was right for Wales at one point might well be completely wrong in the future, an argument I will address in chapter five.

There were further shifts to be reconciled at the end of Thomas's pres-idency: the conventional socialist persona's later conversions to Quango chief (as chair of the Welsh Language Board from 1993) and peer (and later, Presiding Officer of the National Assembly for Wales). His justifi-cation (in the face of much party opposition) for accepting a life peerage in 1992 was that the House of Lords was merely an extension of the institutional representation in the British state which Plaid already had. He argued much later that his underlying strategy had been "to remove all the oxygen of cultural nationalism" from the party to help it to further political advances. That is, he saw his membership of the House of Lords as part of a strategy for underlining the relevance to Plaid of its participation in *all* UK institutions, with the principal objective of gaining concessions for political nationalism. He conceded that "this was not understood by the party, that was a big disappointment". That is an understatement: many of his former allies on the left of the party vowed they would never forgive him for this 'act of betrayal and treachery'.

Thomas describes his presidency as signalling the pursuit of a "developmental" or "gradualist" strategy for changing the party. He recognised that there could be no single, simultaneously out-reaching and inclusive solution to Plaid Cymru's needs. Thus, his strategy was to relocate Plaid Cymru within the Welsh, British and European political arenas. As well as suiting his own priorities as a politician, he recognised that this had to be a long-term project.

Although aware of the conservatism of a large part of Plaid's membership, Thomas hoped for more than an incremental advance towards his goal. This was probably unrealistic; partial progress in this ambitious project was always more likely to be the outcome of Thomas's presidency, especially given his own admission that "I wasn't very good at explaining what the strategy was".

In any case, there are many facets to such a strategy. It is interesting, for example, that Thomas was amongst the first backers for the original idea in the mid 1980s to change the party's name to "Plaid Cymru The Party of Wales", an attempt to reinvent and popularise the party which was to bring considerable success when adopted formally in 1998 and used in the Assembly election campaign of 1999. Thomas recalled the original proposal as being hugely unpopular with many of the party's members at the time. It may be another example of setting an agenda which the rest of the party was not quite ready to follow.

In the context of his presidency, the second term of a Thatcher government and continuing reverberations from the rejection of devolution, Thomas was keen to avoid a 'cataclysmic' analysis of political events and solutions. He supported moves to relocate and redefine the party's strategy to achieve a government for Wales. He later conceded that the Plaid Cymru Commission of Inquiry (which, at the time, he subjected to a highly critical attack[11]) that had reassessed many aspects of Plaid internal organisation and management, together with its external strategies for political progress, was an important part of this: it helped "to digest the 1979 experience". Drawing on the ideas of Raymond Williams, Thomas argued that political situations did not change substantially; hence there was a need for constant reformulation and redefinition, rather than whole-sale abandonment or change. This has interesting reverberations for some of the themes developed later in the book.

Thomas was also a driving force in the new, heightened European focus of the party. He saw the European elections of 1984, and then in 1989, as a crucial means of bypassing Plaid's difficulties in challenging at Westminster general elections: they were "a way of breaking out of the morass of UK politics". The added appeal of Europe at this time was that it offered an arena in which Plaid Cymru's nationalism could sit more easily. There were progressive nationalist and regionalist groups within Europe which offered far more amenable bedfellows, and the elections also allowed access to an arena within which the normality and legiti-macy of the quest for self-government could be emphasised. No wonder this appealed to Thomas, who recalled his campaign for the North Wales seat in the European elections of 1989 as being one of the happiest elec-tion contests for him personally. Europe was clearly the place where Thomas felt most at home.

A further source of Thomas's strategies came from New Left politics. They provided another arena in which he felt comfortable, perhaps rather more so than in the limited one of Welsh nationalism. The Thatcher years were an era where movements or pressure groups were often seen as more attractive, flexible and radical than political parties. Such bodies were also enjoying a period of some growth and influence within the policy-making field for Plaid. Thomas recognised that "movement poli-tics was to become an increasing political focus" and embraced it enthusiastically. He describes the opportunities at the start of his presi-dency to take new ideas forward by a positive effort to include some of the new groups in the fields of environmental, peace and women's issues in particular: "I was keen to turn things back to the national question through developing the social movements and class politics that were emerging during the Thatcher period".

Thomas's own links with many of these organisations meant that, for the first time in its history, Plaid Cymru was the most popular political option for the feminist, environmental, gay, socialist and generally radical elements in Wales. Thomas can take much of the credit for this, for his image was of a radical, inclusive, alternative politician who sought the construction of the new Wales on quite different foundations.

There is a certain irony here though. Later, Thomas was to eschew this pressure group or campaigning role for Plaid Cymru, criticising Plaid's attempt to appeal simultaneously as a pressure group and a political party: "I think it's [Plaid] got to give up the former role (as a pressure group) now... It's not fair on people – the electors". This signals another shift in Thomas's priorities. Later still, Thomas advocated a different role for politicians to pressure group activists. The priority for Plaid at the beginning of the twenty-first century was the "opening up of political institutions". As we shall see, Plaid has shown some reluctance to adopt a straightforward political party role. It is ironic then, that it was during the Thomas presidency that the pressure group role of Plaid was at its most developed. Of course, the two roles need not be contradictory; indeed, they may well be complimentary. Even more significant is the fact that Thomas, of all the post-war presidents, was best equipped to develop and enhance this pressure group role. Thomas admitted: "What I didn't address sufficiently throughout all that was the reaction of, as it were, the nationalist members – whatever you call them – to that project, who had another view... of the national question".

Dafydd Elis Thomas is a pivotal figure in Plaid Cymru's post-war development. His principal legacy was to launch a new epoch in the location of Plaid Cymru as a credible left of centre political force. Like his predecessors, he laid further foundations for Plaid's subsequent maturing. Thomas differs in that this involved uprooting some of the work of Wigley and Evans.

Thomas's own verdict was that he was guilty of "trying to do too much" as president. His efforts were certainly spread thinly as he attended rallies, marches, and campaign meetings for a plethora of organisations aside from Plaid Cymru. He was pulled in many different and, at times, contradictory directions as a result of his enthusiasm for the range of New Left ideas at this time. Whilst he himself felt that "the party failed to understand the strategy" for broadening its appeal, it is a fairer appraisal that he was insufficiently focused in structuring this new strategy. That is, a more staged and partial approach to broadening Plaid's appeal might have worked better than the all-embracing one Thomas pursued. He concedes he "antagonised lots of people through my way of doing it". However, there is also a question mark over whether he was the right person to pioneer this shift: "Some people think I'm a bad manager because I don't persuade people of change, but I try to show the change and then demand it".

There were no great successes electorally under Thomas, but neither were there any disastrous failures. Thomas's presidency laid foundations for future breakthroughs, particularly the successful alliance between Plaid Cymru and the Wales Green Party which saw Plaid's Cynog Dafis elected as MP for Ceredigion in the 1992 General Election. It was also to see Plaid's Ieuan Wyn Jones capture Ynys Môn at the 1987 General Election.

Thomas's own interpretation of his presidency is exactly thus; the ideas and embryonic strategies for progress that he started were taken up by others subsequently and contributed in no small measure to the party's later successes (hence "I was right ten years too soon!"). Also in his own words, "I wanted two terms as president not one". A second term might conceivably have shifted the party further to the left. Yet, his successor, the returning Dafydd Wigley, proved capable and committed to this identity for Plaid Cymru and, if anything, Wigley's methods and style were more widely acceptable than Thomas's.

One of Thomas's most important legacies was to open up Plaid Cymru, both its membership and its ideas, to a wider audience than ever before. Much of the scepticism about nationalism's association with socialism was diluted through Thomas's emergence as one of the doyens of the British Left which was bristling with indignation at some of the more strident activities of Prime Minister Thatcher: "In other institutions, I was seen as representing the majority view". Events like the Falklands War and the Miners' Strike added grist to the mill and Thomas quickly became a key voice in the British Left's alliance against Thatcher (he agrees that he had more success in persuading outsiders of Plaid's relevance than he did party members). The overspill of Thomas's reputation was a simultaneous mainstreaming of Plaid Cymru.

That Thomas was clearly more successful in convincing those outside Plaid of his ideas for Wales than he was within the party begs the question of whether, with his British Left credentials, he was the best person to push this strategy to reinvent Plaid. There are two possible answers. First, it needed someone with his intellectual vision and undoubted charisma to convince the party of the priority for change. The second suggests that what was also needed was a more conciliatory figure to carry the diverse and often conservative local Plaid membership with it.

Nevertheless, there is essentially a symbiotic relationship between the public image of Plaid Cymru and the view taken by its membership. The party's external image as a left of centre party particularly, came from its relocation in the wider public mind and an adjustment of the party's own members to this role. Thomas may not have succeeded in bringing about the fundamental reinvention of Plaid that he desired, but his period as president at least forced the party itself, the other political parties and the media in Wales and Britain, to reassess their views of Plaid Cymru. That, in itself, was no mean feat and will probably count as Dafydd Elis Thomas's greatest legacy.

Dafydd Wigley, 1991-2000

Dafydd Wigley returned as party president for the second time in 1991, and the period until his resignation in 2000 was to signal one of the fastest periods of growth in Plaid's modern history. As its most successful electoral era, the 1990s offer another dimension to the story of Plaid Cymru's development as a political party.

Watching Thomas lead the party after 1984 was difficult for Wigley. There is no doubt he was unsuited for a place on the sidelines. He was party vice chair in charge of elections for some of the period and thus a member of the *Pwyllgor Gwaith*, but was clearly frustrated at not being in charge. This period was an exasperating one for Wigley: "I became more and more frustrated... so much so, I seriously considered a career outside politics". Wigley recalled being 'headhunted' for several senior jobs in the public and voluntary sectors in Wales. The source of his frustration was that he "didn't believe the party was addressing issues of concern or campaigning on them". A more detached appraisal might say that, under Dafydd Elis Thomas, Plaid Cymru was not campaigning in the way Wigley understood political campaigning, but more on that later.

The start of his second term as president required "some rebuilding work to be done", in particular the reconstruction of those who had been out of favour under Thomas. His assessment was based less on antipathy to Thomas's strategies for broadening the party than on his methods and intellectual style.

The basis for Wigley's presidential strategy in 1991 was to make the breakthrough the party had long sought in the south Wales valleys: "it had to be based on taking votes from Labour". This marks another point of departure from his predecessor. Although firmly on the left himself, Thomas was realistic about where Plaid votes came from. He was quite happy to see Plaid Cymru adopting the role as alternative choice for any disaffected voters, Labour, Conservative and Liberal Democrat. Wigley saw the way forward for Plaid as challenging, and then replacing, Labour in its heartland areas of south and northeast Wales.

Wigley's second term witnessed a more dramatic spurt of growth from Plaid, especially in the electoral sense. The 1992 General Election saw the party capture Ceredigion with a joint Plaid/Wales Green Party candidate, Cynog Dafis. However, Plaid's strategy for fighting this General Election had been based on the assumption of a Labour victory. The Conservative win meant there was no route for any measure of devolution and the subsequent context in which Plaid had to operate was not at all what it had expected.

One of the greatest achievements of his second presidency was the party's growth at local government level. Wigley oversaw a rapid spurt in the number of Plaid Cymru councillors on Wales's local authorities. It began to emerge as a real challenger to Labour hegemony in the south particularly. In 1991, the party had entered into a ruling coalition with the Liberal Democrat and Independent members of Taf Ely Borough Council in south Wales. This was Plaid's first real test of government since a difficult period in charge of Merthyr Tydfil Borough Council in 1976, during which the party had been exposed for its inexperience and naivetë. At the 1979 General Election, Plaid was subsequently swamped in Merthyr by a massive Labour turnout, some felt in retaliation at Plaid's temerity in wresting control of the local council. The Plaid leaders of Taf Ely, Councillor Janet Davies (now also an AM) and Clayton Jones, her deputy, were a little more streetwise than their Merthyr counterparts: "we had to show Plaid Cymru councillors could govern. We had to deliver to the local people".

In the first elections to the new unitary authorities in 1995, Plaid made its first, and some would say long overdue, breakthrough in Gwynedd, the area where it could already boast three MPs. Plaid took control of Gwynedd County Council and retained it in the next elections in 1999. That year, Plaid also won control of two valleys authorities, Rhondda Cynon Taf (the unitary structure which absorbed Taf Ely, Rhondda and Cynon Valley), and Caerffili. Both councils were located in the traditional heartlands of Labour support. These gains, coming on the same day as successes for Plaid in the first National Assembly elections represented a significant breakthrough in the party's challenge in electoral politics. It was now a real threat to Labour throughout Wales, not just in the Welsh-speaking north and west. By 1999, Plaid held 206 seats on the new unitary authorities and controlled three local councils. Wigley saw the benefits of "strong leadership at a local level" in Plaid's gains, but also harboured doubts that "local government control would sweep us through to success at other electoral levels". However, these gains confirmed and strengthened Wigley's strategies for a valleys breakthrough. He was frustrated "at the unwillingness of Plaid Cymru to put resources into organising... in the valleys". He saw the absence of a field worker in the valleys as a major obstacle to the party making earlier advances there. The party had always been ambiguous about balancing its efforts in the valleys with the need to consolidate in seats it already held like Ceredigion and Ynys Môn.

The European sphere remained central, with Wigley following his presidential predecessor as candidate for the North Wales seat in the Euro elections of 1994. This candidacy was part of a wider strategy to make Plaid Cymru the second largest party in Wales. The North Wales seat spanned Plaid's Gwynedd heartlands as well as the English-speaking northeast. Wigley believes the European campaign "laid the ground for breakthroughs later in the 1990s" in the eastern and less-Welsh speaking areas of Clwyd especially. The 1994 European elections saw the party's vote increase to over 17% of the Welsh total, despite proving insufficient to provide Plaid with its first MEP. However, in 1999, Plaid captured 29.6% of the vote and gained its first two MEPs.

The 1997 General Election saw a continuation of its strategy and in the face of massive Labour swings, Plaid managed to hold its four seats, whilst the Conservative Party lost all six Welsh MPs. Retaining its MPs was "essential to maintain [Plaid's] profile as the second party – however defined".

The election of a Labour Government in 1997 brought a fresh political context and challenge. Wigley's period in charge of the party had occurred entirely under Conservative governments. Facing a New Labour administration which had its own constitutional agenda posed different problems for Plaid Cymru, especially as Labour pushed ahead with its plans for a Welsh Assembly. In the subsequent devolution referendum in September 1997, Wigley was forced to play a relatively low-key role in the 'Yes' campaign: "It wasn't a natural one for me to take, not taking a leading role". It was, however, a bid to both disassociate the devolution measures from the nationalist agenda of Plaid Cymru, and on the latter's part to "flush out Labour people to defend their own policy and to work for it". The experiences of the first referendum in 1979 were central in all of this. It is to Wigley's credit (and the party's) that Plaid members carried out plenty of groundwork without its leader assuming a prominent role in the all-party Yes for Wales campaign. He may have been disgruntled about his lack of involvement, but his discipline in keeping a low profile shows another side of Dafydd Wigley.

The first elections to the National Assembly signalled Plaid Cymru's 'coming of age'. Wigley's leadership of the party and his broader popular appeal was a critical component in Plaid's success.[12] Campaigning is Wigley's forte and the first 'Welsh general election' offered the perfect opportunity for him to impress: "I like to be out there barnstorming".

Dafydd Wigley's leadership was a significant factor in the electoral achievements of the party in the 1990s. He handed over a far more successful, modern organisation to his successor as president, Ieuan Wyn Jones, the AM and MP for Ynys Môn, in August 2000.

Wigley was a charismatic leader. He enjoyed a high popularity amongst the Plaid membership and, as importantly, amongst the wider electorate. However, his direct (and, at times, abrasive) style gained him enemies too, especially within the smaller band of Plaid activists. Some deemed him headstrong and unstrategic in his management of the party and saw his leadership as energetic but undirected. This was to be a popular criticism levelled at him during the first twelve months of the National Assembly's operation. One Plaid AM described Wigley's leadership in the Assembly as "lacking a clear strategic direction which would have helped us form a constructive opposition to Labour". Not surprisingly, Wigley disputes this: "I would question that without doubt".

Wigley's special strength lay in his wider motivational qualities and few would dispute the value of these to Plaid Cymru during his periods as president. He also showed an underlying understanding of the need for a clear strategy to advance the party, at least in the electoral arena: "I favoured a step by step approach, but there was always an awareness that the train goes further than the next station".

Wigley often spoke of the primacy of establishing a strong local government base as the foundation upon which to build success at other electoral levels: "it is an experience which is practical and confidence-building for the party". He was also committed to advancing the party in the southern, English-speaking areas: "the aim has to be to drive a wedge into support for the Labour party in Wales". The eventual successes in prising Rhondda, Islwyn and Llanelli from Labour in the Assembly elections are testament to the earlier, preparatory work.

Wigley's problem was essentially the same one his predecessors as president had faced; how to introduce and manage a strategy that suited the south when competing pressures were constantly being made from within its heartland areas to speak to their distinctive needs and to ensure further electoral advances there. This is an unresolved dilemma. Despite claims to the contrary (" I had little complaints from Arfon, other than on matters of emphasis"), as a representative of one of its heartland areas, Wigley was drawn in at least two directions. This, more than anything, accounts for the criticisms of lack of direction and focus in the party's strategy during Wigley's presidency. Against this, it must be remembered that Wigley presided over the most successful electoral period in the party's history and he played a pivotal role as leader in these achievements.

Looking at the hallmarks of each president's term of office helps explain the nature of the party's growth. In marking out some key individuals and related events in Plaid Cymru's modern history, the foundations are laid for the interpretations of the party's development in the chapters that follow.

The present chapter has also introduced what will prove to be one of the book's principal themes – the significance and influence of personalities in each stage in Plaid Cymru's growth, and the relative malleability of the party. It is not all about party presidents, either. Similar influences have been exerted by certain groups within the party membership itself, as we shall see.

In the light of considerable changes in focus, the relative cohesion and internal harmony that characterise the party throughout its modern history are quite remarkable. This is another important theme in the maturing of Plaid Cymru.

Notes

1. Information included in this table is compiled from a range of party reports, records and receipts.
2. This part of the chapter is based on a series of interviews conducted with each party president. I am grateful for each's frank and helpful co-operation with this chapter especially. Unless otherwise specified, all quotes in this section come from these interviews with Gwynfor Evans, in October 1991, April 1992, September 1996 and November 2000.
3. Butt Philip, A., *The Welsh Question, Nationalism in Welsh Politics, 1945-1970,* (University of Wales Press, 1975).
4. Plaid Cymru Research Group, *Economic Plan for Wales,* (Plaid Cymru, 1969).
5. Emyr Wynn Williams, interview, June 1998.
6. All quotes in this section come from interviews with Dafydd Wigley in 1992, 1994, and August 1998, when he was party president, and in January 2001 after he had relinquished the post.
7. The party president was elected for a two-year term.
8. This is covered in more detail in chapter five.
9. The Wigleys' two young sons, Alun and Geraint, died in 1984. They had been suffering from a rare genetic condition.
10. All quotes in this section come from interviews with Dafydd Elis Thomas, in 1991, 1994, 1995 and in November 2000 when Thomas was Presiding Officer at the National Assembly for Wales.
11. See Williams, E.W. & Thomas D.E., "Commissioning National Liberation", *Bulletin of Scottish Politics,* (1981).
12. See McAllister, L., 'Plaid Cymru's Coming of Age?', *Contemporary Wales,* vol. 14, 2001.

TWO

4. The Electoral Perspective

Its work as a pressure group would alone justify Plaid Cymru's existence[1]

Plaid Cymru is only part of the nationalist movement, and is that part which is most constrained to a moderate course. The reward for such restraint should be in electoral success.[2]

These two statements about Plaid Cymru's status were made at almost the same time and give some indication of the debate inside the party as to its proper role in Welsh politics.

This chapter offers an electoral perspective on Plaid Cymru's development in its consideration and contrasting of Plaid's participation in elections and non-electoral campaigns. This exploration of its status helps identify the characteristics that explain the nature of the organisation and, in turn, decides how best to describe Plaid Cymru: as a conventional political party, as a pressure group, as part of a broader movement, or as an organisation containing elements of all three.

There are two possible answers to the question, what is Plaid Cymru? The first says Plaid Cymru is a political party, like Labour, the Conservatives or the Liberal Democrats; the second response is that Plaid has some characteristics of a political party, some of a pressure group and some of a constituent part of a broader movement. These potential answers emphasise the essential problem of identity: for much of the post-war period, Plaid Cymru itself could not decide what it was, or what it should be. The gradual clarification and emerging consensus as to its status mark important stages in the party's development.

This review of Plaid Cymru's involvement in some of the landmark elections and non-electoral campaigns since 1945 does not just give clues as to its status; it also questions the suitability of some of its strategies and priorities. These are related themes: to what extent is an ambiguity of status reflected in Plaid Cymru's strategies for Wales? Have strategic choices about the activities pursued forced Plaid to behave simultaneously as both party and pressure group?

We can judge Plaid Cymru against the core characteristics of political parties and of pressure groups. Matching Plaid against these criteria helps us first, to understand the priorities it has given to elections and campaigns at different points in its history, and then to explore shifts in its strategy.

Identifying a Political Party

What makes a party different to other political organisations? In *British Political Parties*[3], Ball posits three general characteristics that distinguish political parties: definition; function; organisation.

The political party is an institution central to representative democracy. The origins of parties in Britain lay in the growing complexity of the political system, emerging in the seventeenth century from the Whig/Tory divide after the Reform Acts of 1832 and 1867 which widened the electoral franchise. The growth of a party system was seen as a direct reflection of the division of political society into mass and elite; political parties were the means by which the new, expanded political mass could express its interests and concerns. Modern parties are the agencies which represent the masses. They combine aims, values and methods in a vision of how society should operate. They attract members and voters on the basis of this vision.

As politics developed, so too did the nature and organisation of politics itself. Today, political parties are seen as "powerful organizations that seek to monopolise mediation between the governed and those who govern". Organisations that were formerly loosely structured "are managed with a view to winning and exercising political power".[4]

On this basis, we may define a political party as a component of representative democracy which: has a recognised degree of permanence; contests elections and seeks to place its members in positions of influence in the legislature; occupies executive positions within the political system, such as in the cabinet, or exercises influence on those occupying such offices by virtue of its position in the legislature; has a distinctive vision which distinguishes it from other political groupings.[5]

The second characteristic of a political party is function, or role. Ball regarded the four main functions of a political party to be: representative; electoral; governing; policy-formulating. Meny & Knapp, in *Government and Politics in Western Europe* agree, listing the functions as: office-holding; policy-making; communication; integration of constituent organs.[6] Other commentators, however, offer an alternative group of functions: integration and mobilisation; influencing voting patterns;

recruitment of political personnel; elaboration of policies.[7]

There is some overlap between these classifications and, taken as a whole, they help identify a party's typical functions within a political system.

The way in which a political party is structured or organised reveals much about its status. Writing in the early 1950s, Duverger explored parties within Western political systems on the basis of their organisation. His main distinction (between 'cadre' and 'mass' parties) is shaped by structure, not size.[8] Thirty years later, Ball argued that a party must have a degree of permanence, or continuity; that is, the organisation of a party must be sustainable beyond the life span of its leadership.

The organisation of a party should also have a formal structure and a clear programme designed to achieve specific political objectives. A party has members locally, as well as a central leadership, all of whom are committed to the party's defined aims. It should also have a distinctive vision which separates it from others, and should meet regularly to facilitate consultation and improve relations between members and leaders.

Identifying a Pressure Group

Parties and pressure groups perform different but complementary functions. Whilst most bodies in a political system are established to further or protect one interest or more, the term 'interest' or 'pressure' group refers specifically to those organisations which promote a particular interest, but do not aspire to take power or control government. Pressure groups are "unlike parties in that they rarely stand for office and have no aspirations to form a government. They do not put forward candidates at elections and they do not seek to exercise power directly".[9] A pressure group is distinctive in that it interacts with the various institutions of the political system to influence public policy, ultimately to achieve its interests or ends.

Some commentators distinguish between parties and pressure groups by focusing on the difference between interest aggregation by the former, and interest articulation by the latter. Thus, parties gather various concerns and try to represent them. Pressure groups, meanwhile, articulate specific issues and lobby other agencies to act upon them.[10] Thus, parties aggregate interests in their quest to gain power, whilst pressure groups speak for different sectors sharing the same goal in an attempt to influence the holders of power.

Yet for all these distinctions, the two organisations sometimes perform similar functions in the political process. The key factor is power. According to Ball's framework, a party aims to occupy power positions, or influence those who are already in power. This is important for it broadens the definition of the role of a political party and helps explain the regular duplication of some of the functions of parties and pressure groups.

More or Less a Political Party?

Whilst it is possible to test Plaid Cymru against these characteristics, it is worth remembering that the inclusion of a nationalist party within this framework is, by definition, problematic. Its *raison d'être* is often not to control the existing structure, but rather to gain power for its own territorial unit, the nation, within or outside that system. Traditional understandings of nationalism have been based on the idea of the nation and the state becoming coterminous. This often involves challenges to the existing state and an attempt to replace it with a new and separate one. However, Plaid Cymru has never sought to form a government at Westminster, an impossibility when it can realistically contest only forty seats. Instead it has campaigned for the election of Plaid Cymru MPs in order to influence the agenda there in Wales's favour. Gwynfor Evans talked about a very specific rationale: "by fighting every Parliamentary by-election in the first half of the sixties and by contesting local elections on an increasing scale, Plaid Cymru at least made it impossible for the English parties to forget Wales". It is legitimate to ask whether this is the role of a pressure group or a political party.

Throughout its history, Plaid has been aware of the need to define its role within Welsh politics. In 1970, it warned: "Plaid Cymru must realise that a political party, seeking a popular mandate, cannot act as an umbrella for every nationalist faction. Plaid Cymru is only part of the nationalist movement, and is that part which is most constrained to a moderate course".[11] Subsequent shifts in the party's status reflect important developments in its political strategy. Gwynfor Evans argued that: "Plaid Cymru has been more than a party and more than a movement". Others, like Phil Williams, former party chair, emphasised: "The distinction is important: a pressure group is dedicated to specific aims and seeks to achieve those aims by influencing the people who hold power; a political party seeks to hold power itself". Dafydd Williams, former party general secretary, described Plaid Cymru as "at one and the same time a national movement, a political party and a pressure group for Wales".

Others have suggested that the best way forward for Plaid was "to start being a real political party, developing and promoting its ideology and programme". There is some disagreement as to whether the party's electoral success since 1966 had encouraged it to tone down its campaigning activities to the party's detriment; some claimed it signalled a 'maturing' of Plaid, whilst others saw it as a lost opportunity to recruit a different kind of activist to the party fold.

Tension over the status and role of Plaid reached its peak during the 1960s and 1970s. However, the issue was not fully resolved then, and there remains a certain ambivalence about its status amongst Plaid's members and leaders. Yet, such tensions about status are not uncommon amongst nationalist parties. Just as the rather indeterminate, amorphous origins of Plaid Cymru in 1925 are unexceptional for newly formed political parties, particularly nationalist ones, it is also true that most nationalist parties fail to fit a definitive check-list of criteria for either political party or pressure group. This is because nationalism cannot be codified simply in terms of electoral success, for the desire for national self-government is multi-faceted. Organising a variety of campaigns to gain additional support for the ultimate political goal of a Welsh government has been as crucial as winning seats on elected bodies.

"Nevertheless a small organised party persisted in thinking Welsh, in putting Wales first in politics and in actively seeking the conditions which would make possible a continued national identity" recorded Gwynfor Evans[12]. Plaid's leaders were aware of the need to elaborate its status as a political party from the start: "the hour had come to change the [economic and social] system".[13] But this awareness was not matched with a will to formalise a political programme for the new party. The issue is by no means resolved in the modern party, which has regularly revisited this debate on its status and role within Welsh politics. The advent of the National Assembly was the greatest modern stimulus for breaking the cycle:

> ... in the context of the Assembly, Plaid Cymru will have a different existence from the party of protest which has existed in the House of Commons – and so, yes, we will be a new party.[14]

Given the size and resources of the party in its early years, it is no wonder that many regarded the prospect of electoral success as optimistic. Yet, as I recorded earlier, Plaid adopted some of the characteristics of a political party from its very inception. However, there was always a sense in which it had to act principally as a pressure group, exerting indirect influence on the holders of power.

In 1962, Harri Webb, the editor of the party's newspaper, *Welsh Nation*, criticised Gwynfor Evans's comment that Plaid Cymru was "a powerful catalyst" within Welsh and British politics pointing out: "This is consistent with an overall strategy... which sees the party as still principally a pressure group, exerting indirect rather than direct influence on the processes of political power".[15]

In the same paper, thirteen years later, it was suggested that, for Plaid to act as a political party, it required a definite philosophy or ideology. To be a movement, its perspective could operate "across boundaries". The argument was made that, in promoting 'a world order', Plaid was at this time behaving as a movement.[16] The significance of this lay in its implications for Plaid Cymru's operation. For example, as a movement, Plaid could eschew policy; as a political party, a coherent ideology and a broad base of policies were required.

Of course, it is possible to argue that the role of nationalist parties is to influence other political parties to support national autonomy. Essentially, this is a pressure group function, although the mechanics of influencing can involve electoral challenges and the provision of a detailed political programme, making the relationship more complicated than it might first seem. Several of Plaid's leaders, including party chief executive Karl Davies, reinforced the importance of the new context ushered in by devolution, suggesting that it emphasised that, until its first real national campaign in the General Election of 1959 and its first electoral success in 1966, Plaid was a pressure group "that just happened to put up candidates for election". The traditional context of Westminster, with Plaid inevitably marginalised, had encouraged the party to sustain a parallel campaigning character which was as significant as its electoral identity.

Members' motivations for joining Plaid throw further light on the party's status. When questioned for my research, many cited concern for the Welsh language as the main reason, whilst others identified specific areas of Plaid policy such as the party's commitment to unilateral nuclear disarmament. Some women claimed the party was more genuinely supportive of women's rights than the others and that this was the main attraction. However, easily the most frequent response was Plaid's status as the sole nationalist party, seeking recognition for Wales encouraged them to join. These replies reinforce Plaid's simultaneous appeal as a party and a pressure group. They also point to some of the problems Plaid faced by trying to fulfil the two roles successfully.

We are now in a position to judge whether Plaid Cymru fits Ball's four defining characteristics of a political party. His first requirement was for a party to have a permanent organisation. We have already seen that Plaid Cymru has a national organisation that is now stable, albeit habitually limited by financial constraints. It also possesses a local structure based on the *Cangen*, or branch. The *Cangen* network has remained relatively static with around 150 branches in 1945, approximately 100 official branches in 1985, 180 in 1992, and around 220 in 1999.

Party membership has grown, with an official 6,050 in 1945, around 7,000 in 1992, 10,000 in 1995 and 16,000 in 1999, although different ways of recording branch membership numbers make these figures a little misleading.[17] There has been an incremental growth in the party's organisation with more national and local office bases and extra paid staff. These additions reflect Plaid's adoption of more of the characteristics of a political party.

Secondly, the political party must "contest elections" and aim "to place its members in positions of influence in the legislature". Since the 1945 General Election, at which it contested just seven seats, Plaid Cymru has made significant and quantifiable advances in its electoral interventions. It has fought every Welsh constituency since 1970, despite the consistent loss of deposits in the southeast and northeast. The party has renewed its emphasis on local government elections, particularly since the 1960s when local politics were seen as a way of heightening the relevance and profile of the party in all parts of Wales, as well as providing a foothold for success at other levels. The number of elected councillors in all forms has risen. Also, since the first direct elections to the European Parliament in 1979, Plaid Cymru has contested each of Wales's four seats (five since 1994).

This second part of Ball's conditions poses more problems than the first. A nationalist party like Plaid Cymru is unlikely to seek places in the legislature of the state whose legitimacy it rejects. Yet there is evidence that Plaid has fulfilled part of this criterion too, with Dafydd Wigley's appointment as a Privy Councillor and Dafydd Elis Thomas's acceptance of a peerage the clearest illustrations.

It is the third of Ball's characteristics that causes most difficulty. A political party needs either to "occupy executive positions" or "to exercise influence on those occupying such offices". It is impossible for Plaid Cymru to fulfil the first part of this requirement within the bounds of the dominant state, the United Kingdom. However, the establishment of the

National Assembly, bringing a measure of devolution to Wales, gives Plaid the opportunity to do precisely that. Yet, there have always been instances when Plaid Cymru has tried to "exert influence". Along with its "assertions of policies of self-government, there are attempts to extract limited concessions from the government", according to Lees and Kimber.[18]

Ball's final characteristic is the need for a party to own "a distinctive label which distinguishes it from other political groupings". In both British and Welsh contexts, Plaid Cymru satisfies this condition. Its constitutional commitment to full national status within the European Union distinguishes Plaid Cymru from the other parties competing for votes. It has consciously located itself outside the mainstream of party politics, projecting itself as the only guarantor of Welsh interests. This brought considerable rewards in the first elections to the National Assembly.

Thus, Plaid Cymru appears to fit most of Ball's criteria for a political party. Add to this Lees and Kimber's definition of political party as seeking "to influence the workings of the political system", and it is fair to say that Plaid has behaved as a conventional political party since 1945 – maybe even earlier. However, a survey of the party's campaigning activities shows that the question of Plaid's status is by no means solved.

Plaid Cymru's Campaigning Record

Plaid Cymru's participation in single-issue and broad-based campaigns gives us further important clues as to the party's own perception of its status, its motivations (what stimulates its leaders and members), and its broader impact on the political scene.

Plaid Cymru has been a remarkably successful campaign machine. In its approach and commitment to the campaigns that I discuss here, Plaid shows an uncomplicated enthusiasm for this kind of political activity. Indeed, in some instances, one suspects that this is where the party has felt most comfortable. The reasons for this are evident in the factors which distinguish campaigns from elections. There is more freedom of choice in campaigns. That is, the timing, the choice of campaign and the level of resources devoted to it are not fixed in the same way as elections. Campaigns often involve higher and deeper levels of commitment by the participants throughout their duration. They often inspire greater emotional input. Campaigns straddle the divide between politicians and the public. They may even be perceived as having more direct relevance to the lives of people than an election to choose a political representative.

I have chosen four important campaigns which Plaid has led, or in which it took a prominent role. The context of each is vital, reflecting the pressures and priorities of a particular political era in Plaid's development. The four campaigns are the Parliament for Wales Campaign between 1950 and 1956; Tryweryn (1955-1959); Welsh language campaigns; the Anti-Poll Tax campaign of 1990-1992.

*

No single group, other than Plaid Cymru gave the campaign staunch support...[19]

The active workers in the campaign for a Welsh Parliament were almost without exception nationalists.[20]

It was a Plaid Cymru effort.[21]

The Parliament for Wales Campaign was launched in July 1950 at Llandrindod Wells to lobby for a "Parliament with adequate legislative authority in Welsh affairs".[22] Its clear constitutional focus marks it out from the other campaigns considered here. However powerful the feelings are for constitutional change, there is always less of a spark associated with such efforts than with those campaigns with economic or material motivations.

The Parliament for Wales Campaign (PWC) modelled itself on the Scottish Covenant which had collected nearly two million signatures in support of a Scottish Parliament. The principal strategy of PWC was the collection of signatures for a similar petition to the Westminster Parliament which would demonstrate the depth of support in Wales for a form of self-government. The eventual petition was impressive, containing some 240,000 signatures, around 14% of the electorate, according to the *Western Mail*. The presentation of the petition followed the defeat of a private member's 'Parliament for Wales' bill, drafted by the eminent constitutional lawyer, Dewi Watcyn Powell, and introduced by S.O. Davies, the Labour MP for Merthyr Tydfil in 1955.

Organisationally, PWC floundered from the start and was only rescued from financial ruin by the appointment of Elwyn Roberts as its organiser in 1953. Roberts was Plaid's Gwynedd organiser and a local councillor. He would later become general secretary of the party. Roberts is rightly credited with the organisational modernisation of Plaid in the late 1960s. He proved equally valuable to the Parliament for Wales Campaign.

Despite the large number of signatures collected, the campaign failed to mobilise widespread popular support. Politically, it was damaged by the nature of its support. Apart from Plaid Cymru, there was only a luke-warm engagement by the other political parties in Wales. The campaign's influence on the Conservative Government or the Labour Opposition was thus marginal. Despite this lack of cross-party support, Plaid claimed that the Parliament for Wales Campaign reawakened national consciousness and "helped plant the idea of a Welsh Parliament in the public mind for the first time this century".[23] However, the slow progress by which Wales gained even minimal devolution subsequently would suggest that it was going to take rather more than the Parliament for Wales Campaign to kindle a more sustainable form of national consciousness.

Yet, the Campaign was a significant factor in Plaid's development. First, it motivated it to expand its electoral work. The president, Gwynfor Evans, saw the Campaign as having stimulated a new period of growth for the party. In the 1955 General Election, Plaid fought eleven seats and gained 11.3% of the vote in these constituencies. In 1959, Plaid managed an average of 4,000 votes (10.3%) in the twenty seats it fought. Evans attributed this growth directly to Plaid's involvement in the Campaign for a Welsh Parliament.

In truth, the impact of the campaign on Plaid's development was less straightforward; involving itself in a broad, cross-party campaign offered another strategic dimension to Plaid's activities at a crucial time. It also helped promote some key Plaid politicians to positions of greater prominence, including Dr. Gwenan Jones, Elwyn Roberts and Gwynfor Evans himself.

It also underlined the difficulties inherent in cross-party campaigning, and led indirectly to a clearer electoral focus to the party's work. Plaid had undertaken much of the campaigning work, yet its efforts had been largely ignored by the Westminster Parliament. This called into question the value of this kind of campaigning. In some respects, the Parliament for Wales Campaign was a precursor for events in 1979 which saw Plaid closely involved in the devolution referendum campaign when it took much of the subsequent blame for the failure to secure a pro-devolution majority in the referendum.

*

It [the flooding of Tryweryn] hammered home the fact that one of the richest Welsh natural resources was being exploited without benefit to the Welsh people and that this was possible because of the nation's complete lack of political freedom.[24]

The campaign against a plan by the Liverpool Corporation to flood part of the valley of Tryweryn in Meirionnydd, in the heart of rural, Welsh-speaking north Wales ranks as one of the most significant post-war issues for Plaid Cymru. The project to create a new reservoir to provide water to Merseyside dominated Plaid Cymru's agenda between 1955 and 1962. After some skilful gerrymandering tactics whereby the scheme was sold to the Commons through a private bill sponsored by Liverpool City Council, the views of the local authorities in Wales and of the Welsh MPs (the majority of whom opposed the plan) could be ignored. The bill passed its third reading in the Commons with 175 MPs voting for the measure and 79 against: "The Welsh national community had never been more united, but even a united Wales was powerless".[25]

Events at Tryweryn were hugely symbolic. It was a notable *cause célèbre* for it offered a powerful and dramatic example of Wales's impotence. Despite virtually unanimous opposition from the people and politicians of Wales, the valley was drowned and with it a significant part of Welsh life. Little wonder then that Tryweryn was seen as the perfect illustration of the marginal position of Wales in the existing British system "Plaid Cymru lost the fight. The valley was drowned, the community scattered, the water seized. Nevertheless, the campaign was seminal".[26]

Most importantly, Tryweryn encapsulated the dilemma facing Plaid at this time – how to marry electoral strategies with the kind of direct protest that was firmly entrenched in the party's history. Tryweryn sparked memories of the burning of the Bombing School at Penyberth in 1936, an episode which had revitalised Plaid Cymru at the time. Yet, memories of that campaign (and the folklore which surrounded it) against the establishment of a Bombing School on a site less than forty miles from Tryweryn, also proved a millstone for the party's campaigning efforts over Tryweryn: "One could nearly claim that a number of Plaid Cymru members...were suffering from what may be called 'Penyberthitis', namely the simplistic belief that only through having a new version of the Penyberth action every twenty years or so would it be possible to maintain the momentum of Welsh nationalism".[27]

Tryweryn was different to Penyberth in many different respects. The most important factor was the point in Plaid's development at which it occurred. The ambivalence felt by some within Plaid's leadership at the time of Tryweryn emphasises the dilemma of the emerging political party. There was an acknowledgement that the nature of any campaigning activity on Tryweryn should reflect the fact that Plaid was by now "a growing political party".[28] Little wonder that Tryweryn sparked such debate. By now Plaid was starting to act as a political party and it had to marry this with its traditional campaigning role. There was a feeling that Penyberth, for all its symbolism and emotional reverberations, had not signalled any substantive electoral breakthrough for Plaid Cymru. Again, this is significant for it suggests that, by the 1960s, Plaid was beginning to regard campaigns as mechanisms for pursuing its political objectives, particularly self-government. That is, campaigns were not evaluated just in their own right, but as means to the party's end.

That said, Plaid still led the campaign against the drowning of Tryweryn and mobilised the public, the political community, including fifteen of Wales's local authorities, and the press, including the *Western Mail,* in opposition to Liverpool's plans. This saw Plaid engage in most of the traditional campaign activities including rallies, letters to the press, petitions and lobbies. In the event it was to no avail, but Plaid's involvement tells us something about the party. It clearly had huge emotional symbolism: "Some of the present leaders of Plaid Cymru have said that it was the Tryweryn campaign that awakened their national spirit".[29] One of these was the future party president, Dafydd Wigley, who identified Tryweryn as one of the factors that spurred him to a more active role in Plaid Cymru: "It [Tryweryn] showed how a community could be totally incapable of defending itself. Liverpool had its own way regardless. The Westminster Parliament overruled all local opposition".[30]

The campaign clearly helped recruit some important new members to Plaid, but not necessarily large numbers. According to the party's Annual Report, recruitment actually fell. The number joining in 1964 was around two-thirds of the figure in 1960. Neither did the party's campaigning efforts translate directly into electoral support. Mindful of Penyberth and the party's subsequent public image, Plaid deliberately chose not to adopt unconstitutional or direct action in its campaigning methods, instead opting for a constitutional position. Given that the rewards for this were not immediately felt, members could be forgiven for thinking that the party had effectively fallen between two stools in its campaign strategy. Supporters of direct action saw it as weak-willed or indecisive, while advocates of its firmly constitutionalist position did not gain immediate electoral reward.

The party president, Gwynfor Evans, clearly understood this: "echoes of the campaign are still heard; some of its consequences still remain". Yet, the General Election of 1959 did see Plaid field candidates in twenty constituencies, almost double the number it had in 1955 and in stark contrast to the five (of 71) seats fought by the SNP in Scotland. This increased activity reflected the boost that Tryweryn had given Plaid's more conventional political work. Just as the contribution of J.E. Jones had proved crucial during the Tryweryn campaign, the efforts of the party's next general secretary, Emrys Roberts, proved as crucial to the party's development as those of any political leader in Plaid's history. Roberts added a modernising zeal to the party, organising the party to enable it to expand its electoral and campaigning work.

However, the difficulties of marrying electoral and non-electoral strategies, or at least of expecting healthy dividends from the latter, were highlighted in a hugely disappointing result for Gwynfor Evans in 1959 as the party's candidate in Meirionnydd where Plaid expected to benefit from its work to save Tryweryn. Evans admitted "the Tryweryn campaign did not significantly strengthen the national party in Merioneth, where I was the Plaid Cymru candidate".[31] It is also interesting that he recalled no ambivalence in the leadership's commitment to the twin-pronged strategy of fighting elections and campaigning for Tryweryn.

Tryweryn's significance for Plaid is that it articulated a latent debate about its appropriate political status and proved a cross-roads for the party's campaigning methods. It also forced Plaid to confront the issues surrounding direct action, as well as extended electoral involvement.

*

> While I sit here in comfort, over fifty young Welsh people are in prisons in England and in Wales... because of their attachment to their country and language... They are a small number from a splendid host of the nation's youth who have suffered imprisonment for its sake during the last few years. There is a new spirit afoot in the land.[32]

The author of these words, Gwynfor Evans, recalled that, as a schoolboy, he had argued in a chapel debate for the use of the English language. It was not until he was sixteen, that Evans "fell in love with Welsh history, language and literature". This love affair was to shape both his and his party's approach to political campaigning.

> Most people think of language as a means of communication and no more. Communication is of course its main function, but it is far more than that. It is the vehicle of the nation's culture, the medium through which the nation's values have been, and continue to be, transmitted, the treasury of the nation's experiences and memories, the mind and memory of the nation.[33]

Language is a vital component of national identity. A language as old as Welsh with an associated cultural and social heritage has been an essential component in Welsh identity and its preservation and promotion a crucial part of the party's aims. Plaid Cymru and support for the preservation and advance of the Welsh language have gone hand in hand for most of the party's life: "the success and furtherance of this Welsh concept depends on the Welsh language... The government of Wales must be Welsh in spirit and language".[34] This simple link makes Plaid unique within the scheme of United Kingdom politics, and the language issue has been central to Plaid's perception of itself, as well as how others have viewed it.

The relationships between Plaid and the principal groups campaigning for the language throw further light on how its pressure group and political party roles relate. The formation of the leading language pressure group, *Cymdeithas yr Iaith Gymraeg* (The Welsh Language Society) in 1962 was in response to Saunders Lewis's 'Fate of the Language' radio lecture, which predicted the death of the language without urgent intervention: "If present tendencies continue, Welsh will have ceased to be a spoken language by the beginning of the twenty-first century". The creation of a separate language pressure group presented Plaid with the opportunity to scale down its own campaigns for the language and develop more fully other policies related to the goal of self-government. Concentrating on a more strictly economic focus was widely recognised as a vital next stage in Plaid's development. Thus, Dafydd Wigley acknowledged that: "The formation of *Cymdeithas yr Iaith Gymraeg* facilitated the organisation of a separate political/economic perspective [for Plaid] as language issues were then organised separately".[35] Even Gwynfor Evans stated "...although the language has been a great source of strength to the party, its electoral progress would certainly have been more rapid if it had abandoned the language fight".[36]

Plaid's involvement in campaigns to protect and support the Welsh language encapsulates many of the fundamental tensions within the party's growth. One of these concerns the balance between linguistic motivations for joining Plaid and support for its non-cultural aims. This issue has plagued Plaid, as well as proving a primary source of criticism levelled at it by its political opponents. In addition to the national opinion polls, Plaid's most detailed, professional market research conducted in 1998[37] pointed to its continued close association with the language in the public eye. This spurred the party to address once more in the long-standing challenge of balancing this appeal with one to the majority non-Welsh speakers.

Relevance is the watchword of the discussion of language campaigning and Plaid Cymru. The stance of one of Plaid's former MPs, Cynog Dafis AM, is instructive. He dropped out of active involvement with Plaid in the mid 1960s to immerse himself in the activities of *Cymdeithas yr Iaith Gymraeg*, becoming its chair for part of that decade. The reason he gave was the greater relevance to the nationalist movement of *Cymdeithas* at this time. His switch drew attention to the relative relevance of Plaid Cymru's political contribution at this time: "It was clear in the early 1960s that Plaid's electoral strategy was taking us nowhere".[38] Dafis re-engaged with party politics with Plaid after 1979.

The formation of *Cymdeithas* did not signal the end of Plaid's engagement with language campaigns however. It continued to campaign for parity between the Welsh and English languages. After 1979, around 2,000 Plaid members withheld their television licence fees in protest at a refusal to expand Welsh language broadcasting. Three senior party members, Ned Thomas, Meredydd Evans and Pennar Davies, pursued their own direct action, breaking into the control room of the Pencarreg Mountain television mast and switching off its power.

However, easily the most significant single action in the Welsh language campaigns was Gwynfor Evans's threat to fast to death unless Margaret Thatcher's Conservative Government upheld its promise to establish a Welsh language television service by concentrating Welsh programming at peak viewing times on the new fourth television channel: "The national party's low morale ... convinced me that I would have to take some costly personal action to help restore its spirit... I decided that the action would be a fast which would continue indefinitely unless the government restored its Welsh channel policy".[39] Evans announced in May 1980 that he would fast, Ghandi-like, unless the government kept to its promise when Parliament reassembled in October: "I have said that if Mr. Whitelaw [the Home Secretary] does not keep his word by October 6th I shall start fasting on that day, and will continue to fast until the Government redeems its promise".

The drama and emotional intensity of Evans's threatened fast was a major boost to the party. Here was one of Wales's most senior and charismatic politicians threatening to die for the language: "It is they [the Welsh people] who will decide, through their action or inaction whether the rich civilisation of Wales is to be transmitted or not to future generations. Welshmen make Welsh history".[40] The government eventually yielded to

popular pressure, announcing on 17 September 1980 that a Welsh channel, *Sianel Pedwar Cymru* (S4C), would be established.

What did this mean for Plaid Cymru? Evans claimed: "The case for
Welsh national freedom was given unprecedented publicity in the wake
of the fight for an adequate Welsh television service".[41] That is not
entirely the case. Certainly, there was significant media coverage of
Evans's threat and the saga of the government's response to it, but crucially, this did not relate to a broader justification of Plaid's political
objective of Welsh autonomy. The fourth channel campaign was a language protest with the specific representations of national identity that
this normally entails.

Thus, it would be misleading to call it a success for political nationalism. It clearly proved the strength of both Plaid Cymru and *Cymdeithas
yr Iaith Gymraeg* as campaigning forces, but what it also did was relocate
Plaid Cymru once again at the centre of campaigns for the Welsh language. In so doing, it boosted the linguistic and cultural focus of Welsh
nationalism and validated many members' belief that a campaigning role
was the most appropriate and effective one for Plaid to follow.

There was also a degree of discomfort within Plaid's membership at
the time, among those who wished the party to concentrate on the economic case for self-government. Dafydd Elis Thomas later described the
S4C campaign as prolonging a form of "linguistic chauvinism" within
Plaid, which slowed down its progress as a political party.[42]

By 1999, its former chair Cynog Dafis claimed he "was absolutely
convinced that *Cymdeithas yr Iaith Gymraeg* is an irrelevance now in
terms of the language. The language movement hasn't been able to
reconstruct itself, it does not have a sufficiently sound analysis of social
issues or political trends... it is caught in a no-man's land, being not one
thing or another".[43]

Again, context is vital. There have been many policy developments
which have protected the language by legislative initiatives, such as the
weak Welsh Language Act of 1967, the establishment of a new Quango,
the Welsh Language Board, in 1993, the Welsh Language Education
Committee and the Welsh Language Act of 1993. This new legal protection for the language freed Plaid to concentrate on other matters similar
to the way the formation of *Cymdeithas* had previously.

Essentially what is at question here is the continued uncertainty about
the compatibility of Plaid's profile as a doughty campaigner for the language and its appeal to the wider Welsh population, the large majority of

whom are not Welsh-speakers. This, in turn, relates to Plaid's need to construct an image different to its traditional one as defender of the language. Plaid's success as a credible political party has always depended on it expanding beyond this inherited, but limited, constituency. Actually breaking out has proved far more difficult. As Peter Keelan has said,

> It [Plaid] doesn't relate to cultural politics, say in terms of the language, directly enough to material issues, economic issues and so on. It tends to treat them all as disparate areas with very little connection between them.[44]

At the end of the twentieth century, Plaid had made tangible progress towards this breakthrough but had by no means resolved all of the tensions that have been identified here. Cynog Dafis is right to say that "...if the debate is to be sufficiently muscular and not sentimentalised, it's perfectly possible to marry a commitment to the language and a bilingual Wales with increased support for Plaid Cymru". However, the party does not appear to have found the best way of achieving this.

*

One of the leaders of Plaid Cymru's campaign against the Poll Tax, Peter Keelan described it as "*the* crux issue for Plaid in the early 1990s". Introducing a Poll Tax to replace domestic rates was Margaret Thatcher's grand scheme to transfer responsibility for raising revenue on to individual citizens in each local authority area. Thatcher saw it as a way of linking in the public mind errant, Labour-run councils with high levels of spending. The Poll Tax, or 'Community Charge' as it was officially known, was a way of identifying responsibility, and thus of increasing accountability. It was introduced in 1990 and gave Plaid the perfect opportunity to resurrect its campaigns focus.

By 1990, Plaid had grown into a party committed to fighting elections at all levels. It won a creditable 12.9% in the 1989 European Elections and gained its third MP, Ieuan Wyn Jones, for the Ynys Môn seat in the 1987 General Election. However, electoral breakthroughs had been slow in coming and there was a mood of relative frustration at the pace of progress. There was also a groundswell of opinion amongst the party membership that it needed to enhance its radical credentials by offering the kind of challenge to the more strident Conservative initiatives that a Labour Party led by Neil Kinnock was unable to do. The introduction of the Poll Tax was thus a gilt-edged opportunity for Plaid: "...it was the best way forward strategically and electorally... the party was doing next to nothing in terms of political campaigning as opposed to electoral campaigning... and there seemed to be a general lack of direction about how to take the party forward. We saw the Poll Tax campaign as an obvious way of taking the party forward".

Again, the Poll Tax campaign should be located against others fought during the last quarter of the century, for example, the television licence non-payment campaign which was then overshadowed by Gwynfor Evans's planned fast over the fourth television channel, and the hugely successful campaign against the proposed American radar base at St. David's in Pembrokeshire in 1990.

Most significant among the other campaigns was the water rates campaign of 1982-83. Plaid focused on the public outrage felt in Wales over the higher water rates paid by Welsh consumers compared with those charged in England. Plaid's campaign of civil disobedience included withholding payments. Officially it ended in February 1983, but the repercussions continued long after. Many non-payers faced court cases and Plaid's opponents used its involvement in the campaign to challenge its legitimacy as a democratic political party.

This experience was at the front of the party's mind when it considered its strategy to resist the Poll Tax. There were obvious parallels: the option of non-payment and the issue of the imposition of an unfair policy by the English on a powerless Wales. The severe criticism by its political opponents of its support for 'illegal action' certainly accounts for the initial reluctance of some of the leadership to go down the non-payment path.

Peter Keelan suggests this was used as an excuse to avoid a direct action campaign: "Within the party hierarchy, it was seen as a problem because it wasn't directly related to electoral politics, and I think that was a problem of lack of vision amongst a lot of the senior party, especially the MPs". The suggestion was that Plaid had become wedded to electoral strategies to the exclusion of all else.

The stakes were clearly high. In the face of a Thatcher government and a weak Labour opposition, Plaid tried to establish itself up as the guardian of Wales's poorest people, who were facing a regressive tax which took no account of ability to pay. This was in stark contrast to the stance of a Labour Party enthusiastically toning down its radical image as part of an attempt to capture the middle ground in the 1992 General Election. The theme of Plaid's opposition to the Poll Tax was 'no mandate', asserting that the Conservative Government had no democratic authority in Wales with its small group of Welsh MPs.

> There are many many different ways of fighting the Poll Tax, and it is a cause that unites the vast majority of the people of Wales. There is a place for everybody in this struggle, there is something that everybody can do.[45]

The universality of Siân Edwards's argument was accepted by Plaid Cymru when it set up a Poll Tax Group to organise a campaign of "mass frustration in which all its members can take part". Learning lessons from Scotland, where the tax had been introduced a year earlier, and the actions of its political ally, the SNP, the Plaid campaign initially set up 'committees of one hundred' which would be deliberately composed of people who were in circumstances which would make enforcement orders difficult. However, the campaign soon developed a momentum of its own (especially as there was widespread anger at the tax and Plaid was alone amongst the main Welsh parties in taking this non-payment line) and the Poll Tax Group was forced to set up several different committees and help groups to offer advice and support to a whole range of individuals (inside and outside the party) who were unable or unwilling to pay the tax. The campaign built upon the party's strength in local government, with several Plaid councillors refusing to pay their bills. Geraint Davies (later AM for the Rhondda) was one of these and the Labour-run council swiftly sent bailiffs to his family home.

That the three Plaid MPs decided to stop short of refusing to pay was revealing too. It indicates some of the tensions within the party between its emerging role as a conventional political party and its chequered past as a radical campaigning force. Dafydd Wigley (who was president) was the only MP from the party's three at this time to vote in favour of the MPs' involvement in the non-payment campaign. He recalled his willingness to join in the campaign, but claimed to have been outvoted by his two parliamentary colleagues, Dafydd Elis Thomas and Ieuan Wyn Jones. This may well have been the outcome of their final deliberations, but it was also the case that all three MPs had been equivocal from the start about the legitimacy and advisability of the non-payment element of the campaign. The leaders of the Poll Tax campaign were aware of this ambivalence: "The split... or difference of opinion was between the MPs and certain councillors who thought it wasn't a legitimate campaign for the party to be involved in, for it wasn't directly related to electoral politics and it may jeopardise that later on..."

Keelan interpreted this as a failure to effectively coalesce the twin roles of party and pressure group. He claimed that the campaign offered the chance for Plaid to enhance its radical focus whilst also gaining electoral advantage, and blamed the party leadership, particularly its MPs, for failing to recognise the strategic opportunities presented by the Poll Tax. Keelan subsequently withdrew from a prominent role in the party, partly in frustration at the timidity of the party over the Poll Tax.

By now, the run-up to the 1992 General Election was dominating the party's plans and Plaid was well aware that Labour would use its non-payment stance as a way of associating the party with illegal behaviour, painting it as an unsuitable constitutional choice for the electorate (many local Plaid activists claimed Rhondda MP, Allan Rogers, was still trying to smear Plaid for non-payers in difficulty with the local authority some four years after the campaign was concluded).

> Possibly the success that the party has achieved in elections... has acted as a spur... but as a fetter as well, to campaign only in certain ways and there may well be a contradiction between those – that success requires campaigning in different ways outside of elections and that now is being ruled out..[46]

In the Poll Tax campaign particularly, there is evidence of a crossover between electoral success for Plaid and its campaign efforts. In Ceredigion, the campaign added value and weight to the alliance that had been established between Plaid Cymru and the Wales Green Party. Cynog Dafis, who was later elected MP for the constituency, said: "The Poll Tax campaign in Ceredigion was really very important. That was part of the sort of 'get real' business in Plaid's development".[47]

In the final analysis, the Poll Tax destroyed itself, helped by mass public protests on a scale not seen for some time: "The campaign against the Poll Tax won its greatest victory to date in helping topple Thatcher from her perch".[48] It was a public policy disaster, introduced with no consultation and ignoring expert advice as to inherent problems of collection and cost. It contributed to the downfall of Margaret Thatcher as leader of the Conservative Party and Prime Minister, and a humiliating climbdown by her party. The legislation was eventually repealed and the Poll Tax was replaced with the Council Tax, a property based system of collecting local revenue.

The Poll Tax campaign tells us a number of things about Plaid Cymru's position in Welsh politics at the beginning of the 1990s. First, the party still appeared ambivalent about the most appropriate course to follow – elections or campaigns. It was undecided as to the wisdom of direct or quasi-illegal actions (like non-payment), largely for fear of the damage this would do to its reputation as a mainstream political party.

The campaign forced the party to ask itself serious questions, particularly whether it was an appropriate one for a party with three MPs and a tranche of councillors across Wales's local authorities. There were real concerns that Plaid involvement in such campaigns might threaten its future electoral success. However, the Poll Tax campaign also enhanced Plaid's credentials as a party prepared to fight for all people in Wales.

Plaid Cymru's Electoral Record

Elections are the normal terrain for political parties; in Ball's definition of a political party, contesting elections is a key criterion. In conventional terms, election performance is the primary measurement for the current status and progress of a political party. Historically, Plaid Cymru has approached the electoral arena with some scepticism. At its beginning, the party was ambivalent about contesting elections. For its first five years, it took the Sinn Fèin position of refusal to take up seats in Westminster. Though that policy was abandoned, it was not until after the war that Plaid made a concerted effort to fight more seats and to widen its appeal to gain more votes. Unsurprisingly, this change in strategy took some time to reap rewards.

The defining characteristics of Plaid's incursions into the electoral arena during the period 1945 to 1999, the peaks and troughs of its election performances, tell us a good deal about the party. Plaid began the new post-war era well, gaining a quarter of the vote in Caernarfon Boroughs and finishing second to the Liberals. It followed this with impressive results in by-elections in the southern valleys, gaining 16.2% at Neath and, in 1946, almost a third of the votes in Ogmore and a fifth of the total at Aberdare.

In the general elections before 1966, Plaid averaged 3.2% of the vote, showing some growth from the pre-war years. More importantly, the party started to contest more seats: in 1959, twenty candidates stood; in 1964, twenty-three although this slipped back to twenty in 1966.

1959 – a new beginning?

The 1959 General Election is a hugely significant peak on the graph – "There is a tendency now for people to believe that all good things started after July 1966, but... many of the changes had already started"[49] – of Plaid Cymru's electoral performance. Phil Williams called 1959 the "real turning-point for Plaid Cymru". Twenty candidates (more than half of Wales's total) averaged 4,000 votes and gained 78,000 votes (10.3% of the total) across Wales. The real breakthrough of 1959 was that Plaid gained respectable polls in south-eastern constituencies in Wales, as well as in the Welsh-speaking north and west. Its twenty candidates stood in every county of Wales except Brecon and Radnorshire. This cross-Wales strategy enabled Plaid to argue that it could no longer be called a 'fringe' party. Nor could it continue to act as a pressure group. Williams again: "As soon as Plaid started fighting elections and occasionally winning a sizeable share of the vote, then its role as an effective pressure group was coming to an end". Acceptance of this was a crucial step towards the party contesting all of the then thirty-six Welsh Parliamentary seats.

However, it is not the case that "between 1959 and 1966 Plaid had been totally transformed into a political party", as Williams claimed. The party was involved in campaigns at the same time, sometimes expending more of its resources and energies on them than on elections. 1959 was the beginning of a long transformation for Plaid Cymru. It is better described as "the period when Plaid Cymru was truly gathering its strength for the breakthrough that was to come".[50] The importance of 1959 is precisely that it marked the *beginning* of Plaid's transformation into a party firmly focused on electoral goals.

Table 1: Plaid Cymru's General Election Performance, 1945-1999			
General Election	No. of Plaid Candidates	No. of Plaid MPs Elected	% of Vote Gained by Plaid
1945	7	0	1.1
1950	7	0	1.2
1951	4	0	0.7
1955	11	0	3.2
1959	20	0	5.2
1964	23	0	4.8
1966	20	0	4.3
1970	36	0	11.5
1974 (Feb.)	36	2	10.7
1974 (Oct.)	36	3	10.8
1979	36	2	8.1
1983	38	2	7.8
1987	38	3	7.3
1992	38	4	9
1997	40	4	9.9

Table 2: Plaid Cymru's performance in parliamentary by-elections, 1945-1999

Date	Constituency	Plaid Vote	Plaid % of Total Vote	Position (Victorious Party)
1945	Caernarfon B	6,844	24.8	Second (Lib)
1945	Neath	6,290	16.2	Second (Lab)
1946	Ogmore	5,685	29.4	Second (Lab)
1946	Aberdare	7,090	20.0	Second (Lab)
1955	Wrexham	4,572	11.3	Third (Lab)
1956	Newport	1,978	3.8	Third (Lab)
1957	Carmarthen	5,741	11.5	Third (Lab)
1958	Pontypool	2,927	10.2	Third (Lab)
1962	Montgomery	1,594	6.2	Fourth (Lib)
1963	Swansea East	1,620	5.2	Fifth (Lab)
1965	Abertillery	1,551	6.7	Third (Lab)
1966	Carmarthen	16,179	39.0	First
1967	Rhondda West	10,067	39.9	Second (Lab)
1968	Caerffili	14,274	40.4	Second (Lab)
1972	Merthyr Tydfil	11,852	36.7	Second (Lab)
1982	Gower	3,431	8.7	Fourth (Lab)
1984	Cynon Valley	3,619	11.0	Third (Lab)
1985	Brecon & Radnor	435	1.1	Fourth (Alliance)
1989	Pontypridd	9,755	25.3	Second (Lab)
1989	Vale of Glamorgan	1,672	3.5	Fourth (Lab)
1991	Neath	8,132	23.4	Second (Lab)
1991	Monmouth*	277	0.6	Fifth (Lab)
1995	Islwyn	2,933	12.6	Second (Lab)

* Contested as a joint Plaid Cymru/Wales Green Party candidate

Table 3: Plaid Cymru's performance in European elections, 1979-1999

Date	Turnout	Total vote	% Plaid vote	MEPs elected	Overall placing in Wales
1979	36.0%	83,399	11.7	0	Third
1984	39.7%	103,031	12.2	0	Fourth
1989	40.7%	115,062	12.9	0	Third
1994	43.1%	162,478	17.1	0	Second
1999	28.3%	185,235	29.6	2	Second

Note: the 1979 election was the first to elect Members of the European Parliament; they were previously appointed by the member state government.

Party	% Vote (Constituency Ballot)	No. of Seats (Constituency Ballot)	% Vote (Regional Ballot)	No. of Seats (Regional Ballot)	Total AMs Elected
Table 4: Results of the National Assembly for Wales elections, May 1999					
Labour	37.6	27	35.5	1	28
Plaid Cymru	28.4	9	30.6	8	17
Conservative	15.9	1	16.5	8	9
Lib Dems	13.5	3	12.6	3	6
Others	4.7	0	4.9	0	0
Total					60

There was a real growth in the party's membership, particularly in those areas where the party had previously had no electoral presence. Fighting seats like Caerffili and Cardiff North in the south, and Flint West and Wrexham in the northeast gave the party a foundation upon which to build a broader membership base. Many of these new recruits came from Labour (like Phil Williams from Bargoed, near Caerffili and Robyn Lewis from Nefyn in Gwynedd) and, just as important, many were not Welsh speaking. The developments were used by the party to claim a connection between an expansion in election contests and a growth in the party's membership and organisational clout.

In this way, the 1959 election enhanced the value of fighting elections and indicated that at least some of the electorate was receptive to Plaid's policies. This was later used by Plaid's younger activists, like Phil Williams, Dafydd Wigley and Emrys Roberts, as vindication of a firmer electoral strategy. They argued that fighting the maximum numbers of seats possible was crucial, for it could be proved that the party performed better on each subsequent occasion that a particular seat was contested. This challenges the popular view that the by-election victory of 1966 was the real breakthrough for the party after a period of "drift and fragmentation" from 1959.[51] The period 1959 to 1966 was an important period of foundation-laying for further electoral growth.

The dramatic significance in Plaid's (and possibly even Wales's) political history of Gwynfor Evans' startling victory in the Carmarthen by-election of July 1966 cannot be underplayed: "..it was Caerfyrddin (Carmarthen) that gave us the proper sense of urgency and a very unfamiliar sense of importance". The scale of his success in Carmarthen, with a record swing against the government, was momentous. His victory meant a substantial transformation of both Plaid's self-image, and the way in which other parties perceived it. Evans described the Welsh people "walking with their heads a little higher, their backs a little straighter".[52] Dafydd Wigley, Evans's successor as president, argued: "Gwynfor's victory at Carmarthen set in motion, and gave credibility to, the whole concept of independent political action to save and safeguard the Welsh nation. It was an assertion that if Wales was to have a future, it was one which we had to build for ourselves... It had to happen here in Wales, in the minds and spirits of individual men and women, and the communities within which we live our lives".[53] Others suggested that the by-election victory "rendered the nature of the party's political programme a relevant public issue"[54] Outside the party, Evans's victory was seen to pose a real threat to Labour's hegemony. Plaid had its first MP, its first senior elected representative. We should remember Ball's definition of a political party as having representatives in the corridors of power. The Carmarthen victory meant an inevitable rise in profile, influence and self-esteem for Plaid.

Phil Williams claimed that "the result of the Rhondda by-election was... even more sensational than the result in Caerfyrddin". Indeed, the self-confidence engendered by this win was vindicated with an excellent result in the subsequent by-election at Rhondda West in 1967, when Plaid's Vic Davies cut the Labour majority to just over 2,300 from nearly 17,000 in the General Election a year earlier. This was followed in 1968 at the Caerffili by-election which saw a swing to Plaid's Phil Williams of 40%, and at Merthyr four years later when its candidate, Emrys Roberts, gained a 37% swing and cut the vast Labour majority to less than 4,000 votes. This time, percentage votes higher than Carmarthen, in the case of the first two, were insufficient to displace the Labour candidate; nonetheless, Labour, as the historically dominant party in Wales, was clearly unnerved by these 'close seconds' for Plaid in industrial, non-Welsh speaking areas.

The General Election of 1970 was Plaid Cymru's most successful of the period, despite Evans losing Carmarthen. The party secured 11.5% of the total vote and fought all thirty-six Welsh seats for the first time, performing well in the industrial valleys. Fighting every seat in Wales was further confirmation in Plaid's maturing into a political party.

The twin General Elections of February and October 1974 continued the momentum, with the election of Dafydd Wigley in Caernarfon and Dafydd Elis Thomas in Meirionnydd unseating vulnerable Labour MPs. They were joined in the October 1974 election by Gwynfor Evans, who had missed out on regaining Carmarthen by just three votes in February 1974. The significance of a Plaid group of three MPs at Westminster was heightened by the perilous situation of the Callaghan Labour administration, and by the dramatic success of Plaid's sister party in Scotland, the Scottish National Party (SNP), which polled over three-quarters of a million votes, beating the Conservatives into third place and gaining eleven Scottish seats. This gave the combined nationalist group of fourteen a vital leverage in the period 1974 to 1979, and precipitated the government's plans for elected assemblies in Scotland and Wales.

The 1979 General Election was a hugely difficult one for Plaid Cymru, following so quickly the fateful vote against Labour's devolution proposals. There were huge swings to the Conservatives and Plaid's vote declined to just over 8%. It lost the Carmarthen seat once more.

Historian Gwyn Alf Williams claimed the 1983 General Election "registered even more visibly Wales's presence with The South of the British geography of politics". This was a hugely difficult time for Plaid to progress. The 1983 election was Dafydd Wigley's first as leader, and Plaid was also confronted by the new alliance between the Social Democrats and the Liberals. Its vote fell slightly to 7.8%, although it retained its two seats in Caernarfon and Meirionnydd. The Alliance gained almost a quarter of votes cast in Wales, despite having no organised presence in many areas and undertaking little visible campaigning.

The general election fell between two by-elections, in Gower in 1982 and in Cynon Valley in 1984. Neither brought Plaid even the runners-up slot vital to any party trying to position itself as the challenger to Labour. These elections were followed in 1985 by a predictably poor showing in another by-election in the three-way marginal, Brecon and Radnor.

Celtic Alliances

In 1986, Plaid signed an official agreement with its counterpart in Scotland, the Scottish Nationalist Party (SNP). There had been co-operation between the parties since the 1930s, (Gwynfor Evans met the SNP executive in Edinburgh in 1938) but it was during the 1970s that the two parties began to work closely together.

The agreement was primarily an electoral pact, in which the two parties formed a cohesive group in the House of Commons. It was designed as a show of strength and strategic planning for the 1987 General Election, to give the parties additional leverage in the event of a minority government. However, the Conservatives won easily once again and

Plaid's share of the vote fell further to 7.3%, reinforcing Gwyn Alf Williams's fear that Welsh politics was beginning to ape that in Britain as a whole. Plaid had the consolation of taking the Ynys Môn constituency with 43.2% of the vote. This raised the party's parliamentary representation to three once again.

The SNP won just three seats, which minimised the potential for the Plaid-SNP alliance at Westminster, although there were brave claims that "the six... MPs will use all constitutional means at their disposal to draw attention to the undemocratic way our two countries are being run, and the Tories' lack of mandate in Scotland and Wales".[55] Although the pact subsequently lost some of its profile and momentum, there remained close co-operation between the two parties at Westminster. During the 1990s, the two parties (MPs and staff) met as a group each Wednesday evening to review tactics for the subsequent week's parliamentary business, sharing duties such as supply day debates and supplementary questions. They also tried to pursue a joint approach to major policy debates wherever possible, and the parties' whips often acted on behalf of both Plaid and the SNP.[56]

Even with its extra MP after 1987, Dafydd Wigley admitted "The results were bad for the party, despite the magnificent win in Ynys Môn. The continuing slide in the Valleys is near disastrous". The sought-after breakthrough in the south continued to exercise the party's mind. The left-wing pressure group, the National Left, went further and highlighted an issue which was to dominate debate within Plaid on electoral strategies for the next decade: "In effect the gulf in understanding between Plaid Gwynedd and Plaid Cymru has become wider, deeper and potentially more dangerous for the survival of the party... We have a political party, but we have no organisation outside Gwynedd".[57]

Two further by-elections took place in 1989, first in Pontypridd and then in the Vale of Glamorgan. Despite bordering each other geographically, the two constituencies were vastly different. For Plaid, Pontypridd was the opportunity to test its much-vaunted effort in the southern valleys. It fought to win, hoping to spark the kind of breakthrough in the valleys that the 1960s by-elections had promised, but not delivered. The party's efforts met with only partial success. Plaid's candidate, Syd Morgan, came second, albeit with a creditable 25.3% of the poll and a 20% swing from Labour. However, neither the result nor the campaign suggested Plaid was poised to break through in the valleys. The challenge to Labour hegemony in south Wales had to wait another ten years. The final by-election of the 1980s in the Vale of Glamorgan saw Plaid suffer from the inevitable squeeze between the two main parties, with Labour emerging victorious in a close contest, and Plaid losing its deposit with just 3.5% of the vote.

There were very mixed fortunes for Plaid Cymru in the three by-elections in the first five years of the 1990s, in Neath in 1991 (another potentially fertile valleys seat for Plaid) where it came a creditable second with 23.4% of the vote. This was followed by an unsurprisingly poor showing in the border marginal seat, Monmouth, when the joint Plaid Cymru/Green candidate polled only 227 votes (0.6%), suffering the indignity of finishing behind the Monster Raving Loony Party. In Islwyn in 1995, Plaid's Jocelyn Davies came a distant second to Labour, albeit with a decent 12.7% share of the vote.

The 1992 and 1997 General Elections were also unspectacular, despite the election of a fourth MP in Ceredigion in 1992. The greatest achievement of 1997 was surely consolidation. Plaid held its seats in the face of huge swings to New Labour. Local solicitor, Elfyn Llwyd, took over from Dafydd Elis Thomas as MP for the Meirionnydd Nant Conwy constituency, confirming the relatively sturdy support and organisation Plaid had built up in Caernarfon, Meirionnydd and Ynys Môn (and was beginning to establish in Ceredigion).

The 1980s and early 1990s were hardly successful electoral years for Plaid Cymru. As was the pattern, the party performed well in both sets of elections to the European Parliament in 1984 and 1989, achieving 12.2% and 12.9% of the vote respectively. Nevertheless, it was no nearer a conventionally defined electoral breakthrough at the end of the 1980s than it had been thirty years earlier.

It was the final year of the century that brought the most remarkable electoral breakthroughs for Plaid. The first 'Welsh General Election' for the National Assembly for Wales in May 1999 saw the party gain seventeen seats and 28.4 % of the total vote in the constituency poll (and 30.6% in the vote for regional seats).

The Local Level

There was little real attempt to win seats on local councils in Plaid's early years, largely due to the lack of members and resources to fight elections. However, Saunders Lewis often referred to the potential of council membership for building momentum for Wales's own government.

Local government became a more important part of Plaid's electoral activities from the 1970s onwards. The party's strategy articulates the pragmatic approach of many within Plaid's leadership: it saw the local level as its best chance of success and as a stepping stone to break-throughs at other levels.

Following local government reorganisation in 1974, Plaid placed renewed emphasis on winning seats on the new community, district, and county councils. The argument for seeking control at this level of politics rested on a theory, most vividly expressed by long-standing valleys councillor, Syd Morgan, who argued that when people trusted Plaid Cymru to empty their dustbins, they would begin to accept the party's statements on the need for a Welsh government too. Other advocates of a local government-based strategy pointed to the practical and strategic management of a local council reflecting the power relations of larger government. It was thus a way of proving that Plaid Cymru was a party which, given the opportunity, could govern, and govern well. It offered Plaid the chance to build upon a grassroots empathy for the party. This would then allow it to demonstrate that it could deliver some of its policies for Wales on the smaller stage of the local council.

However, the strategy is slightly flawed. Voters impose their own divisions between different elections. That there is only a tenuous cross-over of loyalties amongst the electorate from local to other elections in Wales is proved by an examination of some of the Plaid-held local government wards within Labour-held parliamentary constituencies (and also by the anomaly of the Plaid by-election candidate in the Vale of Glamorgan gaining more votes in his local council ward than in the constituency as a whole when both elections were held on the same day!). Similar patterns of shifting alignment between different levels were shown in the first elections to the Assembly in 1999.

Of equal importance was the strategy's potential for offering a counterbalance in southern Wales to the party's reputation for representing Welsh-speakers primarily. This was an important recognition of the need to broaden Plaid's appeal and redress the limitations of its public image. Local councillors could act as the public face of Plaid Cymru and were likely to be more representative of the party's true character.

To what extent did this strategy work? Jill Evans, herself a Rhondda councillor at this time, has argued that the contribution of Plaid's local councillors has been ignored in the party's larger strategies. She blamed this on an overwhelming Westminster focus to Plaid's strategy.[58] It is certainly true that the experience of elected Plaid representatives at a local level was never exploited fully. Complaints about the party's over-whelmingly Westminster focus are a recurring theme.

Emyr Williams, who was instrumental in influencing the party's strategies in the 1980s particularly, has argued that Plaid dissipated much of its natural strength by moving away from its location in civil society (that is, in all the informal and formal institutions of local communities) and towards a more entrenched parliamentary position. The dominance of the MPs within the party meant that Plaid diluted many of its long-established campaigning thrusts – on the Welsh language and on constitutional change particularly. The implication of Williams's remarks is that the par-liamentary focus to its efforts made Plaid less political in some respects, whilst more conventionally party political in others.[59]

Yet, once Plaid had made its breakthrough at Westminster and before there was any devolution to Wales, it is inevitable that this should be regarded as symbolising the state of the party's progress. Dafydd Wigley advanced a familiar argument that, despite the importance of local gov-ernment and the European level, "There is only one language that Westminster understands, and that is the election of nationalist MPs from Wales, taking their seats from the Labour, Liberal and Tory parties".[60] This suggests that, before devolution, Plaid's role at Westminster was as much to pressure the other parties as to advance its own policies.

In 1993, prior to local government reorganisation and the introduction of unitary authorities, Plaid Cymru had 41 county councillors and 122 borough/district councillors, supported by a substantial spread of com-munity councillors. After the 1995 unitary elections, Plaid held 114 seats and controlled Gwynedd Council. To date, the local level is where Plaid Cymru can claim most electoral success. Plaid led a coalition-controlled authority in south Wales (Taf Ely Borough Council) between 1991 and 1996, although it failed to make any identifiable headway in this area in the subsequent General Election in May 1997. In the 1999 elections (held on the same day as the first elections to the National Assembly), the party won 206 seats across Wales and added overall control of Caerffili and Rhondda Cynon Taf in the south, to Gwynedd in the north.

Overall, there has been a rather erratic pattern to Plaid's electoral per-formance in all tiers of government since 1945. There is evidence of a gradual progress towards more respectable accumulation of votes (and with it, political profile) but, at best, Plaid's progress before 1999 can be described as tentative. Success was usually been followed by a period of stagnation or regression. Most importantly, the pattern of Plaid's electoral performance reflects shifts in its status as pressure group and political party. Of course, these shifts do not have to be seen as contradictory, for gradual changes in Plaid's status did not always advance it down a uniform path to becoming a conventional political party. Until the devolved elections in 1999, Plaid resurrected its campaigning work at regular intervals, alongside its election focus – on the water rates campaign and the Poll Tax, for example.

This review of its electoral and campaigning activities cannot tell the whole story of Plaid Cymru. Despite officially changing its name to Plaid Cymru The Party of Wales at its 1998 conference,[61] it still does not always behave like a political party. It is equally misleading to describe Plaid Cymru as a straightforward pressure group. Neither is Plaid Cymru just a part of the national movement. Certainly, it is a key component within the wider national movement, but Plaid is far more than this. Its electoral focus and success in achieving elected representatives means it could no longer simply be part of the national movement. Thus, Plaid has been able to behave as a political party, as a pressure group, and as part of the national movement at different times, and sometimes as all three simultaneously. It is also clear that ambiguity of status can be both an advantage and a disadvantage.

> Plaid Cymru, which has been gathering together the creative energies of the Welsh nation, is thus more than a political party... It is a national movement and a moral crusade which has given much of its time to educate people in nationhood.[62]

> Plaid Cymru must realise that a political party, seeking a popular mandate, cannot act as an umbrella for every nationalist faction.[63]

These two versions of Plaid's proper role in Welsh politics underline the party's continuing dilemma. Historically, it has tried to represent the whole national movement (for it is the only nationalist party following constitutional democratic means). At the same time, it recognises that to fulfil its developing role as a political party, it must reject the pressures from other components within the national movement and eschew at least some of its campaigning focus.

Perhaps Plaid Cymru's role in post-war politics should be described as consistently ambiguous: fluctuating between pressure group activity, and behaving as a conventional political party contesting elections in a quest for power. At various points, Plaid has given different priority to both types of political activity, elections and campaigns.

To some extent, Plaid has always been a 'wannabe' political party, focused on winning elections. Sometimes, campaigns were seized upon, as much for their likely electoral fallout as for the saliency of the issue itself: "the party has done a lot of growing up in recent years. It is very much a mainstream political party in the 1990s".[64] There is a clear correlation between the party's election and campaigning activity, and its changing status. There is also a clear decline in its campaigning role and an enhancement of its electoral one as the party has matured.

Why has there been this uncertainty as to its proper and legitimate focus? There are some specific reasons for the tensions: first, the fact that Plaid is a nationalist party. Nationalist parties, as we have seen, do not always fit the neat structural frameworks of other parties. Cultural and linguistic objectives often sit alongside economic ones. The former lend themselves more to pressure group activity than elections, the stuff of parties.

There is also the uniqueness of the nationalist project. Thus, for nationalist parties, the problem is "an exclusive emphasis on policies is difficult by their very nature, their ultimate goal of independence is inherent in their appeal: the goal of self-government for their community is what makes them nationalist".[65] So activities normally associated with political parties can be limiting for those nationalist parties that wish to use every available option to advance their cause.

There are also some more specific reasons for Plaid's ambiguous status. Historically it has shown a lack of confidence to opt for one political role at the expense of the other in its strategic plans. Conscious or otherwise, there are advantages in being able to straddle the divide between party and pressure group.

The debate on status also reflects the importance of the priorities of its broad membership, many of whom quite simply interpreted that membership as an extension of a general, cultural commitment to Wales and things Welsh. Their quiet but sustained influence was to draw the party towards single issue and broad-based pressure group style campaigns.

From its establishment in 1925, there has been a rather basic indecision, or lack of unanimity, about Plaid's role within Welsh politics. In the immediate post-war period, the party began to show an awareness of the inherent tensions in attempts to fulfil the roles of both pressure group and political party. Slowly and incrementally, Plaid began to shed the characteristics of a pressure group, though the issue of status is not completely settled, as Ieuan Wyn Jones indicated: "the issue is not resolved altogether; it hasn't penetrated all of the party".

Plaid's performance in elections (local, Westminster, Assembly and European) mark stages in its metamorphosis. However, it has taken the new context of devolved power to force the party's hand. This was easily the single most dramatic catalyst for change in Plaid self-perception. There were claims that the prospect of an Assembly had forced the party to grow up and to move out of the theoretical and ideological political arena, and into a practical policy-making one. It now had a new responsibility to construct a real programme of government and to put the party's long-standing principles into the realistic context of the Assembly. Before devolution, Plaid Cymru's ambivalence to the constraints and legitimacy of the British parliamentary system affected its strategies: it could not expect to influence electoral politics to such an extent that merited its wholehearted commitment to this kind of activity, hence it combined electoral strategies with a strong campaigning thrust.

Its traditional avoidance of the strategies associated with either a party or a pressure group might be construed as an asset in the political arena. That is, it might obtain the benefits of each. However, Plaid's erratic electoral performances suggest otherwise. Until the late 1990s, Plaid Cymru fell between two stools. If there was a sustainable status which bridges the priorities of party and pressure group, then Plaid clearly had not found it. But by the end of the 1990s, Plaid Cymru was more firmly entrenched as a relatively conventional political party than ever before. The mood now was that "Plaid Cymru's role is to bring about change through conventional political means, gaining control of public authorities".[66]

Yet, there is also a sense in which Plaid may always prove one step away from its ultimate objective of becoming a political party. This will be the case as long as it is the only nationalist party contesting elections within the Welsh arena. Its status as the sole nationalist party has meant an obligation to represent the wider national movement in Wales. Equally, once a party has pledged itself to the electoral arena (as Plaid had done by 1959), then winning seats becomes the single most important motive. This has brought extra problems for Plaid as it has juggled the objective of electoral success with a commitment to advancing the intellectual rationale for self-government as part of a wider national movement. That Plaid has been conscious of these responsibilities can be recognised by its involvement in the campaigns outlined above. The debate about Plaid's status will continue, for it cannot be resolved until there are other, new entrants to the political arena which contest elections on something resembling a nationalist programme:

The entire political context has changed with the creation of the Assembly. The prospect of Plaid actually being a party of potential government or at least a major opposition party is such a huge psychological move along from being a party that could at best muster only forty seats at Westminster. The dynamics change, the focus changes... we're moving out of the theoretical and the idealistic and into the practical and that's a challenge the party may find uncomfortable. I've sensed... there's almost a fear amongst some people that we'll win because winning means a poisoned chalice, winning means the responsibility of governing.[67]

The further development of devolution is likely to prove the catalyst for deciding Plaid Cymru's status one way or the other.

Notes

1. Evans, G., *Wales Can Win,* (Christopher Davies, 1973).
2. Editorial in Triban, *Essays on Welsh Economic and Social Life,* Vol. 4, No. 2, Autumn, 1970.
3. Ball, A., *British Political Parties, The Emergence of a Modern Party System* (Macmillan, 1981).
4. *ibid.*
5. Kimber, R. & Lees, J.D., *Political Parties in Modern Britain, An Organizational and Functional Guide* (Routledge & Kegan Paul, 1972).
6. Meny, Y. & Knapp, A., *Government and Politics in Western Europe, Britain, France, Italy, Germany,* (Oxford University Press, third edition, 1998)
7. Kimber, R. & Lees, J.D., *op. cit.*
8. Duverger, M., *Political Parties,* (Methuen, 1954).
9. Coxall, W., *Parties and Pressure Groups* (Longman, 1981).
10. Von Beyme, K., *Political Parties in Western Democracies* (Gower, 1985).
11. Editorial comment in *Triban*, vol. 4, no. 2, Autumn 1970, p. 2.
12. G. Evans in foreword to D. Williams, *The Story of Plaid Cymru, the Party of Wales* (Plaid Cymru, 1990).
13. Lewis, S., *Y Ddraig Goch*, September 1930.
14. Dafydd Wigley, interview, 03.08.98
15. Webb, H., report on the *Welsh Nation* to National Executive, June-Dec 1962 (Plaid Cymru archive, National Library of Wales).
16. Spanswick, T., 'What is Plaid Cymru?', *Welsh Nation*, 12-18 December 1975.
17. The figures for actual, paid up members in each membership year are likely to be lower in reality. Initially, there were arbitrary methods of collecting this information. In 1999, the total figure includes members from the previous year who had not renewed their membership, as well as some who had not renewed for more than one year. There was also a different system for recording official branches, which makes the 1945 figure of 150 *Canghennau* a little misleading.
18. Kimber & Lees, *op. cit.*
19. Butt Philip, A., *The Welsh Question, Nationalism in Welsh Politics, 1945-1970,* (University of Wales Press, 1975).
20. Evans, G., *Fighting For Wales,* (Y Lolfa, 1991).

21 Gwynfor Evans, interview, 10.11.2000.
22. Undated campaign pamphlet.
23. Evans, G., *Fighting for Wales*, p.191.
24. Evans, G., *ibid*, p. 100
25. Evans, G., *ibid*, p. 97
26. Evans, G., *ibid*, p. 100
27. Davies, J., (2000), *Threequarters of a Century of Plaid Cymru's History*, speech to PC anniversary celebrations, p. 8-9. (this is a translation of: *Bron na ellir honni bod nifer o aelodau Plaid Cymru... yn dioddef o'r hyn y gellid ei alw yn 'Penyberthitis', sef y gred simplistig mai dim ond trwy gael fersiwn newydd o weithred Penyberth bob ryw ugain mlynedd yr oedd modd cynnal momentwm cenedlaetholdeb Cymreig).*
28. Davies, *ibid*.
29. Evans, G., *Fighting for Wales*, *op. cit.*
30. Dafydd Wigley, interview, 22.01.01.
31. Evans, G., *Fighting for Wales*, *op. cit*
32. Evans, G., *Land of My Fathers*, (Y Lolfa, 1992).
33. Evans, G., *Fighting for Wales*, *op. cit.*
34. Lewis, S., *Egwyddorion Cenedlaetholdeb/ Principles of Nationalism*, (Plaid Genedlaethol Cymru, 1926), p. 11-15.
35. Dafydd Wigley, interview, 22.01.01.
36. Evans, G., *Fighting for Wales*.
37. Report for Plaid Cymru from ERES market research agency, Cardiff, 1998.
38. Cynog Dafis, interview, 13.11.00. Plaid's success in the Carmarthen by-election of 1966 caused something of an aberration (in Cynog Dafis's words, "It messed things up a bit.. I wanted to be part of Plaid Cymru when it was doing well."!). Dafis was not alone amongst younger supporters of Plaid in facing this dilemma. Historically, there had been a negative correlation between the success of the embryonic language movement and the electoral progress of Plaid Cymru. Yet here was Plaid gaining its first seat at Westminster at a zenith for *Cymdeithas yr Iaith Gymraeg's* activities.
39. Evans, G., *Fighting for Wales*, *op. cit.*
40. Evans, G, *Life or Death? The Struggle for the Language and Welsh TV Channel*, n.d.
41. Evans, G., (1973), *op. cit.*
42. Dafydd Elis Thomas, interview, 13.11.00.
43. Cynog Dafis, interview, 13.11.00.
44. Peter Keelan, interview, 31.07.98.
45. Edwards, S., *Radical Wales*, No, 25, Spring 1990, p 6.
46. Peter Keelan, interview, 31.07.98
47. Cynog Dafis, interview, 13.11.00.
48. Edwards, S., *Radical Wales*, No. 28, p 21.
49. Williams, P., (1981), *Voice from the Valleys*, (Y Lolfa)
50. Translated from Williams, P., "Plaid Cymru a'r Dyfodol" in Davies, J., *Cymru'n Deffro*, (Y Lolfa, 1981).
51. Williams, P., (1981), *op. cit.*
52. G. Evans, election night speech, quoted in *Radical Wales*, Summer 1991, p. 17.
53. Wigley, D., *Radical Wales*, *ibid*.
54. Williams, E.W., 'The Dynamics of Welsh Identity' in Evans, N., (ed.), *National Identity in the British Isles*, Coleg Harlech occasional papers in Welsh studies, No. 3, (Coleg Harlech, 1989).

55. Parliamentary Report, in annual conference programme, 1987, p. 96.
56. Dafydd Williams, interview, May 2001.
57. National Left Strategy Committee discussion paper, August 1987.
58. Jill Evans, interview, 31.07.98.
59. Emyr Wynn Williams, interview, 17.08.98.
60. Wigley, D., quoted in Coxall, W. N., *Parties and Pressure Groups* (Longman, 1981).
61. In its 1998 conference in Cardiff, the debate which gained by far the most media coverage was over a constitutional change to the party's name registering it under the provisions of the Government of Wales Act 1998 as *Plaid Cymru The Party of Wales*. This translation (or clarification, depending on one's standpoint) was instigated by the leadership, who sought a bilingual identity for the party as it approached the first elections to the National Assembly in 1999. The motion was seen as an attempt to broaden its appeal to English-speaking voters whilst also diminishing its traditional Welsh-speaking image. The motion was passed with a substantial majority, despite some criticism from so-called "traditionalists" who saw it as a dilution of Plaid's historical identity.
62. Evans, G., Wales Can Win, *op. cit.*
63. Editorial in *Triban, Essays on Welsh Economic and Social Life,* Vol. 4, No. 2, Autumn 1970, p. 2.
64. Ieuan Wyn Jones, interview, 13.11.00
65. McAllister, I., in Madgwick, P.& Rose, R., (eds.), *The Territorial Dimension in UK Politics,* (Macmillan, 1982).
66. Cynog Dafis, interview, 13.11.00
67. Marc Phillips, interview, 04.08.98.

5. The Constitutional Perspective

Events, dear boy, events.
– Harold Macmillan.

Plaid Cymru was established to secure a Welsh government. However, the real issue has been the degree of control or independence that a Welsh government might have. What would be the character and autonomy of the new Wales?

As Plaid Cymru has grown, so its specific scheme for self-government has come under greater scrutiny. In addition, changing contexts at domestic and international political levels have necessitated regular refinements to the constitutional and political goals of Plaid Cymru. This chapter explores some of the constitutional debates within Plaid Cymru since 1945, in particular those on devolution, Europe and the House of Lords. These debates expose different constitutional tensions within the party, revealing further levels to the process of its development.

I use the term 'constitutional' to refer to the prototype Wales – its distinctive legal, economic, political and social systems, as well as its external relations – that Plaid Cymru has advocated as its blueprint for a self-governing Wales. We shall see that this vision has shifted many times since 1945, often in response to political events.

The Blueprint for a Future Wales

So let us insist on having, not independence, but freedom. And freedom in this affair means responsibility. We who are Welsh claim that we are responsible for civilization and social ways of life in our part of Europe. That is the political ambition of the National Party.[1]

Whilst Plaid Cymru was established to campaign for a government for Wales, its blueprint was somewhat short on detail. Clarifying the status and authority of a Welsh government has dominated debate within the party ever since. For much of its history, Plaid has pursued vaguely-defined political goals. It has focused on safeguarding, or reinstating, the badges of national identity (sovereignty, language, culture, international recognition), rather than the minutiae of legal and political status.

Tracing the gradual formalising of Plaid's precise scheme for a Welsh government tells us much about the party. The original organisation, Plaid Genedlaethol Cymru, sought freedom for Wales, ensuring "just as much freedom as may be necessary to establish and safeguard civilization in Wales". Its priority was "fighting only for the indispensable, the essential, the necessary things". What the early constitutional stance of Plaid Cymru proved was that the early years of a new party and a virtual blank policy profile poses problems. It faced a wide range of options from which to make a credible constitutional blueprint for the new Wales. The looseness of its earliest proposals became the constitutional inheritance that the party had to deal with later on.

As it assumed more of the characteristics of a political party after 1945, it became clear that more rigorous, robust strategies with greater detail were needed to formalise its political project. It is worth remembering that Plaid has a unique position within Welsh politics. For most of its post-war existence, it has been the only democratic nationalist party of size, which has proved a major factor in shaping constitutional debate within the party.

There is another important dynamic. Nationalist parties, by their nature, focus on changing political and administrative arrangements within their territory. This is often their *raison d'être*. As a consequence, nationalist parties tend to devote more attention to constitutional matters. That is, they must be able to first visualise the kind of political, economic and legal relationships that will characterise the new constitutional status, and second, communicate this to the electorate. This has had to be achieved against a changing background of practical and theoretical politics:

> What is full national status on a Monday, on a Tuesday or on a Wednesday![2]

Throughout its history, three critical issues have dominated constitutional debate in Plaid Cymru: the type and scope of powers a self-governing Wales should have; the terminology to be used to describe this vision for Wales; and the methods for communicating this political scheme to the public.

This look at Plaid's constitutional stance operates from a basic and fundamental assumption: that there is no teleology to the constitutional debate, generally and in the specific case of Plaid Cymru. That is, there is no pre-defined end to the nationalist project. Its political goal is fixed, only in so far as achieving a measure of political independence for Wales. The precise nature of this constitutional project and the language by

Sit down protest at Tryweryn in the late 1950s

Two important, but different influences in Plaid Cymru's development:
Saunders Lewis and Gwynfor Evans

Passionate Plaid politicians: Gwyn Alf Williams, Dafydd Iwan and
Dafydd Elis Thomas

Election successes: President Gwynfor Evans with newly-elected MPs
Dafydd Wigley and Dafydd Elis Thomas, October 1974
Phil Williams, close second to Labour in the 1968 Caerffili by-election
Rhondda councillors Geraint Davies, Jill Evans, Dorian Rees and Larraine
Jones in celebratory mood

Direct action campaigns for the Welsh language and for peace

Councillors protest:
Clayton Jones on the picket line in the 1984-85 Miners' Strike.
Lindsay Whittle leads the symbolic burning of Poll Tax bills in 1991

Rallying cries: Dafydd Elis Thomas addresses students
March against the US Radar Base at St David's, Pembrokeshire

President Dafydd Wigley adds his voice to teachers' protest,
and listens to the concerns of farmers

Ieuan Wyn Jones, newly elected MP for Ynys Môn, arrives at the House
of Commons in 1987
Plaid displays its anti-nuclear credentials

which it is communicated cannot be set in stone. Events and circumstances mean a dynamic process of constitutional review and adjustment is inevitable. Or, as Dafydd Elis Thomas has put it, "It's quite a good thing that we can't be pinned down".[3]

Exploring the changes in Plaid's constitutional proposals is rather like opening the shells of a Russian doll. At its core, the tiniest doll is the plan for a new Wales with sufficient powers and authority to make its own decisions as to political organisation and economic and social priorities. This core remains the same, but the outer layers of the doll represent some of the important shifts in the appearance of this plan, as well as the manner in which it is presented. The different layers show how Plaid has responded to changing political circumstances, updating and moulding its constitutional plans within these new contexts. Some of these shifts have been opportune, some principled. Each has brought a differing measure of success for the party.

"Of course, Plaid Cymru has adapted its constitutional position many times in its history,"[4] stated Ieuan Wyn Jones in 2000. The constitutional position Plaid inherited in 1945 was a commitment to 'dominion status'. This was, in turn, a development of its commitment to 'freedom' which very much reflected the era when Plaid was founded and avoided the language of sovereignty associated with full independence. 'Dominion status' evolved into a commitment to commonwealth status for Wales, along similar lines to Britain's former colonies. This envisaged a close and free confederation between the countries of the British Isles, with them sharing a common economic market.

The end of Plaid's ambivalence about electoral contests proved significant to the constitutional issue. This enhanced electoral context is important, for the party's involvement in various tiers of elections – local, Welsh, British and European – has stimulated many of the revisions to its constitutional programme. From 'dominion status' to 'self-government', through early 1980s support for 'decentralist socialist policies', right up to its later proposals for a Welsh Senate with financial control of the existing Welsh Office budget and law-making powers, Plaid Cymru's constitutional vision for Wales has reflected its growing involvement in elections.

> Political language is designed to make lies sound truthful and murder respectable, and to give an appearance of solidity to pure wind.[5]

Some of these variations in constitutional plans involve little more than shifts in the terminology Plaid has used to communicate its aims.

Exploring them sheds further light on the political priorities of Plaid at various points in its history. There is certainly evidence of some opportunism and pragmatism in the choice of terminology. Other shifts reflect the party's readiness to accept short and medium term progress towards its longer-term objective of a Welsh government. Language is important for answering one of our key questions – how Plaid Cymru communicates its project for Wales. It has used a range of different terms: 'dominion status', 'freedom', 'confederalism', 'independence' and 'full national status' (inside or outside the European Union). They help identify the motors that have driven Plaid's growth and also indicate subtle differences in the way Plaid Cymru's prototype Wales has looked: the relationships between Welsh, UK and European levels, the balance between the executive and the judiciary, and the need for a second chamber in a new Welsh parliament, for example. Overall though, debate on these areas has largely been unsophisticated in depth and detail.

Returning to our Russian doll, there are three layers of particular interest to us: the acceptance of Welsh devolution as a legitimate, interim stage in the party's ultimate goal; the emergence of the European context as a new constitutional framework; and the debate on the House of Lords.

In 1979 Plaid Cymru suffered its *annus horribilis*. The Wales Act 1978 was rejected in the March 1 by 80% of those voting (around 46% of the total Welsh electorate). In the General Election which followed, Plaid's share of the vote slipped to just over 8% and party president, Gwynfor Evans, again lost Carmarthen.

The two most recent and dramatic manifestations of the devolution debate since the war, the referenda of 1979 and 1997 illuminate Plaid Cymru's status by asking some rather fundamental questions of the party. The most important was the extent to which it should compromise its goal of full national status for Wales for a very limited measure of political authority in a devolved assembly.

The logic of devolution depends upon a central authority holding political power and legitimacy. Devolution only makes sense if the authority is granted by the centre to various lower levels. Constitutional control remains at the centre at Westminster, in the UK's case. In practice, rescinding a devolved institution is rare, but that it is possible tells us something about the nature of constitutional change initiated by devolution and the questions it raised for Plaid Cymru.

1979

The referendum held on 1 March 1979 asked for a simple yes or no vote on the terms of the Wales Act 1978. This had proposed a limited form of devolution, its implementation conditional upon a consultative referendum, complete with a 40% rule. This meant that the Act could be repealed if less than 40% of eligible electors in Wales voted in favour of the proposal.

The Wales Act was the product of the Kilbrandon Commission, set up by the Labour Government in 1968 to discuss the issue of limited devolution to Wales and Scotland. The Commission reported in October 1973, recommending directly elected Scottish and Welsh assemblies. Its task had been to seek "to foster democratic control over the increasingly complex processes of modern government and to bring government closer to the people". There were many conditions to the deliberations of the Kilbrandon Commission, most important amongst them, the preservation of "the political and economic unity of the United Kingdom". This is significant, for it set the context, not only for the Commission but also for the subsequent structuring of the Government's devolution plans. Devolution was presented as a method for increasing democratic accountability, not as a means for material and social advancement which it acknowledged "devolution cannot further". Devolution was thus inspired by constitutional not economic motivations. In particular, it was designed to appease the two nationalist parties in Wales and Scotland, whose progress was a cause of some concern to the government.

There was also a minority report from the Kilbrandon Commission, produced by Lord Crowther Hunt and Professor Alan Peacock. Its main differences with the majority findings were three-fold: first, it sought the extension of devolution to the English regions as well (an issue resurrected in 1997); secondly, it proposed greater legislative powers for the Welsh and Scottish assemblies; and thirdly, it argued that legal and constitutional protection should be given to the regional assemblies, to avoid excessive interference from the United Kingdom level. This minority report pre-empted many of the criticisms that were eventually levelled at the Wales Act for its limitations and ill-defined goals. The Act was seen to have originated "from a disharmony of motives and imprecision of aim".[6]

Plaid Cymru had given evidence to the Crowther Committee at meetings in Cardiff and Aberystwyth. Not surprisingly, the rationale behind its submissions was the need for full self-government for Wales with economic and legal competence, rather than the limited devolved schemes on offer.

The devolution referendum was the second such vote of the 1970s. Referenda are devices of direct democracy, which in theory allow voters to decide upon an issue for themselves. This usually means a straightforward choice between supporting the proposal on offer or rejecting it. This simple yes or no option meant Plaid faced a critical dilemma – whether or not to support the timid scheme for devolution that was far removed from its own vision for Welsh autonomy. Could devolution be used as a way of gradually building momentum for self-government, or would it simply assist Labour's efforts to appease the revitalised nationalist parties in Wales and Scotland?

The essential problem was that the terms for devolution were set externally and were presented as an uncomplicated 'either-or', between some more autonomy and the status quo. Crucially for Plaid, this meant it was forced to engage in a debate upon a central plank of its constitutional being, the terms of which bore little resemblance to the party's own priorities.

By the time Plaid Cymru entered the devolution debate, after some understandable soul-searching, the wider pro-lobby was already arguing that a 'Yes' vote represented a straightforward extension of democracy. However, the real truth was that the devolution debate in 1979 offered a multitude of interpretations of democracy and its implications for Welsh politics. In 1977, party president, Gwynfor Evans, had set up an internal, ad-hoc group. After some debate, it decided that Plaid should oppose any referendum proposal on devolution. However, Evans began to speak more favourably in public about the terms of the White Paper. Gradually more of the membership came round to supporting a yes vote. Once again, it was Evans's persuasive influence that helped dilute some of the internal opposition to the devolution proposals.

In 1978, Plaid agreed to support a 'Yes' vote, whilst also trying to keep its longer-term goal of self-government on the agenda. At a hastily convened meeting in Newtown, Powys, the party launched a campaign entitled 'Who Governs Wales?' designed to highlight the broader issues of power at a Welsh level. The logic of this campaign was to offset internal criticisms of Plaid's acceptance of the limited devolution on offer. It was also a way of trying to portray devolution as an important stage towards self-government. The strategy clearly did not work, for there was prolonged internal discord over the party's position. This meant Plaid entered the campaign with an unprecedented degree of dissent within its own grass-roots, as well as general ambivalence as to the wisdom of supporting the Labour-led 'Yes' campaign.

There is no real history of effective party co-operation in British political campaigns. In 1979, longstanding party tensions further complicated
the issue. For Plaid to support to the 'Yes' campaign meant working
alongside its longstanding political rival, the Labour Party. What is more,
because the proposals originated from the Labour Government, it was
guaranteed the upper hand within the 'Yes' lobby.

In addition, deep divisions within Labour ranks, both amongst its MPs
and at grassroots level, meant support for the 'Yes' campaign involved
Plaid in an already bitter, internecine row. Scepticism from Plaid's own
membership towards the terms of devolution offered, as well as the
wisdom of joining forces with Labour, hinted at the difficult campaign
that lay ahead.

The huge 'No' vote is recalled by senior party figures as "a gigantic
blow to the party's credibility and strategic direction".[7] The overwhelming
rejection of devolution was a watershed in Plaid Cymru's modern history.
The party was forced into a long-overdue review of its political and constitutional strategies. The immediate focus was the hastily convened
internal Commission of Inquiry. It met in the knowledge that the referendum and devolution were not responsible for constitutional tensions
within Plaid Cymru – they already existed. The 1970s debates merely
exacerbated these tensions. Supporting the government's devolution
scheme meant tacit acceptance of the legitimacy of the process of devolv-
ing power, something fundamentally at odds with the party's primary
objectives. Thus, the first major devolution debate of the post-war period
signalled a cross-roads in constitutional debate within Plaid Cymru.

More immediately, the internal Commission sat in the context of
Dafydd Wigley's claim that "the morale of Wales as a nation and Plaid
Cymru as a party" was "at rock bottom". The party acknowledged that
"The period ahead is ... bound to be one of deliberation ... the next Plaid
Cymru conference in the autumn must face up to some searching ques-
tions concerning the party's future".[8] Aware of previous indecision about
its political strategies encouraged the party to treat strategy, possibly for
the first time in its history, as a serious priority.

The *Cyngor Cenedlaethol* instructed the Commission to stage a comprehensive review of the party's organisation, strategy and finances. It
became a highly structured body with strict, self-imposed terms of reference. It met between 1979 and 1981 with detailed agendas for discussion
at each meeting. That the Commission assumed a formal structure is

important, first because it was untypical of Plaid at this time. Secondly, there was criticism from some members that its establishment was a knee-jerk reaction to events of 1979, designed to convince its members that Plaid was doing something, at least. As a consequence, it had to prove its worth.

The Commission's format and brief suggested clear and conscious objectives. The five-man Commission (Dafydd Wigley, Eurfyl ap Gwilym, Phil Williams, Owen John Thomas and Emrys Roberts) were asked:

> to consider and report back on the position of Plaid Cymru following the referendum and elections of 1979, and on the steps that need to be taken to facilitate the attainment of Plaid Cymru's goals of securing self-government for Wales, safeguarding the culture, language, traditions and economic life of Wales and securing for Wales the right to become a member of the United Nations.[9]

The question of commissions and their application to politics is an interesting one in itself. Regular checks on the course of political progress are crucial for a political party. However, commissions are often conservative in intention, used as mechanisms for preserving the status quo. This was to be a criticism directed at Plaid's.

After nearly two years of deliberation, the Commission presented its report in 1981. The most striking feature was its scope and depth. It was surprising because internal party reviews rarely set complete, comprehensive agendas; they more often start from an assumption that the party philosophy or ideology is entrenched and sacrosanct, as it forms the essence of the party's existence. The findings of the Labour Party's policy review in 1991, for example, scarcely duplicated Plaid's candour. Despite its claim that the review "is not an election manifesto", the Labour document was drafted to show "how our convictions apply to the challenges and changes confronting the United Kingdom in the final decade of this century and beyond". This made it little more than an adjustment of policy positions. There was virtually no analysis of Labour's ideology or political philosophy, although this did come later under New Labour, though with little of the consultation and engagement shown by Plaid in 1981.[10]

That a substantial part of the Plaid Cymru report dealt with 'Political Philosophy' tells us two things: first, the seriousness with which the commission approached its task and its structured method of operating, and second, the previous lack of a detailed exposition of where Plaid Cymru stood ideologically. One section of the report encapsulates this:

Those who argue that the pragmatic approach is inadequate maintain that the party can never have a clear-cut identifiable and projectable image until its policies are more firmly rooted in socio-economic theory and that such a development is essential if we are to achieve any widespread support in the more highly politicised parts of the country. We sympathise with that point of view.

Having agreed that a broad egalitarian tradition is an important element in Welsh identity, it follows that our political philosophy should take account of that fact. That means that we must seek to establish a society which not only recognises our right to enjoy freedoms enjoyed by other nations but also recognises the right of local communities and of individuals to equality of opportunity based on a fair distribution of wealth and power.

The report's other main concern was to formulate an appropriate strategy for Plaid to follow. It started with the assumption that:

A political party implicitly recognises the authority of the constitutional structures that exist and within which it works. As our aim is radically to change if not to destroy those structures, by acting as a traditional political party, we partly compromise our position from the outset. If, by gaining control of local authorities and forcing concessions at parliamentary level, we get the present system to work more in harmony with the needs of Wales and its local communities, we are in effect strengthening the system of government that we seek to replace. Our very success, therefore, can easily lead to negative long-term results.

This is a succinct statement of the tensions that have plagued Plaid Cymru throughout its existence. It returns us to the psychological tug-of-war between the methods of a political party and those of a pressure group. In many ways, it is also a reflection of the heavy dose of realism apparent in the party after the blows of 1979.

Despite its grand claims, the report did not offer a solution, largely because there was no clear-cut solution. One member, Dafydd Wigley, had argued elsewhere that Plaid Cymru "had to fight not only for self-government for Wales but also for the best possible deal for the people of Wales within the status quo".[11] It is not difficult to spot the contradictions. The report recommended Plaid's involvement in more pressure group activities at the expense of its traditional electoral strategy. Yet, it also went on to warn that "we must be wary of throwing away too readily the advantages of an increasingly effective political machine that has been built up in a painstaking manner over the years".

Due to an unavoidable absence from meetings on his part and then, to a criticism of lack of originality in the commission's main report, one of its members, Phil Williams, produced his own minority report which added to the debate about the nature of Plaid. In it, Williams identified something the main report had failed to: Plaid Cymru faced a very clear choice; it must decide between acting as "a movement to win a better deal for the Welsh people within the existing framework" or as one "totally determined to end English rule".[12]

Williams continued: "I do not believe that the National Movement can make progress until the role of Plaid Cymru is properly defined. The future of Wales is too important to be jeopardised by muddled thinking".

It would appear that the commission was hamstrung by a basic inability to agree on Plaid's best role in Welsh politics. Other strategic issues could not be resolved until agreement was reached on this fundamental matter.

There were other attacks on the relevance of the majority report. Two leading members of Plaid's left, Dafydd Elis Thomas, MP for Meirionnydd, and Emyr Wynn Williams claimed that "commissions are set up to find out what they want to find out".[13] To ensure any meaningful self-analysis, evaluation must be conducted by the body or membership of an organisation, and not by a coterie of specialists. The latter, they argued, was elitist and would invariably be governed by conservative instincts. They claimed that the Commission of Inquiry was designed to prevent any real directional change in strategy and position after the devolution referendum. Neither was there an identifiable historical context to the commission's appraisal of Plaid's status. The report thus became a snapshot picture of Plaid Cymru in the early 1980s, rather than a serious contextual analysis that might have come up with a clearer class-based analysis of the plight of Wales and Plaid.

Thomas and Williams went on to argue that the commission had abjectly failed to investigate the source of the party's current dilemma, and as a result, was seeking solutions to an, as yet, unspecified problem. In a sense, they were right; unless Plaid could confirm its status as a political party or pressure group, then developing an appropriate strategy was like building a castle on shifting sands. Their final criticism centred on the language of the report, claiming its simplistic vocabulary and references proved the lack of an ideological position. The report's conclusions were therefore superficial, ahistorical and unfeasible. The Commission was an exercise in confirming what the party already knew, rather than a serious evaluation of its problems, with proposals for their resolution. It showed "intense conservatism", and worse still, "nauseating paternalism". The

General Secretary, Dafydd Williams, agreed that "its approach pre-empted the outcome. The report said what everyone assumed it would in 1979".[14]

Yet for all this, there is evidence that the commission did influence the direction and pace of Plaid Cymru's development. It generated clear outputs and did, at least, rehearse the debate about Plaid's status in the aftermath of the referendum, even if no concrete solutions were offered. It led directly to a monumental motion at the 1981 party conference and, indirectly, to a prolonged period of infighting about party ideology and aims. Most importantly, it forced the party to take stock at a crucial time in its history.

This was recognised much later by Plaid's leaders. Despite his criticisms of the commission at the time, Dafydd Elis Thomas later emphasised the importance of any attempt at analysis which helped redefine the party's objectives and strategies, and avoided "a cataclysmic view" which would have been easy after the 1979 rejection of devolution. Thus, the commission at least "enabled the party to refocus".[15]

Ieuan Wyn Jones (who was vice-president at the time of the commission and took over as president from Dafydd Wigley in August 2000) suggested that too much had been expected of the commission: "it could never have provided all the answers". What it did do, he felt was offer an opportunity to conduct something of a SWOT analysis of the party.[16] The commission was more than this, however. It served as a reminder of many of the important issues that still surrounded the party's development.

Dafydd Williams doubted its lasting relevance and remained convinced that it "is difficult to think of a single positive aspect for Plaid politically".[17] Certainly, there was little immediate, tangible benefit from the review, yet its success lay in exposing the need for Plaid to address some rather fundamental issues that it had previously avoided. The Commission of Inquiry began a process of change, rather than resolving any of these challenging questions on status and strategy.

1997

The second referendum on devolution, in September 1997, was an altogether different affair to 1979. It occurred in a radically changed context and brought quite different results.

I have linked Plaid Cymru's maturing as political party to shifts in context and changing opportunities. The election of a Labour Government in May 1997 (the first for eighteen years) and its decision to press on immediately with its plans for devolution marked one such important new context. It also presented Plaid with a new set of opportunities and challenges.

The most important factor was motivation: for the Labour government in 1979, devolution was driven by expediency, based upon a desperate self-preservation; in 1997, the New Labour government saw devolution as part of its wider programme to modernise the UK's constitution. Constitutional reform was a key component in the broader process of political modernisation. Advantages could be accrued by presenting the rationale for devolution within a framework of wider administrative decentralisation, and alongside proposals for reform of the House of Lords and a review of the voting system for European elections. This time it was not a sop to the nationalist parties in Scotland and Wales. Rather, it was part of New Labour's vision of a modern and mature United Kingdom.

Plaid Cymru's approach to the two campaigns differed quite considerably too. In 1997, Plaid was, officially at least, a partner to a determined Labour effort, which this time had a degree of strategic integrity in its planning and operation. A key difference was that the pro-campaign was led by the "cross-party and non-party" Yes for Wales campaign, established in February 1997, which differed from the prominently Labour-run and Plaid-operated campaign in 1979. It meant there was an air of non-partisanship in the yes campaign, a feeling that it was not being led entirely by the usual party politicians. It was to prove crucial.

The background to the referendum is also important. In the lead-up to the May 1997 General Election, against a backdrop of Labour deliberations on the advantages of holding a referendum, Plaid pledged to campaign for a multi-option referendum (with the status quo, limited devolution and self-government in Europe as choices). However, it was quickly acknowledged that this kind of referendum was unlikely to be conceded by the Labour leadership ("we recognised the *realpolitik* that Labour would not contemplate a multi-option ballot".[18]) In reappraising its stance, Plaid took some time to decide to offer its official support to the 'Yes' campaign for the 1997 referendum, no doubt memories of 1979 haunting many within its ranks.

Its involvement in the devolution campaign took a variety of forms. Many members contributed at a local level to the activities of Yes for Wales and party leaders offered valuable advice and back-up to the central machinery of the campaign. Plaid's MPs, however, were forced to make a less tangible and visible contribution. It was decided early on (by both Labour's ministerial team at the Welsh Office and, to a lesser degree, by Plaid Cymru itself) to "restrain or limit" president Dafydd Wigley's contribution, largely for fear of associating the yes camp too closely with Plaid. Labour was anxious to avoid its plans being "tainted by association" with nationalism. Wigley did participate, although the general impression was that the Plaid president "had effectively to be gagged throughout the campaign". Plaid's other MPs also played a role, but some concern was expressed by Yes for Wales leaders that Ieuan Wyn Jones and Cynog Dafis failed to operate within the agreed structures of the organisation, preferring instead to make *ad-hoc* additions to the campaigning effort as it went along.[19] This was thought to reflect a "frustration on Plaid's part that they weren't running the show".[20] However, Plaid's contribution to certain aspects of the campaign was widely acknowledged (despite tensions with Labour which were apparent throughout) and the outcome was even seen to be one of mutual respect between Labour and Plaid for each other's special contribution.

Some of Plaid's own members criticised the party for having conceded the political and ideological leadership of so vital a Welsh campaign to Labour, but most of the party's mainstream (both leaders and members) understood that the party had little option other than to support Labour's devolution proposals, for opposition would have meant permanent exclusion from one of the most critical debates on Wales's political future.

There remained an air of partisanship throughout though, with Plaid arguing that it was its contribution that pulled the vote back on course for the eventual narrow victory, with its members conducting the bulk of the telephone canvassing and leaflet distribution (even delivering a Labour-produced newspaper, *The Rose*) during the latter stages of the campaign. Whilst this Plaid effort was acknowledged by the Yes for Wales leadership, Labour Party members also put in colossal efforts locally, in areas like Ogmore in the south Wales valleys, as did "non-party political virgins" in areas like Pembrokeshire.

In a dramatic, nail-biting finale, the results in the early hours of Friday, 19 September 1997 saw 50.3% (558,419 votes) in favour and 49.7% (552,698) against. This meant a majority of just 6,721 supporting the establishment of an assembly. Turnout was just 50.1%. In the light of this, the contribution of Plaid Cymru activists to the campaign becomes even more significant.

However close the result, it still meant that the first all-Wales elected institution for some six hundred years would be established. The first elections to the National Assembly for Wales (as it was to be called) offered Plaid the chance to contest a Welsh, rather than a British, General Election for the first time.

The party could hardly have wished for a better climate in which to fight its first Welsh general election. The dynamics of the campaign and the party's successes in the elections to the Assembly on 6 May 1999 offer a further insight into the role of devolution as a catalyst for Plaid's growth.

The largely colourless, lacklustre lead-up ('campaign' is too forceful a description) to the elections hardly prepared Wales for the excitement that was to follow when votes were counted (nor, indeed, during the first year of the Assembly's existence).

The scale of the electoral upheaval that occurred in these elections surprised all observers. They effectively unravelled the historic pattern of voter allegiance to the four main political parties in Wales. It was the "quiet earthquake"[21] that turned Welsh politics on its head. The electorate, for so long Labour's most reliable source of votes, abandoned the party in droves. There was a concomitant switch of support to Plaid Cymru that allowed it to move for the first time beyond its traditional electoral heartlands in the north and west to a decent foothold in the southern valleys.

The themes underpinning these elections help us understand how the second act of the devolution play affected, and was affected, by Plaid Cymru. Against a background of Labour leadership election fiascos, criticisms of "control-freak" tendencies in shaping the campaign's strategic direction and a series of long-standing scandals in Welsh local government, centring on mainly Labour-run councils' mismanagement, inefficiency and, in some instances, corruption, Plaid had almost perfect conditions for the Assembly election.[22]

Here again, the issue of a symbiosis between Labour and Plaid reappears. Throughout their histories, Plaid and Labour have experienced a close relationship. On many occasions, it has been Plaid's downfall; on this occasion, it was to its not inconsiderable benefit. Two traumatic leadership contests in the Welsh Labour Party, ongoing disputes over candidate selection and the controversial policy of 'twinning' to ensure better gender balance in the Assembly, plus the general unpopularity of Tony Blair and his lieutenant in Wales, Alun Michael, were all grist to Plaid's mill. Thus, a policy of distancing itself from, whilst also juxtaposing itself to Labour was a hugely successful election strategy, and employed very deliberately by Plaid. The party was further assisted by Labour borrowing an 'off the peg' onslaught on Plaid from Scotland and the SNP-inspired attacks there. One size clearly does not fit all and this strategy backfired with a sympathetic Welsh electorate.

For a number of reasons, this was the election at which Plaid Cymru successfully played its trump card. The party conducted the most impressive election campaign in its history . First, the new context provided by the National Assembly offered the perfect opportunity for Plaid to display the coherence of its long-standing, all-Wales political programme. Secondly (and perhaps more importantly), the party had succeeded in modernising itself internally. Senior party figures identified the immense advances made in information management and communication at the party's new headquarters in Cardiff, and the successful switch to telephone canvassing as key factors in this modernisation. Plaid was also helped by an injection of cash from two sizeable individual bequests which enabled the party to employ additional staff in the run-up to the election. It spent close to a quarter of a million pounds on the Assembly election (a figure in sharp contrast to the £40,000 spent on the 1997 General Election campaign). This internal modernisation was a key factor. Put simply, the party began to transform itself from a well-intentioned but shambling, amateur organisation into a more modern, competent and professional show.

Plaid was further boosted by the high morale of its activists, motivated by the prospect of the first elections to the new devolved institution and later by Plaid's consistently high standing in the opinion polls leading up to the election. One senses that Plaid's grass-roots members were less truculent than usual! There was a feeling that they were actually prepared to be led and thus happy to follow the party's campaign strategy, often to the letter. Huge electoral prizes were on offer for the first real time in Plaid's history and it was easy to engender internal unity as a consequence.

In addition to a sound financial footing, the location of the campaign strategy on a firm research foundation was crucial too. Quantified data had been collected through a major independent market research project conducted in the summer of 1998. Now strategy and the ongoing tactics of the campaign were not based on the traditional guesswork or anecdotal evidence, but on hard, measurable data. It was another first for Plaid. Data acquired from the market research also sparked the party's first serious attempt to rebrand itself. The marketing of the name change to Plaid Cymru The Party of Wales' was an important element in this and had a quiet, but successful, impact upon English-speakers, adding legitimacy to their decision to switch to Plaid.

In the matter of campaigning methods, large-scale, properly managed telephone canvassing proved crucial and, more importantly, the manner in which this information was utilised emerged as a huge contributory factor in Plaid's success. The party purchased an SNP-commissioned software package that had first been used in the Perth and Kinross by-election in Scotland. This ensured that the data generated was regular and enriched. Longitudinal information was then employed tactically to determine ongoing strategies in all of Plaid's key seats.

The party was also helped by its long-established, all-Wales policies. For Plaid, it was not a question of bolt-on or adaptation, since the party had always had such policies, although some had hardly been robust (and, in some cases, not entirely practical or realistic). In the event, any remaining flaws were to prove incidental, for there was no vigorous dissection of policy during the election campaign.

Finally, there was the role of Dafydd Wigley as leader. Wigley clearly brought Plaid enormous benefits, especially when contrasted with the other party leaders. Throughout his time as president, Wigley represented the image Plaid Cymru wished to convey, both to the electorate and its own members, as a compassionate, honest, articulate, all-Wales leader, with popular appeal across the different linguistic, socio-economic, geographic and cultural divides. This was enhanced by his media appearances in the campaign and reaped hefty dividends at the polls.

Independence: the 'Never, Ever' Controversy

Although the election campaign was largely a damp squib, with little rigorous scrutiny of policy, it did stimulate another important constitutional debate within Plaid Cymru.

In response to questioning at an April campaign press conference, Dafydd Wigley tried to distinguish between 'independence' for Wales and the party's newly worded commitment to 'full national status in Europe'. Plaid's 1983 General Election manifesto had talked openly of "an independent Welsh state" and the party's official website had until recently called for "full self-government and an independent voice", providing Labour, in particular, with plenty of ammunition. Its campaign organiser, Peter Hain, MP for Neath, claimed that Plaid had abandoned one of its long-standing political commitments in the middle of the election campaign and was engaged in "a clumsy campaign to censor their beliefs". Wigley claimed that the party had "never, ever" sought Welsh independence, arguing that in a modern context "there is no such thing", whilst accusing Labour of "Millbank McCarthyism" for what were perceived as

London-inspired attacks on Plaid.

This provides an interesting update on devolution's impact on the constitutional debate in Plaid Cymru. There has been regular discussion about the appropriateness of terms such as 'independence', 'freedom' and 'self-government' to describe its political project, but Wigley's 'never, ever' declaration allowed Labour and Liberal Democrat researchers to trawl through Plaid publications, gleefully recording plenty of appearances of the 'i-word'. At one level, the issue did not affect Plaid too adversely. Voters may well have been sceptical of Plaid's protestations of independence innocence (indeed, a HTV/NOP poll showed that nearly half did not believe the party) but that did not deter them from voting for the rather pragmatic and cautious manifesto offered by Plaid. This situation reinforces the appropriateness of different language to communicate its constitutional scheme, and the need to be consistent about the terminology used.

The 'never-ever' controversy formed an interesting diversion from an otherwise lacklustre campaign. Plaid's formal aim was not independence, but full national status within the European Union, although clearly the former had been used frequently in party literature. The wider significance of this was that it forced the party to re-engage once more with the constitutional blueprint it had for Wales.[23]

Plaid Cymru's Coming of Age?

The elections to the National Assembly were Plaid's most successful ever. It won seventeen seats, at least four more than party leaders suggested to me on the eve of the poll.[24] That it exceeded even its own expectations owed much to its campaign managers expecting the usual fallback in support during the week of the election. However, the elections replicated the pattern of a successful by-election, with Plaid's support increasing right through to the moment when people cast their votes.

This saw Plaid capture the historically rock solid Labour seats of Rhondda, Llanelli and Islwyn, with swings of 30-35% in much of the southern valleys and a decent share of the vote virtually everywhere. Not surprisingly, it gave a huge confidence boost to the party. It had broken out of its traditional heartlands, offering a satisfying retort to its opponents' traditional taunts of 'Plaid Gwynedd' (referring to its north west fastness). By June 1999, everyone in Wales had a Plaid representative at one or more elected levels.

In some respects, Plaid's performance should come as little surprise. It was clearly the party most prepared for the first, modern Welsh General Election. Plaid had been waiting seventy-four years for this moment. Nevertheless, it *was* a surprise – to insiders and outside commentators alike – that the party produced such a professional and strategic campaign to bring about this success. The Plaid campaign was the only instance in the party's history of a successful synthesis between enthusiasm, commitment and professionalism. Effective management was the basis of the party's triumphs, along with a more robust set of policies for which Cynog Dafis MP and Simon Thomas (who had been political advisor for the Plaid-run Taf Ely Borough Council and was Dafis's successor as MP for Ceredigion when he stood down in February 2000) were responsible.

Thus, Plaid effectively maximised its strengths, and simultaneously minimised its weaknesses. It benefited from its new-found confidence, showing admirable restraint and a lack of premature euphoria in the conduct of its campaign. It also showed a skill in maximising benefits for itself from Labour's sizeable predicaments at the time. The result was a realistic, confident, understandable and popular campaign that yielded hugely impressive electoral rewards.

79:97 – Fortune Reversal

What has this overview of the two main debates on devolution since the war revealed about the constitutional question in Plaid Cymru? In one sense, they show the extent of the party's maturing between 1979 and 1997. Plaid's response to the devolution proposals, the nature of its participation in the two referendum campaigns, as well as its performance in the 1999 elections, indicate how far it had developed into a conventional political party, able to plan and execute a strategy for success.

Equally, devolution forced Plaid to reassess the significance of the various stages in its long-term constitutional project. Returning to our metaphor of the Russian doll, Plaid looked again at its inner layers to isolate short and medium term strategies for achieving its ultimate goal of a self-governing Wales. The manner in which Plaid embraced the limited form of devolution on offer in 1997 with little disharmony amongst its own members suggests that the party was prepared to concede the importance of the first step on a much longer journey. Plaid's readiness to accept the legitimacy of the Assembly with its limited powers, together with its declared commitment to make it work, illustrates how devolution had become one of the constituent shells of Plaid's Russian doll.

The European Dimension

> From its foundation the Welsh national party has had a lively con-
> sciousness of Wales as a European nation.[25]

The 'Europeanisation' – the making more European in outlook – of Plaid
Cymru is the second important constitutional dynamic in the last quarter
of the twentieth century. An examination of the party's shift in attitude to
Europe and the European Union illuminates further the pattern of its
growth.

> Wales can understand Europe, for she is one of the family.[26]

In a very real sense, until the 1970s and the start of a serious debate on
UK membership of the European Economic Community (EEC), Plaid
Cymru had been able to maintain an uncomplicated commitment to
Europe. From its beginning, Plaid looked to Europe as the natural political context for a small nation like Wales. The party's leaders, from
Saunders Lewis (Wales "should have a seat in... European society by
virtue of the value of her civilization") to Gwynfor Evans ("The hope of
a national future for Wales lies in her becoming an equal member of the
European Community. The people of Wales must learn to think of themselves not as British but as Welsh Europeans, members of the
international community") had used Europe to justify the case for Welsh
self-government. There were plenty of romantic interpretations of
Wales's world location. A sharper and more practical focus to the debate
did not come until the major experiment in European integration had
begun in earnest. The question of the United Kingdom joining the EEC
posed important questions for all the political parties in Britain. Many of
these questions concerned Plaid's central constitutional beliefs.

Plaid had traditionally looked to countries like Canada and New
Zealand as models for the kind of constitutional status it sought for
Wales. It had long campaigned for Welsh membership of the United
Nations. Now it had to consider the issue of membership of a different
organisation with a supranational character.

Debate on the United Kingdom's prospective membership of the EEC
dominated Plaid's annual conferences in the early 1970s. It raised a
number of sensitive questions, relating particularly to Wales's constitutional status and to issues of national and supranational sovereignty.
Since sovereignty involves notions of political autonomy, authority and
self-determination, it is little wonder that the issue of UK membership of

a supranational body with a primarily economic and trade focus posed such dilemmas for Plaid Cymru.

In its early discussions on EEC membership, the party divided on traditional left-right lines, with the left arguing against joining what was viewed as a 'capitalist club'. But the split was not complete, for some mavericks did not line up with their usual allies. The debate was deep and complicated. There now occurred a realignment within the party as the constitutional implications of EEC membership became apparent.

The announcement of the referendum on UK membership in 1975 placed under scrutiny Plaid's long-established but rather unsophisticated position of 'pro-Europe, anti-EEC'. Some focus was given to a broad debate on the pros and cons of membership in an important paper by Gwynn Matthews,[27] which helped formalise Plaid's position. Matthews's paper was widely regarded as a "balanced, sensible document" in its outline of the advantages and disadvantages of the UK joining the EEC from the perspective of a small nationalist party like Plaid.

The party's two newspapers, *Welsh Nation* and *Y Ddraig Goch* also tried to stimulate a more meaningful analysis to remove the 'in or out' focus of the debate. There were trenchant pieces by Emrys Roberts, former chair of the party, in which he described the trends of the Common Market as bringing "a paucity of job opportunities, heavy migration, low wages, high unemployment and the near extinction of our language and national identity". The argument against membership focused on the incorporation of Wales by another institutional structure which, like Westminster, was not democratically elected by the Welsh people (interestingly an early form of the 'democratic deficit' debates that appeared in the EU much later). In the absence of national institutions of its own, Wales's interests would surely be as badly misrepresented in Europe as they were at Westminster ("Wales' bitter experience as part of the UK underlines the danger of incorporating peoples into a large multinational state..."). There were references to the terms of the Treaty of Rome which, it was claimed, would establish a centralist and bureaucratic alliance, rather than the prototype 'Europe of the Regions' that Plaid sought even then: "Britain's continuing membership of the Community would mean the end of Wales becoming a complete self-governing nation and the end of our democratically elected parliament as the supreme law-making body in Wales".

Argument also centred on the perceived lack of economic benefit to Wales. It could not secure economic growth and prosperity "within the straitjacket of EEC membership". Instead, Plaid should campaign for a "loose European confederation" or a "free trade association of self-governing European nations to replace British membership of the EEC". The party suggested re-joining EFTA as an alternative to the EEC, offering "most of the advantages of economic association with few of the disadvantages". Thus, "Decentralisation of power rather than Common Market membership was the most effective way to tackle Britain's economic problems...". It was also widely agreed that "to change the EEC from the inside would be a Herculean task". Clear parallels can be seen here with debates on Europe in wider Left circles. Several leading members of Plaid saw this aping of Labour as a source of internal tension, sensing that the party was duplicating Labour debates.

How did this translate into a strategy for the referendum of 1975? Together with Labour party left-wingers like Tony Benn and Michael Foot, Plaid initially pledged to campaign for the referendum question to be phrased with a clear reference to Wales ("It must be organised on a Welsh basis, and the result declared constituency by constituency"). Plaid's MPs vowed not to lend support to the referendum bill if this demand was not forthcoming (although the poll was eventually counted on a county-by-county basis).

In its conference early in 1975, Plaid decided to campaign for a no vote in the referendum. It set up a six-strong group, led by Dafydd Elis Thomas MP, and affiliated to the 'Wales Get Britain Out' group, sharing membership with the Wales TUC, the Welsh Communist Party and the Welsh Council of Labour. Involvement in the campaign required membership of one of the groups that represented different sides on the referendum choice. The statutory terms of the act also meant funds were provided for each side in the referendum campaign. This made the EEC referendum campaign fundamentally different to the devolution referendum campaigns of 1979 and, later, 1997 (although interestingly, the issue of campaign funding was also raised in 1997 and in the findings of the Neill Committee on Standards in Public Life).

Eventually, Plaid agreed a sixteen-point policy document setting out its position on the EEC and its stance in the referendum campaign. There were three crucial prongs to Plaid's argument against EEC membership; first, that the EEC was a club designed to protect capitalist interests and would bring no economic benefit for Wales; second, that it had the potential to become a nuclear bloc; and third (and perhaps most important) that the institutions of the EEC allowed for no direct Welsh voice. Each betrays a balance between the pragmatic and ideological motivations that shaped Plaid's constitutional strategies at the time.

The debate on EEC membership is also revealing in terms of the language used to communicate Plaid's plans. The prevailing themes were sovereignty, political autonomy and democratic accountability, all of which feature centrally within Plaid's political vision. Later on, the distinction between the terminology of nations and regions was given some intellectual input in the debate over an emerging 'Europe of the Regions'.

The complicated nature of Plaid's European stance was highlighted by its referendum campaign slogan, "Europe – Yes: the EEC – No". Opposition was firmly directed at the EEC's institutional framework. Plaid's own credentials as a European focused party made it important for it to distinguish between opposition to the EEC, and opposition to Europe itself. The EEC was portrayed as "anti-democratic in its institutions and so exclusive as a club". However, the nature of the ensuing debate on EEC membership, both inside Plaid Cymru and beyond, made it difficult to separate the institutional flaws of the Community from wider European issues.

The party's decision to argue against EEC membership was not without its internal critics. There was also grass-roots opposition: one letter to *Welsh Nation* complained that "Plaid Cymru was behaving like a Left-wing rump of the Labour Party", and argued "whatever its faults – and there are many – the EEC offers Wales a wider and freer atmosphere, where its voice can be heard".

Opponents included Eurfyl ap Gwilym, director of the party's research group, Robin Reeves and most notably, Dafydd Wigley, the newly elected MP for Caernarfon, who argued that EEC membership was to Plaid Cymru's strategic advantage in the pursuit of a government for Wales. When Plaid confirmed its line on the referendum, Wigley withdrew from the campaign, crucially leaving it without the support of one of its new MPs. It is difficult to assess the impact of Wigley's withdrawal, one leading figure described it as negligible, claiming Wigley was "almost quiet on the matter". Others argued that Wigley was conspicuous by his absence from the campaign trail. He later described his frustrations at his alienation, claiming he had felt "very lonely". His arguments, he said, rested on the "basic common sense" knowledge that European integration was going to happen with or without Wales, and it was thus the duty of a nationalist party like Plaid to develop its constitutional arguments within the context of a new European framework. He referred back to Plaid's European inheritance, claiming he was following previous

Plaid leaders, Saunders Lewis in particular: "He [Lewis] would be very pleased at the way Plaid Cymru has [later] discovered the importance of Wales's place within the European context – something that was very close to his heart".[28] Wigley's comments illustrate how new situations and different political circumstances relating to Europe forced Plaid to reconsider this issue, and with it the way self-government might be achieved.

Ambivalence within its own ranks minimised the damage of the eventual vote in favour of the United Kingdom's continued EEC membership. Plaid interpreted the result as necessitating a new European dimension to its basic campaign for self-government ("as a defence mechanism for the people of Wales, self-government has become a necessity following the Referendum"). The party lost no time in producing draft policy proposals for full national status "on the same basis as Denmark and Ireland" within the EEC, calling for the EEC to eventually move towards a confederal association of self-governing European states, rather than political union. It also challenged the iniquity of proposed Welsh representation in the European Parliament by just four MEPs, claiming Wales would thus be marginalised. The party drew attention to Wales's low profile within the EEC, and called for a Welsh representative on the Council of Ministers and the Economic and Social Committee, as well as a right to nominate European Commissioners.

Plaid drew frequent comparisons in *Welsh Nation* with member states like Ireland "which has won a net benefit from the EEC" and Luxembourg which enjoyed full representation in the EEC's structures "with a population the size of Gwent!" Yet it remained ambivalent, constantly implying that the achievement of self-government would give Wales the opportunity "to decide whether to remain within the EEC or pull out and negotiate free trade arrangements (similar to the favourable terms secured by Norway)".

The European issue again exercised the party's constitutional thinking during the 1980s. The 1984 European elections saw a change in Plaid, to support for the idea that the existing institutional framework of the EEC might be the platform from which Westminster could be bypassed and self-government advanced. As the 1984 manifesto stated: "Without national status, Wales has no voice in the EEC: no representative on the Council, no Commissioner, and only four members of the European Parliament". By now, the European ideal was regarded as adequate compensation for its existing institutional flaws. Plaid quickly augmented its pro-European position, suggesting a both pragmatic and principled motivation, in contrast to Labour's opposition to the EEC. In the 1980s and 1990s, Europe became the arena for a rethinking of Plaid's constitutional plans for 'full national status within the EEC': "The new start for Europe will succeed if the voices of the small nations and regions are heard ... The Europe of the future will be the Europe of a hundred flags, and the Red Dragon of Wales must fly among them". From the mid 1980s onwards, and as a member of the Democratic Party of the Peoples of Europe – the European Free Alliance (DPPE-EFA), Plaid began to for- malise a more robust case for reform of the existing framework of the EU. It called for the transfer of Council of Ministers' legislative powers to a two-chamber Parliament, one directly elected by citizens and the second representing the regions and nations.

One result of actual engagement with Europe through elections was criticism by leading European candidates Jill Evans and Peter Keelan of the party's policies as 'unfocused' and spurred by *realpolitik* more than ideological commitment. The party did commit itself to a more compre- hensive, realistic and rigorous analysis of both the opportunities and pitfalls of the EU, but this was scarcely fulfilled by 1999. The election in June that year of the party's first MEPs, Jill Evans and Eurig Wyn, was the most significant fillip for the party's European focus. Plaid benefited from the new system of proportional representation which treated Wales as one region with five MEPs. It followed its National Assembly suc- cesses with a highly creditable 29.6% of the total vote (compared to Labour's 31.9%) in the European elections one month later. Within the European Parliament, the two Plaid MEPs joined the merged Greens/European Free Alliance group which was a broad alliance of green and regionalist parties, like Eusko Alkatarsuna from the Basque Country, Union Democratique Bretonne from Brittany, Volksunie from Flanders and the Scottish National Party.

Even with its first full-time European politicians in place, the party was still gathering a portfolio of responses to new EU policies as they affected Wales – for instance, the impact of the single currency and the accession of new central and eastern European countries, as well as reform of the Common Agricultural Policy and regional policy, and the rights of workers. It had also to consider the formulation of a new posi- tion on the National Assembly's relationship with EU institutions.

Overall, the 'Europeanisation' of Plaid Cymru has been an incremen- tal process originating in some strong, historically European-focused credentials, an area in which Plaid leads in comparison with the other

Welsh political parties. Its position in the 1970s complicates that assessment, but it is clear that Europe features prominently in Plaid's constitutional thinking. Latterly, the debate on a more decentralised Europe with a more powerful Committee of the Regions, contrasts with Plaid's former position on gaining for Wales the same kind of member state status that other small nations within the EU had (although this debate lingers on). It also reinforces the tensions between the hard-line and reforming schools of thought on Plaid's constitutional plans.

The House of Lords

The idea of the Plaid MP for Meirionnydd and former president, Dafydd Elis Thomas, taking up a peerage was first mooted in 1991. The issue sparked considerable argument in the party, which persisted to some degree after Thomas took up his peerage in 1992. Many regarded it as the ultimate betrayal of Plaid Cymru's constitutional aims and political beliefs. Though they were prepared to accept compromises about devolution and the European Union, witnessing a leading figure in Plaid join an institution deemed by many to be elitist, anachronistic and discriminatory was too much for some. Prior to its reform, 775 of a total 1200 accredited peers were hereditary and there were only 79 women peers.

A number of Thomas's former allies on the left of the party, like Phil Williams, Peter Keelan and Siân Edwards, together with former vice-president, Dafydd Iwan, criticised him publicly in an open letter to the *Western Mail* in April 1992. It was suggested that Thomas was attracted by the status a peerage would bring, as much as by its the potential for influencing legislative and policy initiatives. There were other suggestions that this was the latest stage in Thomas's journey towards becoming an establishment figure.

Although acknowledging that his decision to accept a peerage lost him many long-standing supporters in the party, Thomas offered various reasons for his action. He argued that membership of the Lords was merely an extension of the party's long-standing existing activities in the Commons, another British state institution: "it is another part of the British state apparatus". Thomas later pointed to the legislative and policy role that he had been able to play there in relation to the 1993 Welsh Language Act in particular. He also viewed his peerage as being part and parcel of the general modernisation of the Lords: "as far as I was concerned, I was going in there as part of the reforms".[29] However, at the time he accepted the peerage, the reforms of the chamber were in their infancy and much of its elitism remained.

The issue was resurrected in 1999 when the National Assembly offered political parties the opportunity to have additional peers in a 'Transitional Second House' as part of the institution's reforms. A Royal Commission under Lord Wakeham had set out a far-reaching programme of reform. New Labour intended to reform the Lords, in the first instance by ensuring that most hereditary peers lost their seats. The next stage would see a second chamber which could be directly elected or representing the new devolved 'regions' of the United Kingdom.

> ...the relationship between the future Westminster Second House and the National Assembly for Wales could be of [sic] pivotal relationship in assisting or blocking further progress towards self-government in Europe.[30]

> We wish to remove Westminster control over Wales ... But we cannot achieve that by a policy of boycott, which would be portrayed as negative and immature ... We participate in many structures with obvious weaknesses.[31]

Again, there was a groundswell of opposition to the move in Plaid which called for a boycott of involvement in both stages of the reforms. The leadership countered accusations of a sell-out with claims that to avoid representation within the changed Second House would be an abdication of Plaid's representation role. As a political party, it also pointed to the "practical advantages" of "a strengthened team" at Westminster, to help with "monitoring legislation, ensuring a flow of bills, amendments and interventions, as well as assisting with the constant stream of lobbies, delegations and visiting constituents". It also attempted to link the issue to other compromises made by the party during its history, such as taking the required oath of allegiance to the Queen in the Commons and the National Assembly.

Elections were held for Plaid Cymru's possible members in the reformed Second Chamber, with former party general secretary, Dafydd Williams, gaining most votes. In the event, the 1999 party conference threw out the proposal to take up new peerages by a convincing majority.

This issue of membership of the House of Lords illustrates the extent to which Plaid has been prepared to compromise its principles for the opportunity to gain further access to power. It also indicates the growing pragmatism of the party's leadership and its flexibility on a number of key principles, and reveals that, despite the avowed focus on the Wales and European level of influence, the party remains firmly locked into representation in the British political system and its principal institutions.

A Journey Without an End?

> I favoured a step by step approach, but there was always an awareness
> that the train goes further than the next station.[32]

This chapter has looked at Plaid Cymru's development from a constitutional standpoint. It is an important perspective in view of the party's preoccupation with the goal of establishing a Welsh government. Shifts in the party's constitutional thinking in response to events offer another interpretation of its development. The areas discussed here are by no means self-contained; those on devolution and Europe clearly overlap.

Plaid has reconsidered and redefined its constitutional stance during the post-war period. Its early commitment to variations on the objectives of 'dominion' and 'commonwealth' status for Wales were refined gradually, then replaced. The need to express aims differently to the electorate, have dictated revision. Thus, the Senate proposals drafted in the mid 1980s were a reflection of Plaid's readiness to present to the electorate a medium-term objective as a step toward a greater degree of independence at a later date. Similarly, Plaid's scarcely tempered enthusiasm for the National Assembly suggests a willingness to compromise on devolution.

Traditionally, Plaid has focused on constitutional questions to a far greater extent than the other, non-nationalist parties, sometimes to the detriment of properly developed economic and social policies. As the party assumed more of the characteristics of a conventional political party – after 1959 particularly – so it developed a more balanced portfolio of policies.

Nevertheless, there remains some justification for Plaid's reputation as a party preoccupied with the details of Wales's constitutional future. It is a perennial feature of nationalist parties, and especially one with a unique role as the only nationalist party in Wales. The position brings problems and opportunities. Plaid has a huge responsibility in the first instance, as the only political party campaigning democratically on a nationalist agenda. However, the lack of competitors or rivals under the banner of 'nationalism' means that the party can act as a broad church, appealing to many different nationalist perspectives. It may be that Plaid is happy to retain this broad membership: splits over controversial policies would alienate certain sections.

There is another important issue. The party has spent considerable time and energy debating the nuances of its constitutional position. Yet, polls show that most of the electorate's ideas on Plaid are unchanged (and relate little to the party's policies). It gains higher scores than any other party on working for Wales and being honest and caring, yet receives greatest criticism for being a party for Welsh-speakers and having insufficient experience. Polls also identify Plaid as a party campaigning for independence for Wales, despite its protestations to the contrary.

> Plaid Cymru should have no ultimate constitutional aim...The idea that politics is always a road towards somewhere is a simplistic one and I reject it.[33]

It is virtually impossible to identify a clear end to a constitutional project, for the goal shifts as circumstances change. By 1999, most of Plaid's leadership shared this view. The party has been travelling on a constitutional journey since 1925, the final destination of which remains impossible to define firmly. Until the party is satisfied that Wales has sufficient control over its own political destiny to manage its economy and social policies in the manner it chooses in relation to European and global commitments, then the finishing post will not be visible.

Indeed, would the party recognise the finishing line if it were reached? Would this be the culmination of Plaid Cymru's role within Welsh politics? Few within the party believed it would disappear in a self-governing Wales. The most frequent response to this question was that "its role would change quite substantially". Clearly, the party's status would alter dramatically if Wales were to gain a more significant measure of self-government and exercise real independence in its relations within the European Union. It might also face more rigorous competition in the party political arena in the future. Its status as the only nationalist party in Wales is by no means guaranteed, a further factor in the constitutional debate within Plaid Cymru.

Notes

1. Lewis, S., *Egwyddorion Cenedlaetholdeb/Principles of Nationalism,* (Plaid Cymru reprint, 1975).
2. Dafydd Elis Thomas, interview, 13.11.00.
3. *ibid.*
4. Ieuan Wyn Jones, interview, 13.11.00.
5. Orwell, G., *Shooting an Elephant, Politics and the English Language* (Penguin, 1950)
6. Foulkes, D., Jones, J.B., and Wilford, R.A., *The Welsh Veto: The Wales Act 1978 and the Referendum,* (University of Wales Press, 1983).
7. Janet Davies, interview, 01.09.99.
8. Plaid Cymru, *Commission of Inquiry Report,* (Plaid Cymru, 1981).
9. *Cyngor Cenedlaethol,* minutes of meeting on 16.10.79.
10. Labour Party, *Meet the Challenge, Make the Change, A New Agenda for Britain.* 1991.
11. Wigley, D., in Coxall, W.N., *Parties and Pressure Groups,* (Longman, 1981).
12. Williams, P., *Minority Report from Commission of Inquiry, Commission of Inquiry Report,* (Plaid Cymru, 1981).
13. Williams, E.W., & Thomas, D.E., 'Commissioning National Liberation', *Bulletin of Scottish Politics,* 1981.
14. Dafydd Williams, interview, 14.05.01.
15. Dafydd Elis Thomas, interview, 13.11.00.
16. Ieuan Wyn Jones, interview, 13.11.00.
17. Dafydd Williams, interview, 14.05.01.
18. Janet Davies, interview, 01.09.99.
19. Mari James, Yes for Wales campaign, interview, 08.09.98.
20. James, *ibid.*
21. Dafydd Wigley described the Assembly election results as *"daeargryn tawel"* – a quiet earthquake.
22. See Morgan, K., and Mungham, G., *Redesigning Democracy, the Making of the Welsh Assembly* (Seren, 2000).
23. Plaid recognised that it needed to resolve this issue and launched a review after Ieuan Wyn Jones was elected as its new president, taking over from Dafydd Wigley in August 2000. Internal discussion papers were drafted by Jocelyn Davies AM and Cynog Dafis AM. Based on interviews with Karl Davies, chief executive and Janet Davies, director of elections, during the week beginning 3 May 1999.
24. For further details, see McAllister, L., 'Changing the Landscape? The Wider Political Lessons from Recent Elections in Wales', *The Political Quarterly,* Vol. 71, No. 2, 2000; McAllister, L., 'Plaid Cymru's Coming of Age?', Vol. 14, *Contemporary Wales,* pp 109-114, 2001.
25. Evans, G., *Fighting for Wales,* (Y Lolfa, 1991).
26. Lewis, S., *Y Ddraig Goch,* November 1927.
27. Matthews, G., *Wales and the Common Market,* (Plaid Cymru, 1971).
28. Dafydd Wigley, interview, 22.01.01.
29. Dafydd Elis Thomas, interview, 13.11.00.
30. Plaid Cymru position paper, 'Representation and Reform, An Analysis of Plaid Cymru Representation in the Second House at Westminster', 1999.
31. *ibid.,* p. 2.
32. Dafydd Wigley, interview, 22.01.01.
33. Dafydd Elis Thomas, interview, 13.11.00.

6. The Ideological Perspective

I began by describing Plaid Cymru as a nationalist party, its principal aim being to ensure the historically-defined nation called Wales takes control of its own affairs. However, the term nationalism has several different interpretations and applications. This chapter examines how Plaid Cymru has tried to clarify its political objectives. It offers another perspective on Plaid Cymru's growth by exploring the party's efforts to explain its nationalism.

My starting-point is that Plaid Cymru's nationalism has a distinctive character. Whilst nationalism is easily its principal ideological identity, Plaid's politics have also been associated with other ideologies like republicanism, socialism, and environmentalism. This chapter reviews some of the significant debates within Plaid Cymru about the nature of its political identity and discusses the relationship of other ideas to Plaid's core nationalist project.

Lewis Valentine, Plaid Cymru's first president, saw Plaid as "... more than a party – it is a faith". This religious metaphor is rather useful. If nationalism is the 'faith' to which Valentine (himself a clergyman) was referring, it can be better appreciated how difficult clarification or elaboration of that faith has been for Plaid Cymru. That is, its commitment to the fundamental cause of Welsh nationalism has made it, at best irrelevant, at worst sacrilegious, to entertain linking Plaid's nationalism to other political ideas.

Two related questions have shaped Plaid Cymru's debates on ideology since 1945: whether it should formulate an ideology for itself, aside from the historic and fundamental commitment to national self-government; if so, what kind of ideological slant this should be.

> An ideology ... is a complete and self-consistent set of attitudes, moral views, empirical beliefs and even rules of logical discourse and scientific testing.[1]

A political ideology may be described as a set of values promoting a particular political system or a distinctive organisational form. It is essentially a way of seeing the world or expressing how it should be. Yet there have been many different interpretations of ideology in politics. Plamenatz's understanding of an ideology as a set of closely related ideas or attitudes characteristic of a group claims: "Ideology is primarily 'persuasive' and is only ... secondarily 'prescriptive'."[2] A political ideology, therefore, does not have to present a coherent and systematic scheme. Indeed, those that do are the exception, rather than the rule. Instead of expecting to find a rational ideological package which hangs together neatly, Groth has suggested that ideologies are better approached as 'clusters'.[3] By this definition, 'belief-clusters' like nationalism, conservatism or socialism signal the gathering of biases towards or away from a certain form of political organisation. This idea of an 'ideological cluster' (a shared outlook or opinion on the best form of organisation) may prove to be the most productive way of exploring Plaid Cymru's ideology.

In *The Communist Manifesto*, Marx and Engels claimed that "The ideas of the ruling class are in every epoch the ruling ideas". Since Marx's view of ideology as projecting a selective (and therefore false) view of politics and the world, the modern usage of ideology has seen it lose many of its political connotations and become simply "an action-orientated system of thought".[4]

Ideology and Parties

> An ideologist is like a shopkeeper bound to keep only one brand of goods; whatever he says is suspect because we know that for him some conclusions are fixed beyond argument.[5]

In saying this, Minogue understands ideology as presenting a fixed set of values about the proper operation of politics. It is true that a clear ideological identity is a defining characteristic of political parties. Most parties compile a programme of policies that convey a sense of their overall vision and values. Many subscribe to an identified ideology such as socialism, liberalism, conservatism or nationalism. This represents their vision of the principles upon which society and politics should be organised.

Nationalism has been treated as an ideology with a difference. Some argue that nationalism is merely a neutral set of ideas that takes real shape only through its association with other distinct ideologies.[6]

> Socialism is simple. It is working-class men and women collectively and democratically running society for themselves. It is not a new idea ... Ideas don't suddenly leap out of history fully formed. They grow from earlier ideas and are shaped by the society in which they develop.[7]

Like socialism, nationalism draws on a number of different historical perspectives about the nation and about political power. However, nationalism has had a troubled and inconsistent relationship with other ideologies.

There are two reasons why ideological identity may be more difficult to establish for a nationalist party. First, there is a resistance to doing so. Nationalism is seen as sufficient in its own right and therefore not requiring any qualification or addition. Adding a further ideological dimension to its politics compromises the fundamental nationalist stance. Secondly, nationalism can take a variety of forms. This might make it even more important for a nationalist party to adopt a 'qualifier' to explain its specific vision and to distinguish it from other types of nationalism.

At the core of this debate is an acknowledgement of the variety of nationalisms that exist. Nationalist parties do not have uniform positions on how a society should be organised once the national question is resolved. This has made it important for a party like Plaid Cymru to distinguish its own particular brand of nationalism.

The core dilemma for a nationalist party is whether its nationalism explains its political views and policies sufficiently and satisfactorily. Debate within Plaid Cymru over the need or otherwise for an ideological qualification to its nationalism underlines the tension described above, between those who view Welsh nationalism as a free-standing ideology and those who argue for a more explicit and detailed political location for Plaid. The tension between these approaches tells us something of the growing pains of the party. At the outset, it was possible to concentrate on a straightforward nationalist appeal, largely because Plaid was scarcely a political party. As it developed into a more conventional party, the non-nationalist element of economic and social policies assumed more importance.

In practical terms, Plaid's problem has been related to its increasing electoral focus, that is, how to broaden its appeal to a range of people with different cultural and socio-economic backgrounds and political viewpoints. Its goal of full national status for Wales is clear, but the electorate requires a set of policies which explains the precise type of government Plaid proposes.

For most of its early years and certainly up to 1945, Plaid Cymru had no consistent social and economic platform for its nationalism. Its thinking reflected the predilections of its most influential leaders like Saunders Lewis and D.J. Davies. It was in the changed post-war political landscape that the party began to develop a clearer stance on key policies from which an ideological identity, beyond nationalism, might be built. Even then, this platform was by no means consistent and holistic. The gradual accumulation of such policies runs parallel to the ideological debates reviewed here and Plaid only began to clarify its precise blueprint in earnest during the 1970s when the party was beginning to modernise.

I identified 1959 as a key electoral turning point in Plaid's modern history, when it began to operate on an all-Wales level for the first time. As we have seen the party had to wait for its first electoral successes until the Carmarthen by-election of 1966, and the General Elections of 1974. Having MPs focused the party on the need to develop a solid policy platform. It also faced pressure in earnest from its political rivals for the first time

It became clear that there was a general lack of understanding as to what Plaid Cymru stood for. Apart from its commitment to Wales and the Welsh language, there was little public awareness of the rest of its political aims, like its co-operative economic policies and commitment to the nationalisation of industries. It was no surprise that Plaid Cymru suffered serious image problems. Its own polls (internal, and externally-conducted) have shown that the public associate Plaid with all things Welsh, particularly the language. This is easily its most distinctive badge of identity. However, the problem with this is that the vast majority (81.3% in the 1991 census) of people in Wales do not speak Welsh.

These concerns acted as a stimulus for Plaid to explain its nationalism. By clarifying its position, it could also reaffirm what it *did not* stand for. This proved a powerful motivation for the debate on ideology. The party needed to declare clearly what it represented, beyond Welsh self-government; it had to develop a consistent package of policies ,beyond constitutional issues and then decide how best to communicate it.

"The party has changed from being a sect to being a denomination" wrote John Davies.[8] The matter of ideology is further complicated by the diversity of Plaid Cymru's membership. I have already said that it is a broad church whose members hold a wide range of political viewpoints. Agreeing an ideological label for the party's programme is inevitably problematic. Davies's religious metaphor is useful. Plaid's membership resembles the range of non-conformist denominations in Wales who all have slightly different perspectives on religion and wish to retain their own chapels, services and identities.

"If it is a party, what is the nature of its philosophy, its ideology?"

asked a *Welsh Nation* article in the mid 70s.[9] The question struck at the very heart of the debate at a time when Plaid was beginning to consolidate its status as a fully-fledged political party, rather than a pressure group, and reveals the expectation that a party should have a clear ideological identity.

Socialism and Plaid Cymru

Socialism can be described as a current running throughout the development of Plaid Cymru. Its influence has ebbed and flowed, but from the party's beginnings, it has been a strong presence. In the 1920s and 1930s, it was represented by the likes of Kate Roberts and D.J. and Noelle Davies.[10] Roberts fought hard to add a socialist dimension to the early economic policies of Plaid. The Daviess' argument for a leftward slant to Plaid policies that would help distinguish Welsh nationalism from less democratic strains elsewhere in the world is discussed earlier. Theirs was a crucial argument, repeated later by those who wanted Plaid to more fully commit to socialism.

Republicanism and Plaid Cymru

There were two important flows in Plaid's socialist tide: the rise of the republican movement in the 1940s, and again in the 1980s; and the debates on including socialism within Plaid's constitutional aims that began in the 1930s, but reached their peak in the early 1980s.

Essentially, a republican position in UK politics is an anti-establishment one, which argues for a radical reorganisation of society without a monarchy and with sovereignty vested in the people. That there have always been republicans within Plaid Cymru's membership is not altogether surprising given the influences it has historically drawn from Ireland, as well as the powerful anti-royalist strand to its politics. The republican element has never been a dominant force within Plaid Cymru, but its almost continuous existence does underline the persistent left-leaning, anti-monarchist and anti-establishment inclination of at least part of its membership.

After the Second World War, a specific republican organisation, Mudiad Gwerinaethol Cymru (the Welsh Republican Movement – WRM) was established within Plaid Cymru. The formation of the WRM gave a more cohesive structure to what had previously been a loosely organised republican influence. It emerged from a general dissatisfaction with the pace of Plaid's development, particularly in industrial south Wales.

We were young cubs being very impatient with the older politicians.[11]

The leading members of the WRM were predominantly based in the south-east and included Harri Webb, Cliff Bere, Ithel Davies, Ifor Hughes Wilks and Gwilym Prys Davies. Many of its members had not been attached to any existing political party. There were also strong branches elsewhere, especially at Bangor University.

Some WRM members were ex-servicemen and hugely resistant to the overwhelmingly pacifist stance of Plaid Cymru at this time, though again, this was not new. Plaid had seen protests against its pacifist leanings during the war, from activists like John Legonna, a Cornishman, and Trefor Morgan and Ted Merriman from the Ogmore Valley. Morgan and Merriman were also imprisoned for 'insulting behaviour' for deliberately turning their backs at a summer show at Aberystwyth when 'God Save the King' was played.

Many prominent individuals in Plaid had been conscientious objectors during the Second World War and Plaid had led a campaign against conscription, calling it "a badge of our national slavery". The WRM also argued strongly against peacetime conscription.

The WRM was particularly critical of the "preachers and pacifists controlling Plaid Cymru" who had created a party that was, for them, insufficiently militant and assertive. The president, Gwynfor Evans, was singled out for special criticism for failing to offer a strident edge to the national struggle: "We in the republican movement were inspired by anti-Gwynforism as much as anything".

Within this atmosphere of disaffection, a motion calling for a republican basis to Plaid's ideology was put to the party's summer school in 1949 (which at this time took place immediately after the party's annual conference). When the motion was defeated, the republicans staged a mass walkout. This was the stimulus to mobilise independently. Members of the newly formed WRM were henceforth forbidden to be members of any other party. This effectively created a political movement from a loose splinter or pressure group.

Gwynfor Evans later claimed their departure was a huge regret to him, but felt it was a crucial part of Plaid Cymru's development at this time, in order to sustain the party's pacifism: "we clearly disagreed as to the methods for achieving our goals".[12]

There were various strands to the WRM's activities. A militant, anti-imperialist and trade union focus drove it. It published its own newspaper, the bi-monthly, *Welsh Republican*, which survived for thirty-seven issues between 1950 and 1957 and contained some trenchant comment on the pace of Plaid's development, by D.J. Davies amongst others. The WRM attempted to produce a news-sheet, *Llais y Gogledd* (Voice of the North) and tried to establish a network of local branches, especially in the southern valleys.

In the 1950 General Election, the WRM fought the Ogmore seat with its candidate, Ithel Davies, gaining 613 votes. Pedr Lewis remembered fighting the whole election on a budget of £250, "largely borrowed off friends and relations" (this was not, in itself, unusual for even much later on, elections were often fought on a shoe-string). The WRM did not direct its criticisms at Plaid Cymru alone. Its obvious target was Labour's monopoly on Wales and the disregard with which the republicans perceived Labour was treating Wales and things Welsh. It is worth reminding ourselves that Plaid Cymru was a small, fairly insignificant organisation at this time, scarcely able to call itself a political party. Labour was a worthier target.

The WRM had effectively run out of steam by 1954, and Gwilym Prys Davies led the move to disband it as a separate party. He argued that the republicans should return to pressure group agitation within the other parties. Davies duly joined the Labour Party (where he was later to became an influential advocate of its devolution policy), Harri Webb went first to Labour and then to Plaid, and Bere and Lewis back to Plaid Cymru.

> "Our success was to keep Plaid Cymru on the straight and narrow...
> they didn't dare tone down their stance whilst we were around".

The WRM was able to force Plaid to address the issue of its own political ideology and its strategies for self-government more directly. Theirs was a small but significant contribution to the process by which Plaid Cymru became more of a political party with firmer policies. Indeed, the real success of the republicans was in acting as a pressure group.

The investiture of Charles as Prince of Wales in 1969 gave further impetus to the republican sympathisers, of which there were many in Plaid. This republican wing came to the fore again in the early 1980s, this time against a backdrop of a ten-week conspiracy trial, one of the most significant in Welsh political legal history. Eight defendants were accused of having conspired to attack thirteen targets (mainly government and Conservative party premises) between 1980 and 1982.

The police inquiry (one that was later accused as being the real conspiracy) centred on members of the small organisation called the Welsh

Socialist Republican Movement (WSRM). The defendants were all members of the WSRM, some were also members of Plaid Cymru.

> The Welsh Socialist Republican Movement was born in reaction to the politics of the 1970s in Wales, particularly the devolution movement culminating in the 1979 Referendum".[13]

It had been set up in January 1980 as a ginger group seeking to "inject new militancy into socialist and nationalist politics in Wales". There was an ongoing debate as to the strategy the movement should follow, the main issue centering on constitutional versus revolutionary tactics. The WSRM was split ideologically between those who were nationalists first and foremost, and those who were predominantly socialists.

Despite being held in custody for sixteen months without bail, the trial verdict saw all defendants cleared of conspiracy, although two were eventually found guilty of other charges. The trial effectively destroyed the WSRM.

Much of the debate about the type of nationalism Plaid Cymru should represent has centred on positioning the party on a conventional left-right political scale. There have always been moves to label Plaid's politics as explicitly socialist. At its very beginning, there were attempts to explain Plaid Cymru's political position and how it differed from that of the other parties, by activists like D.J. Davies who described Plaid as "a genuinely Radical party and a champion of workers, without succumbing to the fallacy of centralised Socialism...".[14] Examination of some of the earliest moves to debate socialism in Plaid Cymru indicates why the debate on ideology recurs so frequently in the party's history.

I have already described the distinctiveness of Plaid's early political and economic philosophies. They were based on decentralism and co-operative economics, and drew heavily on the research of D.J. Davies who warned, "If we are going to apply the term 'Socialist' to our policy, we should be ready to define the ways in which it differs from the conception of Socialism cherished e.g. by ... the Welsh Labour Party".[15]

In 1938, a conference motion from the Bangor College branch urged the party to switch its campaigning to an explicitly socialist economic and political platform. The motion criticised "cruel capitalism" for Wales's ills, and called for equality of the sexes, a social basis to property ownership, the abandonment of co-operativism and adoption of "a policy combining Nationalism with Socialist principles". Although this sought to move the party on to a more strictly orthodox socialist agenda, it made clear connections with nationalism. The "cruel capitalists" were the English who exploited Wales as an internal colony.

The Bangor motion was overwhelmingly rejected (only two delegates voted in favour). Saunders Lewis preferred the party to reiterate "its policy of co-operation and widespread private property, *perchentyaeth,* is the only one which can assure democratic freedom to individuals, trade unions, and society in Wales". Others, among them Dafydd Jenkins, urged the party to tap into disillusion with Labour's rearmament policy with a specific appeal to Welsh Socialists: "Wales cannot be won for Home Rule unless the Socialists of Wales are won over". These statements illustrate the kind of tensions surrounding the clarifying of Plaid's politics, and indicate the strength of the party's commitment to the ideas of co-operative democracy and *perchentyaeth* at this time.

There were further attempts to explain Plaid Cymru's nationalism immediately after the war. In 1947, a letter to the party's *Welsh Nationalist* newspaper pointed out that Plaid was "an intelligent political party which would bring to Wales the logical results of the aims of the early socialists". This was rather romantic, but it did stimulate further moves to substitute Plaid's existing economic policy with a more trenchant socialist one.

There was also a backlash. In 1960, a motion from the Newport branch warned the party against emphasising a left or right dimension to its politics, claiming it should instead appeal to all those who believed in a parliament for Wales. The idea that Plaid should assume a kind of ideological neutrality on economic and social matters was to be at the centre of internal discussions on the ideology.

At the 1963 conference, a motion from the Bridgend branch, this time explicitly entitled 'Socialism', sought to give greater prominence to "the democratic socialist nature of our policy in our pamphlets and addresses and relocate the people as far as the real meaning of socialism is concerned". The motion also urged Plaid to "devote more time and thought to the economic aspect of workers' control and the practicability of smaller units of industry in present day circumstances". The language normally associated with socialism was now being used by members of Plaid.

That this call so alarmed the party's leadership is also revealing. The motion was discussed at length by the National Executive Council (as it was then termed) which tried to amend it by substituting the word "democracy" for "socialism". The executive amendment deleted that part of the motion that explicitly referred to socialism (this was supported by a similar amendment from Aberystwyth College branch) and the motion was then passed with its amendments. This was an indication of Plaid's sensitivity to incorporating specific references to socialism in its statements.

The party conference was not the only forum for discussing ideology. Party newspapers were also used to provoke debate. There were claims that "it is time for Plaid Cymru to define its philosophy", with suggestions that the party's philosophy was best defined as "neither liberal radicalism nor 'orthodox' socialism, but community socialism".[16] Significantly, this reflects the main thrust of the debates on socialism, which centred on the type of socialism that Plaid Cymru should adopt. The debates focused firstly on whether Plaid should explicitly label itself a socialist party and secondly on the attempts to clarify the specific type of socialism its politics represented. The most important aspect of this was distinguishing it from that of the Labour Party, a recurring theme in the discussion of socialism in Plaid Cymru.

There were further motions during the 1970s on socialist policies, but it was the 1980s that gave the debate its most explicit and structured airing at successive party conferences. We should first explain the political context. Wales has never elected a majority of Conservative MPs. Indeed, the highest number of Conservatives ever returned from Wales was in 1983 when the party held thirteen of thirty-eight seats. In 1929, there was a single Conservative MP from Wales. Seventy years later there were no Conservative MPs. Since 1945, Labour has easily been the electorally dominant party with an absolute majority of all MPs returned from Wales. It gained less than 45% of the vote only once, in 1983.

Wales has been a Labour fortress since the early 1920s, making its twentieth century political culture overwhelmingly red. Plaid Cymru's ambition to become the new party of Wales thus meant it addressing the question of its commitment to socialist values. To challenge Labour as the dominant party, it had to address the nature of Labour's successful appeal to Welsh people.

> There is no hope for the Blaid to win self-government as long as it sticks to its current economic and social policies. Only a nationalist party with valid socialist policies can hope to win the support of the majority of the people of Wales.[17]

In many ways, the debates on socialism in Plaid mirror those on the constitutional question. Parties evaluate their ideological images, often on the basis of shifting political contexts and the pressures of new electoral demands. The immediate stimulus for Plaid was the findings of the party's Commission of Inquiry that reported in 1981. The Commission's report furnished a motion to the annual conference at Carmarthen, which focused on changes to the party constitution designed to hasten the party's recovery from the disasters of 1979.

The motion was long and detailed, taking up around nine hours of debate from a conference total of twenty and a half hours. It was split into ten parts, amounted to several thousand words and attracted a total of twenty-two amendments: "its size alone caused utter chaos! ... It was effectively a wish-list for changing all of Plaid Cymru".[18]

A large part of the motion (and several of its amendments) dealt with the internal structure and organisation of Plaid Cymru. However, another significant chunk – largely set out in the motion's 'Introduction and Declaration' (its preamble) – set out the methods for achieving Plaid's aims:

> Conference believes that these aims can only be achieved by the adoption and implementation of policies which are nationalist, decentralist and socialist. Conference also believes that Plaid Cymru must reorganise its structures and procedures in ways that maximise the participation of the whole membership in decision-making, a reorganisation that demands improved political education of the membership and improved channels of communications within the party.[19]

The motion made explicit reference to socialism as a description of its policies, alongside its long-standing nationalist commitment. It forced the party to confront the question of ideology head on at a particularly opportune moment. The events of 1979 not only forced it to reconsider its strategies and aims; they also created an atmosphere more receptive to a fundamental review of what Plaid stood for.

Three amendments were submitted; one from Dinas Powys branch which aimed at deleting the reference to "decentralist socialism" – this was defeated; one from Pontypwl constituency which tried to strengthen the commitment to socialism (also defeated); one composite amendment from Cardiff North and Dyffryn, Aberpennar branches which elaborated the reference to a "socialist state" to include "the widest measure of democracy in industry and administration" (also defeated).

These amendments give an idea of the nature of activist engagement. Behind the simple division, the membership split between those who favoured a socialist location and those steadfastly opposed. Yet there was also a level of relative sophistication to this debate on the kind of social-ism Plaid Cymru should advocate, as well as the best language for communicating it. The eventual amended motion was passed with a two-thirds majority enabling the constitutional change to be put into place. Plaid Cymru's constitution (and its membership cards) thus included a commitment to socialism for the first time.

This was not the end of the debate, however. Another motion, 'Declaration of Aims', was submitted to the Carmarthen conference by the Newtown branch referring to the "difficult period" the party had experienced since 1979, and proposed a "decentralist socialist basis" as the basis to the party's new economic programme for Wales. It argued for the use of "primarily... orthodox political means" to achieve it. The underlying current of the Newtown motion was the need for better con-sultation with the grassroots of the party in its efforts to reinvent itself. This motion was also passed by the conference.

There was a response to this consolidation of its socialism from Arfon, warning: "that Plaid Cymru should not isolate itself in one corner of the left/right political spectrum, but should build on foundations that recog-nise the Welsh tradition of egalitarianism, social justice and the value of the local community". This articulated the unease felt by some of the membership at the drive towards an explicit inclusion of socialism in the party's aims. In aggregate, the motions show the divide between those arguing for a generic appeal on the basis of nationalism and those urging a firmer ideological focus, based on socialism. They set the terms for a nascent debate on ideology that was to continue through much of the 1980s.

*

The Carmarthen conference motion was by no means decisive however. Further confusion ensued as to the implication of labelling the party explicitly 'socialist'. Dafydd Williams, who was General Secretary at the time, argued that the complicated motion and amendments indicated "the perils of 'in-depth' navel-gazing, producing an enormous document and conference resolution, with unpredictable amendments", and "the most disastrous things were passed by default".[20] Williams was seen by some of those responsible for the explicitly leftward push to be personally uncomfortable about such moves.

At the following year's conference at Llandudno, a motion from Caerffili on 'Devolution and the SDP' was submitted but not discussed.

However, its contents highlighted grassroots concern that the party might dilute its freshly-confirmed socialism through expedient links with the new SDP, hinting at the covert approaches rumoured between individuals in both parties to establish closer co-operation. There was also a composite motion on 'Plaid Cymru Aims' which produced seven amendments, again reflecting the polarisation caused by the socialist tag. By now, terminology had become the principal focus for discussions on ideology with another wide-ranging debate on the appropriateness of the term 'decentralist socialist state' to describe Plaid Cymru's strategy for self-government.

At the Lampeter conference in 1984, two further motions were discussed on 'Plaid Cymru Ideology' and 'Plaid Cymru Beliefs', which tried again to remove the commitment to socialism in the party constitution. Two successful amendments reaffirming the party's commitment to socialism, submitted by Bridgend and Llanharan/Brynna/Llanhari avoided an embarrassing u-turn.

In some respects, the real issue underpinning these debates was the extent to which the commitment to socialism assisted the 'marketing' of Plaid Cymru to Welsh voters. Challenging Labour was Plaid's preoccupation, and how better to do this than to set itself up as a rival socialist party?

Dafydd Wigley discussed the problem of labels in the context of his own presidential campaign: "I would not have gone around describing myself as a socialist, although anyone looking at the programme I was supporting, would have called me one".[21] There was scepticism, expressed by Wigley but felt by others in the party, of the simple faith that some placed in applying a definitive label to Plaid's politics. There was also an understanding that the focus on ideology came from the desperation felt at the party's slow progress and the need to challenge Labour, but that Plaid was in danger of becoming weighed down by ideological obsession.

Wigley was one of these, arguing that the labelling of a political party often confused as much as it illuminated. A bottle of fine wine with no label does not taste better by adding a label to the bottle, while some drinkers may be attracted or put off by clearer identification. That was the risk for Plaid, he argued.

Wigley's own self-image is a factor here. He saw himself primarily as a nationalist, but conceded that other people's conceptions of nationalism might not coincide with his own. If they did not, then the real ideological position of the Welsh nationalist could easily be misconstrued. He too was keen to challenge the criticisms of opponents that nationalism was always located on the right of a traditional political continuum, but was concerned that Plaid attached too much importance to its socialist label. His own nationalism was firmly 'centre-left'. Wigley's comments underline the importance of language and terminology. For him, the language used to communicate Plaid's political vision was the key if the Welsh population was to understand the meaning and significance of its ideological commitment to community socialism.

Wigley described this period in the party's history as being characterised by a form of 'religious fundamentalism'. There is some truth in this for there was a rigid split into two camps over socialism and stormy relations between them. It was a nihilistic, self-destructive period. Members recall a mood of "nastiness" and "confrontation" in the party. The disappointments of 1979 not only stimulated pressure for change, but also apportioned blame.

In truth, the intensity and vitriol of the debates at this time may reveal more about the nature of Plaid's conferences than they do about the depth of ideological schisms within Plaid Cymru itself. That is, by imposing a simple 'for or against' choice confrontational discussion was guaranteed. They also reinforced the pre-eminence of the annual conference on Plaid's development in this period.

Dafydd Elis Thomas was a major player in the debates on ideology, albeit indirectly. His own commitment to New Left ideas and his easy use of the term "socialism" to describe Plaid's economic and social policies was a big influence on the party. Indeed, it was on the back of the Left's ascendancy within the party that Thomas was elected president in 1984.

The exchanges between the two sides made the argument over the inclusion of socialism in the party constitution an intriguing one for the Welsh media. The ongoing coverage in the *Western Mail* portrayed the debate as a threat to the established aims of Plaid Cymru. There was extensive reporting by Clive Betts, the paper's Welsh Affairs Correspondent, which, whilst clearly exaggerating the significance of this debate to Welsh affairs, reflected the newspaper's fascination with internal battles in Wales's political parties, as well as this journalist's interest in Plaid.

Confusion was also a feature of the debates. The party's General Secretary remembered uncertainty amongst delegates about the options that were set before them: "There was little meaningful debate given the vastness of the amended [Carmarthen] motion". However, Janet Davies, who played a leading role in the discussions, claimed that "the party's establishment closed debates down so abruptly that there was little time to elaborate arguments or make positions clear".

There were also stories that, amidst the confusion, the outgoing president, Gwynfor Evans, who carried such influence within the party, voted the 'wrong' way by mistake, thus giving his support to the motion. Such was his influence that it was believed that a bloc of Carmarthen area delegates, and many from elsewhere, followed the president's lead and voted for the change. Hence, some still argue that "socialism was accepted almost by accident".

Like all apocryphal tales, it contains an element of truth. However, others recalled Evans's stance as being "very deliberately supportive" of a firmer ideological commitment. The outgoing president was said to be keen to tighten up Plaid Cymru's ideology. Evans later said he was not "terribly keen on the word 'socialism' – I would have preferred to use the term 'freedom', which is less confined". However, Evans also acknowledged that the debates in the early 1980s 'invigorated' Plaid and he welcomed especially the new groups that it brought to the fore in the party. Whatever the truth, these rumours of Evans's 'accidental support' hint at the wider confusion.

What is the lasting significance of these debates? Some claimed they signalled "a break with Plaid's 'apolitical' past" and "... helped propel Plaid into a political party from a pressure group". They clearly reflected certain new growing pains in the politicisation of the party, but did they push it further towards becoming a mainstream political party?

The case in favour points to the high level of political content in these debates on ideology. At times, there was a relatively sophisticated application of Plaid's policies to the principles of socialism. For those closely involved, the arguments marked "one of the most interesting and exciting periods" in Plaid's history. They were forcing Plaid to clarify its broad nationalist ideology in a more meaningful, strategic way. This was an integral stage in the party's drive to create a credible alternative to Labour.

The case against points to repetitious conference debates, characterised mainly by boredom. The same arguments were raised annually between 1981 and 1985 as the two rival camps exchanged insults in often bitter clashes. Conferences became focused on this issue to the exclusion of all others. There was also criticism that the party never effectively communicated its new socialist identity to the public.

By the end of the 1990s, Plaid's leadership and membership were far less troubled by the terminology of socialism. Wigley's emphasis has shifted somewhat too. He could then claim "Plaid Cymru is a socialist party – in fact, one of the few in Westminster which calls itself socialist", suggesting that he had now become 'the left winger' in the party: "Of course, by now, it's me that's considered the left wing of Plaid ... So it is either me or Plaid or Wales that's changed!"[22] This asks an interesting question: have Plaid's leaders absorbed some of the shifts the party had made or is it just that the term "socialism" has been rehabilitated in the wake of New Labour's move into the political centre ground?

Many Plaid members who had been uncomfortable with the term "nationalist", felt that the opportunity to add an ideological location helped rehabilitate the nationalist label in the public eye. Some suggested that the term socialism should now be loosely applied or "broadly defined as in New Labour's case".

Developing Socialist Policies

As important as the conference motions on socialism was the gradual firming up of a broad-based socialist platform of policies. Again, this had been happening incrementally since 1959. Important conference motions and *Cyngor Cenedlaethol* debates elaborated the party's position on subjects like privatisation, unemployment, disarmament, social policy, a nuclear-free Wales, and opposition to private health provision. In 1969, the party's first 'Economic Plan' set out a radical strategy for Wales's economic renewal based on state redistribution. Later on, there were ambitious schemes for renationalising some of Wales's key industries, like coal, steel and water.

Community Socialism: Plaid Cymru's Brand

> Whenever it is practical for a decision to be made locally or centrally, we believe it must always be made locally, by the people affected. The Labour Party, in contrast, believes passionately in centralism.[23]

The key for Plaid Cymru to distinguish itself and its new commitment to socialism from that of the Labour Party in Wales was its advocacy of *community* socialism. It symbolised Plaid's ideological dilemma: the party needed a form of socialism that had to be distinctively Welsh *and* distinguishable from that of Labour. Adding the term 'community' was a way of Plaid branding its socialism. It also allowed the party to avoid the associations with the state that socialism traditionally conjured up, and built on the decentralist traditions of the party and the "small is beautiful" and communitarian philosophies historically so important to the party.

Whilst conference debates focused on distinguishing Plaid Cymru's socialism intellectually, this was also conducted through a new quarterly magazine, *Radical Wales*, established in 1983. The party helped fund the magazine to add more sophisticated levels to the debate on the future of both Plaid Cymru and Wales. *Radical Wales* stimulated discussion of the terminology to best describe Plaid Cymru's socialism. One of the party's vice chairs, the academic Phil Cooke, sparked the debate by arguing that "the moral basis of decentralisation is indissolubly tied to the moral basis of a democratic society". He claimed that the idea of decentralist socialism was entirely in tune with the new political and economic character of Wales: "decentralist socialism is morally superior to any other kind of social organisation that I can think of".[24] Another *Radical Wales* article discussed the question from an economic perspective: "understanding the sources of market failure is essential to a proper critique of capitalism as well as an appreciation of the possibilities for decentralised decision-making in socialism".[25] Reynolds and Elis Thomas used the terms, 'decentralist' and 'socialist', interchangeably to refer to Plaid Cymru's newly-formulated ideological commitment.[26] Owen and Howells pointed to the need to define community in the context of Plaid's ideological location, arguing that: "Plaid must be more specific in its general aims, the Welsh public need a clearer lead and party image".[27] Marshall, meanwhile, praised Plaid's "refreshing and original commitment to decentralised and community socialism" within a broader libertarian tradition. This, he argued, should be developed through anti-state terminology with the ultimate objective of "a free nation without a state".[28] We can see from these debates that 'decentralist' and 'community' had equal value in distinguishing Plaid's new brand of socialism. Their specific importance lay in adding a Welsh slant that was designed to give Plaid the edge over Labour.

The strength of the concept of community socialism for Plaid was its flexibility. As we saw earlier, community has many understandings, and using the term community socialism allowed Plaid to adjust its ideology to suit different conditions. But it had its critics, too. Rhodri Glyn Thomas, who became AM for Carmarthen East and Dinefwr, doubted that community was a useful term to apply to Plaid's political philosophy, suggesting it carried "an image of being localised without any real power" which implied a weakness in the practical application of community socialism as a serious and understandable political ideology.

However, for others like European and Westminster election candidate, Peter Keelan, the addition of community to socialism brought "a social dimension to an otherwise economistic concept", and also gave "a Welsh historical location to an appropriate ideology".

Helen Mary Jones, later the Plaid AM for Llanelli, interpreted community socialism in a wider sense to include "communities of interest as well as geographical ones". As a consequence, Jones, like Keelan, saw community socialism as the most reflective position for Plaid Cymru. However, she also suggested that the party needed to be "less naïve" in its use of the term, implying that Plaid used the term 'community' to by-pass a more serious elaboration of its politics. For her it skirted the vocabulary of class and gave scope to add a distinctive Welsh identity to its socialist commitment.

Others, like chief executive Karl Davies, saw community as referring to a unit with "the political and economic power to influence the material and aesthetic quality of people's lives". For him, it was a huge help in conveying the idea of decentralist, as opposed to state, socialism, stressing "the importance of people in their communities". Penni Bestic, a former general election candidate and women's section activist, saw her nationalism as being "all about community" since it was driven by affecting local change based on wider, global principles. On this basis, she felt Plaid had internalised the notion of community socialism in its grassroots operation. Former party chair, Marc Phillips, meanwhile, claimed that, whilst he understood the difficulties with using community in Plaid's ideology, it was far from being a sop, for the term had a real meaning in Wales that it may not have elsewhere. Phillips also suggested that the term 'social justice' best represented Plaid's notion of community socialism, based on principles of fairness and equity. The result is a clever compromise: an anti-state, decentralist, community form of socialism that was presented as Plaid's distinctive brand.

Wet or Dry? Hydro and the National Left

The long-running debate on ideology gave rise to two ginger groups, representing each side of the argument about the inclusion of socialism in Plaid's aims. Tensions were high: the motions confirming Plaid's commitment to socialism prompted a walkout during the 1984 Lampeter conference by a section of the membership fiercely opposed to the leftward shift of the party.

At the 1982 Llandudno conference, opponents of socialism had set up a group called Hydro (named after one of the resort's hotels where it first met). The group's leading members included long-standing party maverick, Brian Morgan Edwards, members of the party's London Branch such as Stuart Cole and John Lewis, as well as some locally based activists like Clayton Jones of Pontypridd and Keith Bush of Cardiff. Bush became the group's official spokesperson.

Hydro argued that Plaid's nationalism required no qualifying or explanatory terms. It's central objective was to "re-establish self-government for Wales, unqualified by ideological dogma, as the main aim of Plaid Cymru".[29] It saw its wider role in Welsh politics as being to advertise "that Plaid Cymru was not a monolithic left-wing organisation but had room for all shades of opinion of those whose political framework was primarily that of Wales".

Whilst we should not exaggerate the influence of groups like Hydro, which, after all, had a very small membership, it did contribute to the ideological debates. The position it took encouraged a healthy dialogue on Plaid's ideological identity. Although at times, the debate was scarcely mature in style or presentation, Hydro's challenge to the left did at least help the party engage in some important self-analysis. It also forced the party to acknowledge the breadth of viewpoints held by its members.

Hydro's own supporters acknowledged its partial success. Bush later admitted that Hydro had failed in its specific aim of creating an alternative image for Plaid Cymru (after all, it did not reverse Plaid Cymru's official commitment to socialism). However, it halted further moves to the left and gave a platform to those who supported a more neutral ideological position.

Hydro was disbanded in 1987 when: "The approach of the 1987 General Election made it undesirable that divisions within the party should be accentuated".[30] Whilst this was the official line, it is more likely that, by then, the question of socialism's appropriateness for Plaid Cymru was less of a burning issue, leaving little mileage for the group. Some have hinted at a number of splits within the group which made many of Hydro's original members more than a little uncomfortable with its hardline position.

The other ginger group, the National Left was set up at a fringe meeting during Plaid's 1980 Porthcawl conference. The idea of a left-leaning, non-party affiliated organisation was the brainchild of Dafydd Elis Thomas and Aled Eurig, Thomas's researcher and later Head of News and Current Affairs at BBC Wales. It was a brave move to establish a non-party political organisation, and some Plaid Cymru members attending the inaugural meeting refused to join the new group when it was decided that non-Plaid members could join. The National Left's founder members included Thomas and Eurig, as well as Syd Morgan, Siân Caiach, Phil Cooke, Janet Davies, Robin Reeves, Emyr Wynn Williams and Robin Okey.

The National Left was designed to be a broad-based movement representing all strands of left opinion in Wales, including members of other parties and those without party affiliation. In the event, it was always dominated by Plaid members and focused its attention largely on the challenges facing the party: "we were driven by the question 'where do we go from here?'".[31]

Once again, the legacy of events in 1979 is important. The National Left's first chair, Emyr Wynn Williams, claimed that 1979 marked "a sea-change in the role of the state" and was thus a dramatic turning point for every political activist in Wales. Plaid had to reassess the future of the party as well as the opportunities and challenges of the new historical period. Elis Thomas and Williams had been highly critical of the party's Commission of Inquiry, seeing it as an essentially conservative device to short-circuit deeper, more meaningful debate on its future. The National Left tried to offer a more robust analysis of the party's previous failures. The context in which it was established is important, not only in terms of the referendum fall-out. The 1980s represented a period of general renewal for left politics in Wales, coinciding with a revived interest in nuclear disarmament, women's rights, and industrial democracy. This era was, of course, also marked by the year-long miners' strike of 1984-5 which stirred the left, as a reaction to events if nothing else. The National Left was very much a product of the period.

Its aim "to bring people of left-wing views into Plaid" was intended to strengthen and radicalise the party's membership. Despite most of its 150-200 members being party members too, the National Left maintained only informal links with Plaid Cymru. It campaigned for self-government, along with the implementation of a programme of socialist economic and social policies.

The National Left also intended to act as "a forum for debate, to examine new ideas, to take Plaid policy forward and to open the party up beyond its very narrow base in society". The pressure it exerted was meant to propel Plaid further towards a more economic focus to its political strategies and, by implication, away from its traditional cultural nationalism. It sought to redefine the role of the state from controller to enabler, which reflected the ideas of both the New Left generally, and Plaid's new commitment to decentralist, community socialism.

Like Hydro, the National Left made a distinctive contribution to the ideological development of Plaid Cymru – possibly, a larger contribution than Hydro because of the times. It drove some of the ideological agenda, rather than resisting its introduction. An editorial in a National Left newsletter of Summer 1984 identified the group's principal success in informing the development of policy. In particular, it had helped germinate the constitutional proposals for a *Senedd* (Senate) which formed the basis of the party's 1987 General Election campaign (although Emyr Williams later claimed that the Labour Party had been quicker to develop these themes into a credible and operational policy during the 1990s than had Plaid[32]). Nevertheless, "The Senate proposals were the key to shifting the political debate towards practical proposals". This constitutional plan for an elected Senate, with legislative authority and limited tax-raising powers, was seen as a valuable strategic step towards Plaid's long-term aim of self-government.

Janet Davies (later AM for South West Wales) identified the important promotional and educational role of the National Left in raising the "general level of the debate" and intellectualising the argument on ideology. She also pointed to its internal successes: its members won several senior party posts, so that by 1984, it was able to boast that "at least four vice chairpersons as well as the vice-president, four *Talaith* representatives, and seven other members of *Pwyllgor Gwaith* are members of National Left or close sympathisers". The National Left controlled the editorial line of the party newspaper, *Welsh Nation*, between 1984 and 1987 when the newspaper debated party policy in a more rigorous way. This overlapped with the development of *Radical Wales* as a polemical journal discussing the rationale for Plaid's decentralist socialism. Indeed, some argued that *Radical Wales* had a more profound role in the leftward shift of Plaid than did the National Left. The magazine added a level of sophistication to political debate, both amongst Plaid's membership and within the wider left in Wales. It was timely in that it complemented the leftward drive of the National Left.

There is a clear sense in which the National Left both affected, and was affected by, the wider debate on Plaid's socialism. Some of its members draw attention to its successful lobbying role. They also suggest that debate on a socialist label for Plaid "had been taking place throughout the party on many levels", well before the conference motions of the early 1980s. There is no doubt that the National Left added an additional thrust to Plaid's leftward shift. Some wished to further define its role to ensure it was a lasting presence in the party. In 1983, Evans and Mainwaring posed four questions which quantify the dilemma facing the National Left at the time:

1. Should National Left continue to be located within a peripheral political party such as Plaid Cymru?
2. Should National Left establish an independent Welsh socialist party?
3. Should National Left merely be a forum for left groups in Wales – severed from any particular party affiliation?
4. Should National Left locate itself within the Labour Party?[33]

The National Left and Hydro are important because they were significant splinter organisations in Plaid Cymru which made a contribution to the party's development, by articulating the tensions that a party like Plaid faced in adopting a more explicit ideological label. Although at their peak, relations between Hydro and the National Left were hardly cordial, it is worth pointing out that, even at the most acrimonious points in the discussions on socialism, there were only a handful of resignations by party members. This emphasises the cohesive nature of the party, which may result from Plaid being the only mainstream, constitutional nationalist party in Wales. There were significant and deep differences between the members of Hydro and the National Left. The fact that, for the most part, they retained their membership of Plaid is testament to the unity of the party.

Beyond the Conference Debates

I said earlier that an additional motive for the debates on ideology came from the need to extend Plaid's appeal beyond its traditional heartlands. Some in Plaid felt that the conference debates on socialism might have been largely academic exercises, important for the party's internal development, but scarcely touching the minds of the voters. To position the party as a real challenger to Labour, its political image needed to be communicated more effectively, and attempts were made subsequently to develop Plaid's policy profile on its newly clarified ideological foundations. There were moves by the *Pwyllgor Gwaith* in 1982 to advance a discussion paper on the party's new commitment to decentralist socialism but, although a new version of the constitution, complete with decentralist socialism, was printed in 1982, there is no evidence that the discussion paper ever materialised.

In a letter circulated in January 1985 to all *Pwyllgor Gwaith* members, Cynog Dafis (from 1992 to February 2000, MP for Ceredigion and Pembroke North) suggested the setting up of a working party to elaborate the party's commitment to socialism. He also suggested that the group's particular focus should be to develop Plaid policy with regard to the role of the state, international relationships and the public/private divide in a self-governing Wales. It is clear from the context and tone of Dafis's letter that the party's commitment to decentralist socialism was not far further advanced, and that several senior party members were concerned by the need to develop it further. The reasons that Dafis gave for "elaborating one of the pillars of our political philosophy" are interesting. He argued that the ideology is "essential for our political credibility as a means of recruitment and political growth". The establishment of a working party would clarify Plaid Cymru's political position and prevent the party "becoming a dumping-ground for utopian way-out elements at a time of disillusionment on the Left". Finally, Dafis defended the debate on ideology for unifying the party and helping to end "misunderstandings springing from the vague, slogan-like nature of our standpoint".[34] That no working group was established suggests an ambivalence by the party about advancing the debate.

Since then, there has been little effort to resurrect the debate on linking socialism with nationalism. The party's youth movement unsuccessfully attempted to highlight the ideological angle in the late 1990s, and the Federation of Plaid Cymru Students also injected a firmer ideological input to the party's strategic debates in this period. However, by then, there was little appetite for changing the party's socialist objectives, and its immediate concern was with translation of the theoretical position into practice in a new constitutional context. Plaid was now much more relaxed about its socialist label than it had been in the 1980s. It was also beginning to concentrate more on specific policies – another indication of its development as a political party.

The Environmental Question: Opportunities and Dilemmas

The rise of environmentalism and the growth of the Green Party posed another important challenge to Plaid's ideological development. It was during the late 1980s that environmentalism made its most dramatic impact on Welsh nationalism. Yet Plaid could claim a long-standing commitment to the environmental agenda, stemming originally from its drive to protect the land of Wales. Its environmentalism was not simply romantic though. It was rooted in the party's vision of social ownership and economic respect for the Welsh environment. There is evidence of a long-held concern that Plaid Cymru should develop its environmental focus more substantially. The party's green credentials were by no means flawless, but there was a strong basis on which to build. Cynog Dafis, who was later to become the first joint Plaid Cymru/Wales Green Party MP, traced it to discussions on an alternative economic strategy in the late 1970s and early 1980s.

In 1983, a working party was established after the unanimous approval of a conference motion which urged the party "to explore ecological and environmental issues". This was the beginning of the 'greening' of modern Plaid Cymru, which culminated in formal links with the Wales Green Party during the 1990s, the most important manifestation of Plaid's development of a green strand to its nationalism.

In September 1989, Peter Keelan provided a discussion paper for *Cyngor Cenedlaethol* called 'Beyond Thatcher: Wales in a Green Europe – Self-sustaining Self-government' which called for alliances to be established with progressive political forces generally, and particularly with those in the environmental movement. This was a prerequisite for progressing Plaid's 'Wales in Europe' strategy, Keelan claimed,[35] firmly linking environmentalism with the emerging European focus of the party. Keelan argued for "a strategic electoral intervention" at a United Kingdom level between Plaid, the Greens, the SNP, the SDLP and the SLD to achieve "a federal Britain, a thorough environmental programme and PR".

The immediate context to these discussions was the Green Party's renaissance in the European elections of 1989. The party performed beyond all expectations almost everywhere, gaining nearly 100,000 votes in Wales (over 11%). These were elections in which Plaid Cymru had hoped to do well. Although it gained 12.9% of the Welsh vote, the party was clearly squeezed by a UK and Europe-wide swing to the Greens.

At its subsequent conference at Denbigh, Plaid invited representatives from the Wales Green Party to discuss common ground. There were already murmurs of discontent from both sides, with many in Plaid regarding links with the Greens as threatening the purity of the party's nationalism. Wales Green Party members were portrayed by some as "outsiders". In pursuing links with another party which did not have a strongly Welsh dimension to all of its policies, it was claimed that Plaid was thus compromising its commitment to Welsh self-government. There were similar objectives from Green Party members who were suspicious of joining forces with a nationalist party.

The following year's conference at Cardiff saw joint policy discussions which yielded two firm motions, one on economic, social and environmental policies and the other on Europe, within which the two parties set out agreed aims. These statements were based on sustainable economic and environmental development which would allow Wales "to preserve a distinct identity with a world at peace and in harmony with the environment". Wales Green Party representatives spoke from the platform in these debates at Plaid's conference which was itself a significant innovation.

In the Ceredigion and Pembroke North constituency, the two local parties were already collaborating with a view to fielding a joint candidate in the 1992 General Election. Based on a joint policy campaign paper in 1991, the terms for an electoral deal were agreed by an overwhelming majority in a ballot of local members of both parties. The agenda for co-operation was a radical and Welsh environmentalist one. Cynog Dafis, long-standing Plaid activist and prominent environmental campaigner, was selected as candidate. Dafis declared: "We in Plaid Cymru have the chance to set an international agenda, starting the process by co-operating with the Green Party of Wales. Such co-operation, far from being mere tactics, would spring from a deep philosophical convergence of ideas derived from distinct but compatible perspectives".[36] Wales Green Party's Ken Jones also saw the possibilities of the links: "potentially there is a very broad fellowship that can travel the road towards a radical Green Wales".[37]

At the General Election, Dafis won Ceredigion on the joint ticket with a majority of over 3,000 votes and the third biggest swing in Britain. Dafis identified the links with the Greens as "adding another level of backing to his campaign", appealing particularly to English-speakers in the constituency: "The policies and the political initiatives that they will seek to develop need to be as Green as they are Welsh, and not a whit less Welsh because many of those involved are English in-migrants".

However, there remained a core of opposition to the alliance in both parties. Opposition within the Green Party reached a head early in 1995 when the links with Plaid were declared "totally unconstitutional" and "illegal". Although it eventually collapsed, the alliance in Ceredigion had survived for some five years and created some far-reaching policy initiatives between the two parties. There were notable successes, beyond the election of Dafis: common policy development on environmental and related matters, particularly at Westminster, was a lasting legacy, and Green activist (and subsequently a Green Party member of the Greater London Assembly) Victor Anderson, was employed as one of Plaid Cymru's team of researchers. There was also a joint slate of Plaid/Green candidates for the local elections in 1995 which brought some success, but which also saw renegade Green Party members stand against the 'official' alliance candidates. At a European level, Plaid's Green credentials proved instrumental in consolidating the various nationalist, regionalist and environmentalist members of the European Free Alliance to which Plaid belonged in the European Parliament.

There was another loose alliance between the two parties in Gwent which was far less successful at both electoral and non-electoral levels. None the less, *Pwyllgor Gwaith* representative for the area, Helen Mary Jones argued that the Gwent alliance made a significant contribution to the victory in Ceredigion by establishing a breadth to the links. It also promoted a valuable educational dimension on green and nationalist politics for members of both parties. That it was unsustainable was due to "the negative stance adopted by some within the Greens to things Welsh" and the fact that the Green Party in Wales "effectively imploded".

What is revealing about the electoral agreement between Plaid and the Greens is the insight it offers firstly into Plaid's preoccupation with electoral success, and secondly, the party's willingness to pursue links with other parties on a localised, rather than a national level. The Green Party links only really took off in Ceredigion and this was the outcome of highly determined efforts by a small group of members of each party there.

The arrangement gave Plaid the opportunity to combine its historic campaigning activities (this time on the environment) with an electoral strategy geared towards winning more Westminster and local council seats. It also helped solidify Plaid's existing, but latent, Green credentials. Many influential figures – Phil Williams, Cynog Dafis and Peter Keelan – had long pushed a Green dimension to Plaid's economic policy. The 1990s saw Plaid internalising and consolidating this Green focus in its ideology.

As importantly, the heightened focus on environmentalism shifted once more the balance of Plaid's political vision. Some of its anti-growth public statements on the environment may have been controversial (even

Cynog Dafis admitted that this message "may be a little advanced for the time"). However, they also meant that environmentalism became established as a critical component alongside socialism in the party's ideology. It meant this was the first time that Plaid could legitimately claim to have merged the red and the green into a distinctive brand of modern Welsh nationalism.

A Green and Red Ideology

Plaid Cymru's 1926 manifesto claimed that "having secured a free and Welsh Wales with the authority to live her own life, then everyone can join with whosoever he wishes, either to further socialism in Wales or whatever system he chooses".[38] This review of some of the subsequent debates on ideology gives an indication of how far the party has travelled.

Despite the official commitment to socialism not coming until 1981, it is fair to describe Plaid as socialist-inclined for most of the post-war period. Whether it has ever been a fully-fledged socialist party is questionable, since part of its membership has always felt uncomfortable with the label. Nevertheless, the 1980s debates gave the party another opportunity to position itself as an alternative to Labour. It gradually developed a portfolio of socialist policies which were to stand it in good stead when Labour began its move into the middle ground during the 1990s. Plaid was thus able to position itself as a party committed to Wales, firmly to the left of Labour. This would bear fruit in the first elections to the National Assembly in 1999.

Like most European nationalist movements, Plaid includes a diversity of members with the whole axis of left/right opinion reflected in its membership. This is not surprising given the naturally generic appeal of nationalist parties, particularly when it is the only such party in Wales. We can see once more how being the only nationalist party in Wales has brought both advantages and disadvantages to Plaid. It has been free to pursue different directions at different times. However, it has also meant the danger of losing a section of membership by straying too far with its ideological statements on socialism or environmentalism.

When a nationalist party is the only one then it often functions as a broad church, accepting members with a range of political inclinations and ideological allegiances but the common denominator of self-government for the nation. This serves as the key cohesive agent for its membership. When more complex issues connected with economic and social policy are raised, or the further explanation of its nationalism is

The Ideological Perspective

required, disagreement is inevitable. This was the pattern of events in Plaid Cymru in the 1980s and 1990s. However, it is significant that the party readily withstood its problems and emerged relatively unscathed from its ideological battles.

The extent to which the public understood the party's ideological position is less certain. The party's research continues to suggest that, in the public mind, there is ignorance of its policy position on issues other than self-government and the Welsh language. Consequently, the party could be said to have no natural ideological terrain of its own, beyond the core issue of defending things Welsh.

There has been a remarkable tolerance within the party to its ideological shifts. Despite the formation of splinter groups of different status and influence, Plaid's membership has remained united. Yet again, this is an ongoing debate. There is a clear sense in which the debate "hasn't finished yet", as Dafydd Elis Thomas put it. This is surely true, since the discussion on political values and how best they should be communicated is one with no clear or obvious end. Like our previous discussion of Plaid's constitutional positions, a teleological stance on ideology is equally unreasonable, particularly as external circumstances play such an important part. In fact, one could argue that the downsizing of the debate on ideology is a measure of how conventional a party Plaid Cymru has become. That the 1990s saw Plaid far more concerned with electoral tactics and organisational matters than with wider political and ideological questions tells us something of Plaid Cymru's emergence as a relatively mature political party.

Notes

1. Robertson, D., *Penguin Dictionary of Politics*, (Penguin, 1986).
2. Plamentatz, J., *Ideology*, (Pall Mall, 1970).
3. Groth, A., *Major Ideologies: an Interpretative Survey of Democracy, Socialism and Nationalism,* (John Wiley, 1971).
4. Heywood, A., *Political Ideologies, an Introduction,* (Macmillan, 2nd edn, 1998).
5. Minogue, K., *Nationalism*, (Batsford, 1967).
6. Antonio Gramsci interpreted nationalism as class-neutral or non-economic until it was appropriated by a class within a struggle. See also Adamson D.L. *Class, Ideology and the Nation, A Theory of Welsh Nationalism,* (University of Wales Press, 1991).
7. Paczuska, A., *Socialism for Beginners*, (Unwin Paperbacks, 1986).
8. Translated from John Davies's lecture to commemorate the seventy fifth anniversary of Plaid Cymru, August 2000 (unpublished).
9. Spanswick, T., 'What is Plaid Cymru?', *Welsh Nation*, 12-18 December 1975.

10. See Davies, D.H., *The Welsh Nationalist Party 1925-45, A Call to Nationhood* (University of Wales Press, 1983).
11. Pedr Lewis, member of WRM. All quotes in this section are drawn from interviews and correspondence with Lewis in 2000-01.
12. Interview with Gwynfor Evans, 10.11.00.
13. Osmond, J. *Police Conspiracy,* (Y Lolfa, 1984).
14. Davies, D.J., *Triban,* Vol. 1, No.1 , Autumn 1956.
15. Davies, D.J., *ibid*
16. Tanner, R., 'Community Socialism', *Welsh Nation,* 24-30 October 1975.
17. Meils, G., *A Free Wales, A Welsh Wales, A Socialist Wales,* (Cyhoeddiadau Cymru, 1973).
18. Interview with Dafydd Williams, 19.02.01.
19. Plaid Cymru Annual Conference programme, 1981.
20. Interview with Dafydd Williams, 19.02.01.
21. Interview with Dafydd Wigley, 03.09.98.
22. Interview with Dafydd Wigley, 22.01.01.
23. Williams, P., (1981), *Voice from the Valleys,* (Y Lolfa).
24. Cooke, P., 'Decentralism, Socialism and Democracy', *Radical Wales,* No. 5, Winter 1984.
25. Mainwaring, L., 'Why Decentralised Socialism?', *Radical Wales,* No. 11, Summer 1986.
26. Reynolds, D., & Thomas, D.E., 'Four Years On: Charting Plaid's New Direction', *Radical Wales,* No. 9, Winter 1985.
27. Owen, D., ap Rhys & Howells, A., 'Radical Wales versus Radical Plaid', *Radical Wales,* No. 9, Winter 1983.
28. Marshall, P,. 'Decentralised Socialism: Enslaved or Free?', *Radical Wales,* No.13, Winter 1986.
29. Keith Bush, correspondence with author, 1994.
30. Bush, *ibid.*
31. Interview with Emyr Wynn Williams, 17.08.98.
32. Williams, *ibid.*
33. Evans, J. & Mainwaring, L., 'Reappraisal of Aims and Strategy of Plaid Cymru National Left', Autumn 1983 (internal discussion paper).
34. Cynog Dafis, letter to members of the *Pwyllgor Gwaith* and *Cyngor Cenedlaethol,* 8 January 1985.
35. Keelan, P., 'Beyond Thatcher: Wales in a Green Europe-Self-sustaining Self-government', paper to Plaid Cymru *Cyngor Cenedlaethol,* 30. September 1989.
36. Plaid Cymru and Green Party, Ceredigion and Pembroke North, *Towards a Green Welsh Future/Tua'r Dyfodol Gwyrdd Cymreig,* (Y Lolfa, 1992).
37. Ken Jones, 'Unite for a Radical Green Wales!', *Radical Wales,* No. 24, Winter 1989.

7. A Woman's Perspective: From the Outside Looking In

> None so fitted to break the chains as they who wear them, none so
> well equipped to decide what is a fetter.
>
> James Connolly, *The Re-Conquest of Ireland*

Here I take a novel approach to the story of Plaid Cymru by looking at its development from a woman's perspective. That this breaks new ground says much about the documentation of Welsh politics. Little attention is paid to women in most accounts of Welsh political history, to the extent that even the women who played an important part in Plaid Cymru have largely been marginalised in accounts of the party. As well as producing an unhelpful imbalance, this deficit also means that many of the most interesting and revealing party debates have not been properly documented. Issues of fair representation in Plaid have significance beyond the promotion of women: the equality debates throw further light on Plaid's vision for a future Wales.

The aims of this chapter are to track the changing status of women in Plaid Cymru, and their contribution to its development; to assess the party's commitment to equality; and to judge the significance of debates on women's equality to Plaid's growth as a political party.

Plaid Cymru: the Party of Males?

> It is the duty of Plaid Cymru, the Party of Wales, to clear a path, to
> win space, to win the terrain on which the women of Wales can free
> themselves.
>
> Gwyn Alf Williams, *Towards the Commonwealth of Wales*

A glance at Plaid Cymru and its leadership at most points in its history would show a male-dominated party. Almost exactly half of its membership is female (49.8% in 1995 and 50.1% in 1999), yet in every other form of measurement the party has been almost exclusively male. Every post-war president and general secretary/chief executive of the party has been a man, as have all of the party's seven different MPs. During this time, the party has had two women national chairs – Siân Edwards (1992-93) and Jill Evans (1994-96). Statistics for 1994 show that only 17% of Plaid's county councillors were women, 21% of its district councillors and 31% of the party's community councillors.

The 1990s saw the most significant breakthrough for women in Plaid Cymru. As well as its first women national chairs and several women joining the party's policy cabinet, women made a real breakthrough at an electoral level. The first National Assembly elections saw nearly 42%, that is, twenty-five, women elected to the sixty-seat Assembly. Of these AMs, six were Plaid Cymru women (from a party group of seventeen) with sixteen Labour women (from a group of twenty eight), and three Liberal Democrat women from its team of six.[1] The following month saw Plaid's first successful European election candidates, with Jill Evans elected as one of the party's two MEPs.

Yet women have been present and prominent in Plaid Cymru since its foundation. From Mai Roberts and Kate Roberts[2] in the early development of the party, Lady Mallt Williams in the 1930s and Noelle Davies in the 1940s (who, interestingly, was responsible for some much-needed economic realism), to senior administrators Nans Jones and Gwerfyl Hughes Jones who were responsible for much of its operation during the post-war period, there have always been women in positions of influence and authority. Yet, despite these and other notable women activists (like Jenny Eirian Davies, and then Janet Davies, Siân Edwards, Phyllis Ellis, Jill Evans, Carmel Gahan, Helen Mary Jones and Pauline Jarman), Plaid Cymru's nationalism has been based largely on traditional understandings of gender, language and culture. The outcome has been an internal political culture that is at least as male focused as that of any other party operating within mainstream politics.

Historically, there have been two rather ambivalent interpretations of women in Plaid Cymru. First, they have been seen as agents for the biological reproduction of the nation and the language. Secondly, there has been a deep-seated antipathy towards those women members who described themselves as feminists, for feminism was viewed as a foreign or external influence on Welsh nationalism.

The first interpretation helps explain the conservative position on gender equality taken by many nationalist parties. There are recurring images in Welsh literature and political writing of women as the guarantors of the language and the nation, and there is little doubt that Plaid Cymru has absorbed some of these.

The second is the more interesting perspective, as it helps us under-stand why Plaid Cymru has fluctuated between championing gender equality, and then resisting the growth of feminism within its ranks. In Plaid Cymru, feminism has clearly suffered from its association with origins outside Wales. Roseanne Reeves, convenor of the party's women's section for most of the 1980s, claimed feminism was interpreted as something foreign or English, especially in Welsh-speaking Wales. There, it was construed as an urban and external invention. Reeves suggested that feminism had been deliberately portrayed as an English concept by Plaid's leadership in an attempt to minimise its influence within the party: "because they don't want to take on board any new challenges to traditional Welshness, they are portrayed as alien to Wales".

This meant that, despite the heyday of liberation in the 1960s and 1970s, the more mainstream feminist ideas on the methods for achieving equal representation were able to make little progress in Plaid Cymru until nearly two decades later. Even the existence of a separate women's section was viewed with suspicion by some. This intensified when the section began to assume a more overtly political role: some in the wider party called for it to be disbanded.

Women – the Invisible Nationalists

Women's almost consistently invisible status in Plaid Cymru gave rise to some interesting comparisons. The leftward tilt of the party during the late 1970s and early 1980s provided a boost to those campaigning for better representation for women. The party was encouraged to take the equality debate more seriously by comparing the plight of women in Wales with the problems faced by the larger national community. The historian and broadcaster, Gwyn Alf Williams, in his role as Plaid vice-chair, was a charismatic advocate of the feminist cause. He famously described women as Wales's new working class: "If the women of Wales do not free themselves, then Wales will cease to exist. But if the women of Wales move, the earth will move".[3]

In 1975 the American writer Michael Hechter presented a neo-Marxist analysis of nationalism, based on a theory of uneven economic development.[4] He pointed to the inevitability of imbalance between the centre (or core) and the periphery (or fringes). It meant local economies were shaped by the demands of the centre, ensuring they acted as its satellites. There is a cultural dimension to this theory of internal colonisation with the cultural development of the periphery stalled by the monopolising of power by the centre. Hechter's application of this to Britain, explained that Wales (along with the other Celtic nations) had been deliberately developed as England's closest internal colony. This theory gained credence within Plaid as a way of explaining Wales's disadvantaged position. Hechter's idea of internal colonisation was also applied to gender: Wales as an internal colony within Britain, and women colonised by patriarchal relations.

During the 1980s, Plaid's left wing manipulated these ideas to highlight the position of women in the party. Parallels were drawn between the inherent contradictions of political involvement by nationalists and by women. In particular, the paradox of engaging in a type of politics that women and Welsh nationalists should reject outright was highlighted. That is, Plaid was expending its energies on elections to the Westminster Parliament, for which it reserved wholehearted disapproval, whilst women were forced to ape the dominant style of adversarial politics in their efforts to gain election within Plaid Cymru.

The irony of this was not lost on women in the party. The impetus for change emerged from a coming together of those on the left of the party and those arguing from a specifically feminist perspective. The Plaid Cymru women's section played a key role in this change, but it was joined by the party's other sections (youth, trade union and the National Left) as well as a number of like-minded individual members who were keen to radicalise the party. It was this informal overlap of personnel and arguments that gave the campaigns for equality their biggest and most timely advance.

The Rise and Fall of Plaid Cymru's Women's Section

The women's section (or *Adran y Menywod* in Welsh[5]) dated back to the party's foundation in 1925, Plaid Cymru has always had an official women's section. However, the role and status of the section fluctuated quite considerably over the decades.

> I identified the women's section with boring meetings and conferences where the key-note guest speaker was always a man!
> Siân Edwards

In 1925, the women's section had a largely fund-raising function, providing general support for the administration of campaigns and, occasionally, elections. The section continued like this during the immediate post-war period. It met irregularly and its political roles were limited.

The section was given new life and direction in the early 1980s by a group of younger women, many of whom were new to Plaid Cymru itself. The reinvention of the women's section was part of wider movement to radicalise Plaid after the severe blow dealt by the devolution referendum in 1979. This revival took place within the growth of the wider women's movement and was influenced by the development of feminism in particular.[6] After 1979, many women joined Plaid and for many of these new recruits, it was the first political party to which they had belonged. They differed from the traditional Plaid member on a number of counts: they were younger, largely English speaking, came from the south and east of Wales (or from outside the country) and, of course, they were female. This meant they were often perceived by other Plaid members as outsiders. The revived women's section's attraction of members from different backgrounds to those of the majority of Plaid's membership, caused suspicion, not to say hostility, amongst the existing membership. As well as being different, many held views that challenged the core ideas of the party. As such they were seen as a threat to the traditional cohesion of the party. This negative attitude was seen as an important reason why many new recruits did not last long as party members.

It translated into resistance to the women's section, not only from men in the party, but also from those women who saw feminism as a foreign import. This would be a problem for Plaid in later discussions on fairer representation at electoral and internal levels, but it is possible that such tensions are typical of nationalist parties.[7]

Many members of the revived women's section were also involved in other radical organisations, particularly the Campaign for Nuclear Disarmament (CND), Women for Peace on Earth and the broader peace movement. One leading activist (both in the women's section and in the larger party) claimed that many women were attracted to Plaid by its opposition to nuclear weapons and its radical stance on nuclear energy. Another identified the anti-nuclear position as a major motivation for her continued commitment to Plaid. There is a history of Welsh women's involvement in the peace movement: women from Plaid were involved in the demonstrations at the US base at Greenham Common (in fact, Welsh women led the first peace march to the base). Consequently, the Plaid women's section placed a heavy emphasis on the peace issue. It held a major conference in September 1987 on peace and East-West relations, 'Visions of a New Europe', with speakers from Friesland, Brittany and Scotland. This further heightened Plaid's profile as a leading anti-nuclear organisation.[8]

As well as this campaigning role, the women's section assumed a far more prominent role inside Plaid Cymru, peaking in the 1980s when the section drove forward the equal representation agenda. It pursued what might be called 'add-on' and 'build-in' strategies simultaneously.[9] First, it explored the various methods of positive action that might be used to achieve better representation for women within the party's structures and as external election candidates ('add-on' measures). Secondly, it identified, and sought to remedy, examples of institutionalised sexism within Plaid (such as exclusively male images of politicians in party literature and the old chestnut of conference debates on unemployment with repeated complaints of married women gaining teachers' posts in Wales) through 'build-in' measures. The section's strategies were designed to show Plaid the need to broaden its membership for its appeal to make any breakthrough.

The section was run relatively informally but functioned successfully due to the high level of commitment amongst its activists. It is fair to say it was driven forward by a small band of enthusiastic and energetic women. The section prioritised political education for its members. It discovered that many women members were discouraged from becoming delegates to the party's decision-making bodies by inexperience and a lack of knowledge of how such bodies worked. Hence the section conducted training sessions before annual conferences to assist women delegates and potential speakers. It also organised regular policy discussions to help delegates to *Pwyllgor Gwaith* and *Cyngor Cenedlaethol*. It encouraged the rotation of the chair for its national meetings to give more women the experience of chairing such events.

The section proved its worth as a training ground, for many of the party's leading women politicians, such as AMs Helen Mary Jones and Janet Davies, and MEP and former party chair, Jill Evans, were active members of the women's section. Many of these women attributed their own confidence and careers to the informal political education and support offered by the women's section. However, Evans acknowledged that it had benefited a few women very dramatically, but had not spread much to other women in the party. This is a fair criticism but the positive effect on the political careers of some women should not be underestimated.

Efforts were also made to build a stronger base for the section. Its meetings were held in different locations across Wales with the aim of drawing more members into the scope of its campaigns. There was close co-operation with the other sections of Plaid Cymru, especially the youth movement, where there was felt to be a better chance of educating young male members. The youth movement was to prove a valuable ally in the conference battles that followed.

The women's section played an important role in Plaid Cymru's internal politics after 1979. Its contribution was not limited to the promotion of gender equality onto Plaid's agenda. In fact, for most of the 1980s, the section exerted an influence far beyond its size and structure. The period was frequently remembered by women for its 'general consciousness-raising' when equality became a live issue. The section contributed to the formulation of a more radical ideological stance for Plaid Cymru and as a result speeded up its modernisation.

The women's section's most important contribution to the advancement of equality strategies came during the early 1980s. It helped initiate what proved to be prolonged debate on the issue of equal representation for women within Plaid's internal structures, as well as in the selection of candidates for external elections. There had been moves to discuss the position of women at party conferences from 1975 onwards. A specific motion on women's rights was discussed at the 1978 party conference. However, it was not until 1981 that more practical support for advancing such rights was formalised.[10]

The rather general motion acknowledging the rights of women to equal status in areas like education, work and the family was passed with a far-reaching amendment (from a valleys branch, not the women's section) which declared that "Plaid Cymru will put its own house in order by giving positive recognition to equal rights throughout the party structure". This committed the party to then "devise a scheme... which will result in the *Pwyllgor Gwaith, Cyngor Cenedlaethol*, and subsequent Conferences having an equality of men and women as members or delegates".

Clearly, this was an enormous task for a party dominated by men in most of its delegate and leadership roles.

> ...I was at Carmarthen in our national conference during the debate on equal representation and saw the vision of not only a real future for women but the Party I loved giving it to the women of Wales. Despite everything, the euphoria of that moment when the vote was carried is still burning in my heart. – Siân Caiach, women's section member, in a letter to the section, no date.

All motions seeking changes to the party's constitution require a two-thirds majority. That this one gained the requisite number of votes was an achievement in itself and signalled the beginning of the ascendancy of the radical wing of the party, prominent within which were members of the women's section and youth movement, and later the National Left.

Plaid's response to putting its house in order was to propose that five representatives from the women's section (rather than the single one to which each official section of the party – women, youth and trade union – was entitled) should sit on the party's principal strategic body, the *Pwyllgor Gwaith*, for a trial period of five years. Elections were held in the women's section and the party embarked on its first experiment in positive discrimination.

In many ways, it is not the practical decision or outcome, but the debates themselves that reveal most about Plaid's attitude to gender equality at this time. They sparked as much controversy inside and outside party conferences as those on ideology had, and saw a range of opinions, from practical concerns as to the implementation of mechanisms to ensure equality, to more traditional prejudices about the appropriate role of women in politics. Former general secretary Dafydd Williams suggested that the equal representation debate prolonged and "replicated divisions in the party over socialism". This is certainly how it was portrayed by some who were unconvinced of the lasting value of either debate.

There is undoubtedly an overlap between the discussions on ideology and the pressure for increased representation for women. The same left-leaning activists, largely, campaigned on both issues. Those who argued for the positive promotion of women were, with few exceptions, those seeking a commitment to socialism in the party's constitution. As is readily acknowledged by women who were closely involved, both campaigns were intended to broaden the base of the party with a wider and more radical appeal. Janet Davies, for example, claimed the 1980s debates on gender equality and on socialism were catalysts for later policy elaborations in both areas.

At the 1982 party conference, a motion from the women's section expressed disappointment that full equal representation had not been achieved and called for further minor constitutional changes to facilitate the equality objectives. That an amendment to the motion was tabled by *Cangen Pontypwl*, calling for the women's section to "be immediately disbanded" in the wake of implementation of parts of the equal representation scheme is an indication of the level of hostility that remained.

Antagonism towards the women's section also surfaced in the selection process for the 1984 Cynon Valley by-election in in the heart of the south Wales valleys. Clayton Jones, a local bus company director, a member of Hydro and a vociferous opponent of the women's section and the left generally, was among applicants for the nomination. Jones threatened court action against the party, challenging the legitimacy of the five women's section representatives on the *Pwyllgor Gwaith* who were involved in the candidate selection committee. Upon his eventual selection, the women's section, together with the youth movement, NOPTU and the National Left, withdrew from the by-election campaign. This response appears to have had little impact on the party's efforts in Cynon Valley. Indeed, the party spent more than usual on the campaign (between £8-9,000 according to the Treasurer's annual report), although it still failed to breakthrough.

The episode encouraged the feeling that the left had to mobilise more effectively if it was to challenge individuals like Jones, who had the power and financial resources to press his case. A National Left editorial, written in the summer of 1984, was even more self-critical: "National Left members are made to look like scouts and guides caught up in a war-zone by the manipulations of an unscrupulous candidate and an obsessed constituency party". What the fall-out over Jones's candidature in Cynon Valley showed was that loose coalitions were operating on either side of the debate about how Plaid should move forward. The immediate outcome was the party's closer scrutiny of the constitutional status of the women's section. Following challenges from Jones, the *Pwyllgor Gwaith* instructed the women's section to draft a formal constitution. It had previously merely had general aims – a deliberate choice, some claimed, to avoid the restrictions of conventional constitutions. The section reluctantly obliged, setting out its goals "to further the aims of Plaid Cymru, to win equality for women in Wales, to educate people in Wales about the needs of women in other parts of the world and support their struggles".[11] There was some discomfort within the section at being forced into a corner on redrafting its constitution, especially as the original executive proposal was to revisit the complete constitution of Plaid Cymru, not just that of one of its official sections. Many felt there was a witch-hunt against the women's section in response to its radicalism. Thus, section minutes record "that this [the revised Women's Section Constitution] was far from the ideal mode of organisation for our Section, but that the further changes desired could not be made without altering the Constitution of Plaid Cymru". The minutes also called for "greater support" for the women's section from the *Pwyllgor Gwaith*, indicating that relations were strained.[12] Indeed, there are repeated references in section minutes to the "difficult circumstances" in which women's section representatives operated on the *Pwyllgor Gwaith*. Several delegates said they experienced resentment from other executive members, who felt they had gained preferential treatment and were operating as a caucus at meetings.

Achieving the first attempt at equal representation did not put an end to the debate. There were subsequent attempts at conferences to reverse this positive action. Sensing that the party leadership would end the trial measure after the five year period, the section continued to pressurise for additional changes to Plaid Cymru's constitution to safeguard the women's section. At the 1984 Lampeter conference the section tabled another motion on 'Equal Representation'. It concentrated on ensuring that all local delegates to each level of Plaid's internal organisation (*Cynhadledd, Cyngor Cenedlaethol* etc.) were composed equally of male and female members. The motion was supported by many leading figures outside the women's section, including Phil Williams and Syd Morgan. Previous motions had fallen by just a handful of votes. The section wrote to former party president, Gwynfor Evans, inviting him to propose the conference motion. Evans's intervention was seen as a potentially decisive factor in ensuring the requisite two-thirds majority. However, he declined, replying that "although I am sympathetic to the motion on Equal Representation, I am not an expert at all in this area".[13] It is more likely, however, that Evans was reluctant to intervene in a debate that was bound to cause complicated splits within the local and national membership.

Evans's decision was even more consequential when the motion, like its immediate predecessors, narrowly failed to gain the necessary two-thirds majority, with 66 votes in favour and 34 against. A single vote prevented Plaid from instituting the most radical and thorough programme of equal representation seen in Welsh party politics.

> All this had made us very focused on internal constitutional change.
> We were terribly consumed by internal elections in Plaid Cymru.
> – Siân Edwards

Although the section became almost unwillingly focused on internal power struggles, it also played a broader part in Welsh politics at this time. The section produced the only Plaid Cymru leaflet addressing the 1984-85 miners' strike ('Wales and the Coal Strike'), which was distributed by many local branches in the absence of anything produced centrally. This was no mean feat for the cash-strapped section. It also organised collecting cards to raise money for the families of striking miners and for the Gwynedd slate quarrymen in their strike of 1985-86. Women's section members from Ceredigion and Gogleddd Penfro (North Pembrokeshire) produced their own newsletter, *Jemeima*, in 1986 (named after the Welsh heroine, Jemeima Niclas, who according to legend, had repulsed the French landing at Fishguard during the eighteenth century). This set out some radical policy positions on social policy, housing and energy. All these activities underline the leftward policy agenda driven by the section at this time.

The experiment of five women's section members on the *Pwyllgor Gwaith* continued until 1986 when the party summarily scrapped the policy. There was little consultation with the section; members claimed it was a shock. However, they had expected something of a male back-lash, and had been urging the section to begin "to work at guerrilla tactics to take over the party structures".[14] The backlash came when the party leadership pointed out that, at one third, the proportion of women members of its principal ruling body was higher than ever before. There had been some grumbling that the women elected to the *Pwyllgor Gwaith* were largely new to the party and had little experience of work-ing for Plaid. Certainly, many of these women were new recruits but the fact that many, like Penni Bestic and Helen Mary Jones, were still active members of the party some fifteen years later challenges the suggestion they were opportunist.

The preferential arrangement was officially rescinded at the 1986 con-ference at Tumble. Members of the women's section boycotted Dafydd Elis Thomas's presidential address, the first split within the left of the party whose representatives had previously shown a remarkable cohesion in the face of some tempestuous debates on both equal representation and socialism. The section accused Plaid of short sightedness and insincerity in its professed commitment to redressing gender imbalance. A five-year time span was insufficient to achieve any structural change, it claimed. The specific time limit imposed on the policy seems to be a recurring fea-ture of the party's approach to positive action. It was duplicated in the party's policy for prioritising women on the regional lists in the first Assembly elections in 1999. Once again, this was deemed a 'one-off', with no inherent guarantees that it would be used again.

There were further motions on women's rights – at the 1987 confer-ence for instance – but little meaningful progress was made on the equality agenda thereafter. This was as much to do with the election of several women to leadership positions within the party and outside,[15] as it was with the continued stubbornness of the leadership to support innovative and sustainable internal reforms.

Perhaps the lasting significance of the debates on equal representation was their challenge to Plaid's long-held idea of what Wales and being Welsh meant. That is, the promotion of women as equal partners in Plaid Cymru and as full citizens in a future self-governing Wales chipped away at traditional understandings of Wales and Welsh identity. The party was forced to reassess the overwhelmingly male notion of Wales, the kind described "as red jerseys hurtling down the pitch to the roar of the crowd, the massed choir resplendent in dinner jackets".[16] Through the growing consciousness inspired by the women's section, a feminist critique of Welsh identity began to emerge. It offered an alternative vision of Welsh society. As Gwyn Alf Williams put it with customary passion:

> ...women in Wales today are the nearest equivalent we have to Karl Marx's original definition of a proletariat in 1843, a class which is in society, but not of society, a class which suffers from no particular wrong but from wrong in general, a class which cannot free itself without freeing the whole of society from class.

The limited impact of the first experiment in positive action forced many within the women's section to reconsider its strategies. Jill Evans, who served as women's section representative on the *Pwyllgor Gwaith* from 1989-1991, argued that:

> We do need to look again at the painful subject of the representation of women within the party which is not improving ... I am inclined to suggest drastic action, such as threatening to boycott elections for all senior posts in the party ... I certainly feel on a personal level that I could not defend Plaid Cymru on the question of involving more women in any public forum. Even a Tory Prime Minister is doing more! ... Do we try and ensure that women candidates and Spokespersons are given prominence in the election campaign, or is that propping up the myth that women in Plaid Cymru have equal opportunities?[17]

This encapsulates the problem facing women in Plaid. Should they prop up the party's reputation by encouraging women to stand for election or should they withdraw and highlight the reality of male dominance in the party? This is an ongoing debate for all women engaged in party politics.

The women's section was relatively active during the early part of the 1990s. It was instrumental in the election in 1992 of Siân Edwards as party chair. Edwards was the first woman in Plaid's history to be elected to this position, beating Rhodri Glyn Thomas of Carmarthen by just one vote. Her experience was not to be a happy one. Edwards's election came in the middle of a plan for major internal restructuring led by Ieuan Wyn Jones, then MP for Ynys Môn. The proposals for modernising the party's organisation were initially supported by the majority of its members. It gradually became clear that moves to change the staffing structure of the party, especially at its Cardiff headquarters, included removing general secretary, Dafydd Williams and administrator, Gwerfyl Hughes Jones, who had been in post since 1971. This aroused widespread indignation amongst some members and was to split the party.

Edwards was seen to be supporting the staff in a debate which became increasingly – and uncharacteristically for Plaid – acrimonious. Lacking sufficient support on the *Pwyllgor Gwaith*, which had returned a majority of Wyn Jones supporters, led by Syd Morgan of Rhondda, Edwards recalls the frustration of facing organised blocking tactics:

> The dispute over staffing became the issue which defined all others, defined one's very political stance. Rational debate became almost impossible, and any efforts to act in areas totally unrelated to the dispute were automatically blocked, in a macho display of political point scoring. It was very depressing, as all real political activity seemed on hold for this whole period.[18]

There is little doubt that Edwards was the victim of timing, caught up in an unusually vicious, internal battle, as well as a form of petty sexism, difficult to define unless experienced, hotly denied by those involved, but sadly familiar to most aspiring women politicians in mainstream parties.

Perhaps Plaid Cymru wasn't ready for a woman to take senior office. Perhaps the slightly anarchistic Edwards, with her self-stated commitment to 'co-operation not coercion', was unsuited and ill-prepared for party in-fighting. In any event, when the *Cyngor Cenedlaethol* endorsed the executive's compulsory staff redundancy plans by a small majority, Edwards regarded her position was untenable, and in view of continuing hostility within the *Pwyllgor Gwaith*, resigned as chair in March 1993.

Beyond this, the women's section's status and its programme of activities began to decline during the 1990s. There is a clear sense of it having run out of steam. After the dramas of the 1980s, the following decade found the section low on morale and looking for new ways of tackling the discrimination agenda. There was a widespread feeling that the section had run out of ideas, having lobbied for a range of positive actions, as well as trying to mainstream equality, all without sustained success. It was also a case of high expectations having been shattered by the party's sudden abandonment of the first scheme of positive action, often a danger when so much energy is invested in one particular strategy.

By 1999, the women's section was described by someone who had been a leading member as "virtually defunct". For most of the decade, it maintained its representation on the *Pwyllgor Gwaith* but met irregularly, with low-key agendas and generally poor attendance. It managed to produce an update paper on equal representation for women in 1992 (in conjunction with the party's vice-chair for political education), but there is no evidence of this having any real impact within the wider party. Plaid maintained an Equal Opportunities Director (Helen Mary Jones) during this time. There were regular attempts to revive the section but it never regained the status and authority it had during its 1980s heyday. It did manage to promote some important conference motions (on increasing women's participation in decision-making processes in 1997 and on women's prisons in 1998, for example). However, these were more the result of individual pressure rather than a collective campaign by a party section.

Indeed, it was the party's youth movement (*Mudiad Ieuenctid*) that picked up the equality ball and ran with it. It was responsible for a series of far-reaching internal discussions on equality issues. This time, the young members linked gender issues with broader questions of age, race, sexuality and disability. The youth movement stimulated a timely debate within Plaid Cymru on issues like discrimination against people with disabilities, the homosexual age of consent, repeal of Section 28 of the Local Government Act and questions of religious tolerance. These issues were not without resistance either, and debates in the early 1990s (again largely conducted through party conference) saw the party engage in some tempestuous arguments that once more highlighted the breadth of political, religious and moral differences that existed among the Plaid membership. That there were no major resignations or splits illustrates the membership's capacity to disagree, but ultimately stick together.

The general decline in the women's section and its influence has been blamed on two factors, the exodus from the party in the early 1990s of a number of prominent female activists (some, but by no means all, as a result of disillusionment at the management of the head office staffing restructure and the treatment of the party's first woman chair), and second, the further promotion of many of the section's senior members to leadership positions in the party. Jill Evans (who herself went on to become party chair and a Plaid MEP) acknowledged the irony of the women's section's role in educating individual women like herself, and then suffering from their subsequent greater involvement in the party's structure. This is an almost inevitable consequence of mainstreaming, an idea that was promoted by the women's section itself.

Still, it is significant that, at a time when Plaid's representation of women in elected tiers was at its highest level ever, the women's section was virtually inactive. Its moribund status was acknowledged to be a potential problem by Janet Davies (now an AM): "women are just not coming forward [as election candidates]. That might well be because there is no women's section to fulfil the training and preparatory function".

There are different assessments of the women's section's achievements. Two leading members at its height, Jill Evans and Janet Davies, both felt the debates on equality matured the party to some degree and produced the conditions for future changes. Evans felt that "it just needed one woman to be elected to a position of power – in Westminster or a senior role in the new National Assembly – for things to change significantly".[19] As one of the women who made the breakthrough in 1999, Evans was able to test the degree of change first hand.

The Gender Balance Commission

Plaid's leadership gave low priority to women's representation until 1993, when a Gender Balance Commission was set up. The context for the Commission was the difficulty in operationalising the party's commitment that, for any contested internal election to be valid, there needed to be a woman candidate. This premise was seen as unworkable and a commission was seen as a way to assess alternative solutions. Its remit was to propose the necessary constitutional changes for the party to address the issue of gender equality (although 'balance' was the term more usually applied by now). Because of the composition of its membership, the Gender Balance Commission took a wider remit than simply changing the form of words in the party's constitution.

The commission was the result of pragmatism as much as principle. The women's section was operating on a skeleton basis and significantly, the idea for the commission came from the party leadership at a special conference held in September 1993, rather than from the section itself. It is also telling that the specific impetus for a commission came from the poor image presented by the party's all-male presence at Westminster. There was some scepticism about its likely impact (two members of the eight-person commission claimed it largely repeated what the party already knew in terms of improving procedures for ensuring better equality and presenting more equitable images, replicating the criticisms of the internal Commission of Inquiry over a decade earlier).

In its wide-ranging report published in September 1995, the commission outlined various ways of redressing the imbalance between the sexes in Plaid Cymru's elected representation. It made recommendations under five headings (policies, presentation, resources, elections, and monitoring/review); its findings added legitimacy to the criticism of internal discrimination against women members and to the calls for further positive action. Many felt the commission at least helped Plaid take the issue more seriously, with the party's leaders beginning to see the need for improvement.

On the back of the commission's report, Plaid introduced a national register of candidates as another way of promoting women, as well as ensuring a degree of quality control in the choice and representativeness of candidates. The number of women contesting the 1997 General Election for Plaid (seven out of its forty candidates – exactly the same number as at the 1992 General Election), plus the fact that all of these women fought seats that required a swing of more than 25% to win, suggests this had limited immediate impact. Interestingly, party president Dafydd Wigley spoke several times in the media about the need to ensure better equality of the sexes in the party's slate of election candidates. This gave the impression that the recommendations of the Gender Balance Commission had been enforced, whereas in fact they had not. It proves two important, related points: first, the role of key personalities in advancing a particular argument within Plaid and second, the way in which a statement (often with little official validation) conditioned the membership's approach to issues like women's equality. One member of the commission, Penni Bestic, felt that many members assumed, because Wigley had repeatedly said so on radio and television, that Plaid was officially committed to ensuring gender equality in its election candidates.

Devolution's Clean Slate and the Potential for Change

> It is always much easier to try and get things 'right from the start' rather than adapt and adjust existing entrenched structures and organisations. The imminent advent of a Welsh Parliament gives a golden opportunity for us in Wales to 'get it right' and Plaid Cymru's contribution towards this must be positive and prominent.

Dafydd Wigley's comments in his foreword to the Gender Balance Commission report in 1995 emphasise the changed context of devolution. The advent of the National Assembly for Wales meant a new impetus for improving the representation of women in Welsh politics. Two specific factors brought about the eventual seismic increase in women in the Assembly: the introduction of the Additional Members System (AMS), a more proportional electoral system for the Assembly's first elections; positive action policies taken by Plaid Cymru (and the Wales Labour Party) to ensure better representation for women amongst their successful candidates.

The first electoral experiment with a form of proportional representation created the conditions for improved representation for women. Importantly, Plaid and Labour took advantage of its potential. The healthy numbers of Plaid (and to an even greater extent, Labour) women in the Assembly were not the result of a natural process. Instead, they were the direct outcome of measures taken by the two parties to ensure that women were better represented. In Labour's case, this was through its controversial 'twinning' policy[20] and in Plaid Cymru's, through a slightly less contentious policy of prioritising women candidates on the party's regional lists (sometimes called 'zipping' to reflect the zigzag structure for promoting women candidates at the top of the lists).

It is interesting that several Plaid women candidates at the Assembly elections claimed the party's commitment to equality was based on being seen to be better than the other parties. Plaid has enjoyed assuming the halo of radicalism as a way of setting itself apart from an increasingly moderate Labour Party and further distinguishing itself from an essentially symbiotic relationship with its electoral opponent.[21]

When it came to the first Assembly elections, there was little specific reference to the tacit commitment made by the Gender Balance Commission that Plaid "should commit itself to the aim of ensuring that 50% of its candidates for the Welsh Parliament are women, and 50% men by the time of the first Welsh Parliamentary elections". The ensuing discussions on candidate selection for the Assembly offer some insight into the extent of Plaid's commitment to equality and to the lasting relevance of the commission's findings. Their object was to achieve a better proportion of women candidates on the Plaid slate without compromising the position of its male leaders who were already pencilled in to fight seats like Meirionnydd, Ynys Môn, Caernarfon and Carmarthen East and Dinefwr.

What emerged was a typical political compromise. A paper to the *Cyngor Cenedlaethol* in November 1997 offered two choices: constituency 'twinning' on a similar basis to that discussed by Labour, and 'top-up' prioritisation, or 'zipping', on the party's regional lists.[22] Stormy debates about these options ensued. Heated discussions had taken place behind the scenes between the director of elections, Janet Davies, the director of equal opportunities, Helen Mary Jones and the party's chair, Marc Phillips, and president, Dafydd Wigley, in which threats of resignation and accusations of blackmail were allegedly made. After much discussion at the *Cyngor Cenedlaethol*, it was decided to defer to the *Pwyllgor Gwaith* for the final decision. It opted for 'zipping', with women guaranteed first and third places on each of the five regional party lists (with a similar method employed for the European elections held a month later). It was claimed that this would see the election of at least five Plaid women AMs to balance the four males likely to win the target seats in the constituency ballot. A basic underestimation of the prospect and extent of Plaid's likely success meant that unanticipated gains in the first ballot ensured the gender composition of the eventual Plaid group in the Assembly was improved, but by no means balanced.

Why then did Plaid not adopt a policy of 'twinning'? There are a number of political sub-texts which help explain this. Janet Davies claimed that 'twinning' was never a reality in terms of the crucial *Cyngor Cenedlaethol* vote. Others agreed it would have been impossible to carry the grass-roots of the party in the pre-election consensus had 'twinning' been adopted. There was a fear that Labour's high-profile problems on this issue would be replicated within Plaid.

There was also clear acknowledgement of the (male) leadership's role in resisting 'twinning'.[23] After the first elections to the Assembly, many of the women elected as AMs were pragmatic about the decision to prioritise women on the regional lists, claiming it was the only option that would not have divided the party at leadership and grass-roots level and thus undermined Plaid's potential success. As well as the possibility of legal challenges, one woman AM pointed to the additional problems of 'twinning' in a small political party, where contests are instantly personalised. This reinforces the pre-eminent role of key personalities in the party's development, as well as the issue of finite access to power in small parties like Plaid.

Clearly, the rationale for positive action can often be concealed by personalities, especially in a small political arena like Wales. After all, there were only sixty seats in the National Assembly, many of the forty constituency seats were outside Plaid's realistic prospects for success and some of the others were earmarked for its male leaders. These issues reached a head in the South East Wales region, where prominent and long-standing party activist, Professor Phil Williams looked likely to lose out to a woman candidate who, according to the gender prioritisation principle, should take pole position on the party's regional list. Plaid anticipated that only the first candidate on this list would be elected and there was long-running pressure to make an exception to the 'woman first' strategy, especially as Williams was not contesting a constituency seat. Suggestions were made (by party president Dafydd Wigley, among others) that, in this region, local members should decide whether they favoured a man or a woman at the top of their list. One woman seeking to become a candidate felt she was forced to stand up to the leadership, which was more than ready to bend an important principle to ensure 'a vital man' be allowed a better chance of becoming an AM. Reference was also made to Wigley's tendency to "pencil in people years before things happen", as well as sometimes pencilling in "several people for the same spot".

There were also allegations that several former leading members of the women's section failed to offer support to those arguing for consistent application of the gender prioritisation principle in all five regional lists. The implication was that once these women had guaranteed nominations for themselves, they were less committed to ensuring the policy of promoting women was applied consistently. In the final instance, the party was persuaded to keep its policy of women in pole position on each party list and the debate was eventually proved academic by Plaid's excellent performance in the two ballots which saw the election of both first and second placed candidates (Jocelyn Davies and Phil Williams).

What light has a woman's perspective cast on the pattern of Plaid Cymru's growth? First, and most importantly, it highlights a distinctive women's experience of Welsh politics and of Plaid Cymru in particular. Talking to women active in Plaid confirms that the political careers of women – from local involvement to candidate selection and election campaigning – differ in substantive ways from those of men.

There are two distinct aspects to this different experience: there is a general pattern of political and social inclinations which favours men. This is as apparent in Plaid Cymru as it is in any other political party; as Plaid has grown in size and influence, so it has internalised many of the restricting and exclusionary aspects of party political behaviour.

Looking at the party from a woman's perspective has helped identify some further dynamics in the party's development. Plaid Cymru has had traditionally limited access to power (winnable seats and internal powers of patronage, for example). This has meant that it has been more cautious and reticent in its adoption of positive action for the promotion of women candidates than has Labour, even when it came to the first 'Welsh General Election' in 1999. A traditionally limited access to power has constrained the party's attempts to instigate improvements in gender balance. This is a distinguishing factor in small parties like Plaid Cymru. One should not ignore the basic factor of the will to introduce change, however. In almost every area considered within this chapter, one can sense a basic ambivalence on the part of Plaid Cymru when a proposal for positive action has (as it invariably will) compromised the political ambitions of influential men within the party.

> They'd like to think we're all 'family', you see.
> – Dafydd Elis Thomas.

The second important theme is internal cohesion and party unity. To an extent, the acrimonious debates on equal representation of the 1980s and then again in the lead up to the 1999 Assembly elections might have threatened Plaid's reputation as a united party. True, the promotion of the equality agenda challenged many of its traditionally held ideas of who and what Wales really is. Yet perhaps the most remarkable thing about this issue (and, indeed, the debates on socialism) was the temporary nature of the disharmony created in its wake. Despite some very real rows over equal representation, the party scarcely suffered the major splits that have afflicted other parties, like Labour over 'twinning'. At one level, this could mean that Plaid Cymru is naturally a more cohesive and united party. This is an appealing and useful concept for the party leadership, which has deliberately encouraged the rather unrealistic idea that its membership is of one mind and voice.

The reality is a little different. At least, some women members, have experienced ambivalence as to their role within the party. Many felt torn between loyalty to the party (or, more accurately, the goal of self-government for Wales) and their feminist beliefs – hence, the debates within the women's section on strategies for advancing equal representation. This also reinforces the advantages for Plaid of being the only nationalist party in Wales. Women disillusioned by the party's short-termism on equality issues might have departed for other political pastures had there been any parties in Wales campaigning on a similar platform.

There is a delicate balance between wishing to convey the right image for Plaid as regards women and acknowledging the reality of a rather superficial and opportunistic commitment to equality on the part of Plaid's leadership. The question of unity also underlies the lack of legitimacy attached to all definitions of identity other than the national. This means that the unity of nationalist parties can often be an artificial, manufactured one. National identity is the critical criterion or *raison d'être* for the nationalist party. This means that other forms of identities, such as gender, are deliberately downplayed. Nationalist parties are traditionally mindful to promote the national variable over and above other forms of self-identity (gender, age, ethnicity and sexuality, for example).

Thus, Plaid has been driven by a need to promote a popular perception of unity amongst its membership. This has proved harmful to the advancement of women within its ranks. Possibly it has been actively encouraged as an internal strategy by the Plaid leadership, which has seen it as a way of circumventing the troublesome issue of ensuring equality. This is clearly problematic for women in Plaid Cymru who may find independent strategies for promoting equality difficult to organise and sustain should gender be downgraded in relation to nationality as a legitimate factor in the political identity of the party's members.[24] "The party leadership is supportive only when it suits them" claimed Penni Bestic, after the Gender Balance Commission had reported.

Plaid has clearly begun to suffer from the removal of the ginger group role of the women's section, in the setting of a radical agenda for mainstreaming equality towards which the party might then make gradual progress. More importantly, without an ultimate goal or ambition, the party has found it harder to push for staged, add-on improvements in the position of women.

Plaid Cymru and the Labour Party

> It is my belief that the leading lights in Plaid saw having women candidates as desirable at last, not because of forces within the party but despite them. It's simply no longer the done thing not to do something about getting women elected. But this was still balanced against the desire to have the 'best team' possible.[25]

There can be little dispute that Plaid Cymru has sought to advance gender equality only when under pressure from within its own ranks or out of concern for its public image. The party has also responded to Labour initiatives in this respect. Although in some ways, the equal representation measures taken by Plaid during the 1980s can be presented as trail-blazing, since then, Plaid and Labour have followed very similar paths. Both have adopted 'add-on', or positive, actions on the assumption that, once women are elected to positions of power, they will demonstrate their ability to perform equally with men. The parties seem happy to acknowledge that positive actions are only part of the solution, and leave untouched the institutionalised sexism that is evident in both cases.[26]

Gaining six women AMs and a woman MEP in 1999 were important first steps for Plaid Cymru. Yet, there was a general feeling amongst women in the party that the next logical stages for ensuring proper equal representation had not been absorbed, either intellectually or pragmatically, by either the party's leadership or grass-roots.[27] There is some recognition of the danger of complacency now that a limited measure of equality had been achieved. Clearly, there are further battles ahead for Plaid Cymru. Making progress towards more equitable representation for women is bound to be difficult, given the constraints outlined above.

"Parties make little progress on gender issues unless they are forced to".[28] As with its electoral performances, the progress of equality for women in Plaid Cymru has been slow and erratic largely because there has been no structure or strategic plan for advancing equality. The party has relied upon a 'trickle down effect', whereby the women who become leading Plaid politicians begin a sustainable process of improved representation. This shows both naïveté and a lack of real commitment to the issue on Plaid's part. The history of gender equality in the party has been shaped by the activities of its women's section (especially when it was at the peak of activism). This has meant a dependency on the actions of the section to spearhead equality proposals. When the section is at a low ebb, the issue of women's equality is correspondingly low or non-existent on Plaid's agenda.

Plaid has merely responded to pressures, rather than developing its own strategy, which suggests a lack of will to institutionalise equality. In this, at least, it is no different to other political parties. Most of the measures it has implemented since the 1980s have been limited, time-specific, positive actions which, whilst making some immediate and quantifiable progress, are too often undone by a return to less equitable methods once the timescale for the experiment expires.

A woman's perspective on Plaid Cymru's recent history is best characterised by basic inequalities of access and opportunity. A look at the party's development through a woman's eyes suggests that, for most of the post-war period, Plaid Cymru has been as much the party of males as the party of Wales.

Notes

1. The Labour/Liberal Democrat coalition that formed the ruling administration in the Assembly after 2000 has five women in its nine-strong cabinet, making it one of the few executives in Europe with a larger proportion of women ministers than men. This picture has led to the Assembly being heralded as the much vaunted, inclusive politics in action.
2. Mai Roberts was private secretary to E.T John, the Liberal MP. Roberts assisted in arrangements for the first meeting of the two groups that eventually merged in 1925 to form Plaid Genedlaethol Cymru. She claimed to be the first to register and to pay her membership fee for the new party! Kate Roberts was initially reluctant to align herself with Plaid Genedlaethol Cymru due to her own socialism and a lack of empathy with Saunders Lewis's political views ("as I am a socialist I really cannot reconcile myself with his ideas."). However, she joined the new party in autumn 1926 and proved instrumental in adding an economic focus to the politics of Plaid.
3. Williams, G.A., *Towards the Commonwealth of Wales*, (Plaid Cymru pamphlet, 1987).
4. Hechter, M., *Internal Colonialism: The Celtic Fringe in British National Development, 1536-1966*, (Routledge & Kegan Paul, 1975).
5. It was formerly called *Adran y Merched*. *Merched* is Welsh for 'daughters' or 'girls', rather than 'women'.
6. See Edwards, J. & McAllister L., 'One Step Forward, Two Steps Back: Women in the Two Main Political Parties in Wales', paper to the 51st Political Studies Association conference, University of Manchester, 10-12 April 2001.
7. Davies, C.A., 'Women, Nationalism and Feminism', in Aaron, J. et al, *Our Sisters' Land, The Changing Identities of Women in Wales*, (University of Wales Press, 1994).
8. When the party started to prevaricate on the issue of nuclear power in the mid 80s, several activists left, including some prominent members of the women's section.
9. Edwards and McAllister, (2001), *op cit*.
10. The 1981 conference motion on Women's Rights read: "Conference recognises the rights of women to have equal status and opportunities with men in education, work, pay, family responsibilities and social activities, and declares that Plaid Cymru will give active and positive support to achieve these rights".
11. Plaid Cymru women's section constitution, circa 1984. There had been some resistance to formulating a proper constitution for the section, with some members preferring to operate in the informal ways associated with campaigning bodies.
12. Plaid Cymru women's section, minutes of meeting held at Blaenau Ffestiniog, 31 March–1 April 1984.
13. Translation of letter in Welsh from Gwynfor Evans to women's section convenor, Roseanne Reeves, 16.10.85.
14. Janet Davies, letter to women's section convenor, Roseanne Reeves, 01.11.85.

15. Janet Davies became leader of Taf-Ely Borough Council in south Wales in 1991 until the council was disbanded in 1996. Siân Edwards was elected party chair in 1992.

16. Aaron, J. et al, *op. cit.*

17. Jill Evans, report to the AGM of the Plaid Cymru women's section, 5 November 1991.

18. From interviews with Siân Edwards, in 1993, 1995 and 2001.

19. This proved a self-fulfilling prophecy for Evans, herself, was elected as a member of the European Parliament in June 1999, a month after several prominent women's section activists (including Janet Davies and Helen Mary Jones) had been elected amongst the six women Assembly Members in the Plaid group.

20. Labour's constituency parties were almost equally divided on the policy of 'twinning'. For further information, see Brennan, K., "'twinning' a Better Balance", *Welsh Democracy Review,* No. 3, no date.

21. However, Labour's adoption of 'twinning' in the Assembly elections challenged Plaid Cymru's self-image, for the policy was a more radical and far-reaching one than it had seen fit to introduce itself.

22. Paper to Plaid Cymru *Cyngor Cenedlaethol,* November 1997.

23. Interviews with Janet Davies and Helen Mary Jones, 1998-99.

24. See McAllister, L., 'Gender, Nation and party: An Uneasy Alliance for Welsh Nationalism', *Women's History Review,* Vol. 10, No. 1, 2001, pp. 51-69.

25. Jocelyn Davies AM, correspondence with author, April 2001.

26. It seems ironic that while Labour and Plaid are taking seriously the mainstreaming of equality at every level of the policy-making process in the Assembly, neither is taking a similarly formal approach to mainstreaming gender equality within their own parties.

27. Hot on the heels of list prioritisation in the Assembly elections, Plaid adopted three male candidates to defend the Westminster constituencies currently held by Plaid in the 2001 General Election, despite commitments to choose women candidates in some of these seats. In the 2001 General Election, Plaid fielded seven women candidates, whilst Labour fielded just five in the forty Welsh constituencies. For further information, see Edwards, J. and McAllister L., One Step Forward, Two Steps Back: Women in the Two Main Political Parties in Wales', *op. cit.*

28. See Lovenduski, J. and Norris, P., (eds.), *Gender and Party Politics,* (Sage, 1993).

THREE

8. The Emergence of a Political Party?

This book has described the dramatic growth of Plaid Cymru from its humble origins to a pivotal position in Welsh politics. It has used a combination of narrative and analysis to tell the story of Plaid Cymru, and to identify some distinctive features of its growth. It has explored Plaid Cymru's emergence as a political party against the theoretical backdrop of writings and theories on nationalist politics and parties.

The contrast between Plaid Cymru in 1945 and 1999 could scarcely be more stark. As I have said, its role in 1999 as the second largest party in the National Assembly for Wales is a far cry from the small outfit that emerged from the Second World War with no elected representatives and hardly any organisational structure. It is impossible to exaggerate the distance travelled by Plaid Cymru during the second half of the twentieth century.

This final chapter focuses on the most important dynamics that emerge from the perspectives from which I have viewed the party's growth. These dynamics have governed the character of Plaid's progression from little more than bit part player to one of the principal forces in the new devolved Wales.

Many of Plaid Cymru's growth spurts have been followed by a slump or, at best, a plateau. This 'stop-start' character has been an important feature of Plaid, not only electorally but also in the party's initiatives like streamlining its organisation and improving the numbers of women in its ranks. The party's uneven development has seen plenty of false dawns, as well as pleasant surprises when the party has exceeded its own expectations.

The Dynamics of Growth

Five important factors help answer the how, when and why questions about Plaid Cymru's emergence as a political party. Together, they have conditioned the pace and pattern of Plaid's modern history. The first is that Plaid Cymru has, for most of its existence, been the only nationalist party committed to a constitutional programme for Wales and to democratic means for achieving its goals. Other parties sharing a nationalist agenda have been largely marginal, not wedded to strictly constitutional methods or short-lived.

The second factor is Plaid's ability to show a remarkable internal unity during the course of its post-war development to which party members and leaders have contributed greatly. That Plaid's political activities have been those of both a conventional party and a campaigning pressure group is the third factor. It has shown enthusiasm for electoral and non-electoral campaigns, although different periods in the party's history see the ascendancy of one strategy over the other. For much of the time however, ambiguity about its proper status has conditioned Plaid's political strategies and the subsequent pace of its progress.

Key personalities, especially but not exclusively its three presidents between 1945 and 1999, and the way they have influenced the pattern of Plaid's development is the fourth factor. The fifth is that for most of this period, Plaid has been a left of centre party and has identified itself as such. Socialism has been a constant, underlying influence on the party's politics. This has resulted in an unique relationship between the Labour Party and Plaid: the issues and challenges that have faced Labour have stimulated similar debates within Plaid, and vice versa.

Has being Wales's only nationalist party been a help or a hindrance? There are two aspects to this: first, the matter of Plaid's distinctiveness from its political competitors by nature of it being a nationalist party; second, the implications of the lack of competition from other nationalist parties within Wales. For most of its post-war history, Plaid Cymru has been the only nationalist party operating within the Welsh political arena. Several organisations with a nationalist agenda have operated at different times: the Welsh Socialist Republican Movement, the Independent Wales Party, Cymru Goch, The Free Wales Army, Mudiad Amddiffyn Cymru (Movement for the Defence of Wales), and Meibion Glyndwr (Sons of Glyndwr). They are all quite different to Plaid Cymru however. Some were short-lived, others eschew elections, some support violent or direct action, and others see their role as pressurising Plaid (and, to a lesser extent, Labour) to take a more radical approach to Wales.

Plaid Cymru is clearly a rather different political party to most. Its priority has been the achievement of a Welsh government with independent powers. Although it has been articulated in a variety of ways, this objective has shaped the party's political profile and strategies. Its distinctive identity comes from this nationalist programme and from its uniqueness as the only nationalist party regularly contesting elections in Wales.

That there have been no concerted challenges to Plaid Cymru's status as the only democratic nationalist party of Wales has been both a help and a hindrance to the party's development: it has allowed Plaid a relatively free run within Welsh politics, but has also brought a responsibility to represent a large and diverse support base, which often holds conflicting views as to how the party should achieve its goal of self-government. Pressed beyond their commitment to a government for Wales, Plaid's membership will give quite different reasons for belonging to the party, ranging from its socialism to support for the Welsh language. Those who vote for the party have similarly diverse motivations.

Plaid's formal relationships with other parties, particularly the Scottish National Party and the Wales Green Party, have been attempts to broaden its appeal; the former through establishing links with similar parties in other countries, and the latter through connecting with a major swing in public opinion on environmental concerns. It has also been helped by the formation of other groups within the broader nationalist movement. For example, the establishment of *Cymdeithas yr Iaith Gymraeg* in 1962 removed some of the onus for language campaigning from Plaid. Whilst this unique status has brought some problems for Plaid, on balance it has proved one of the most significant fillips to its growth.

> We have a movement that has avoided any serious split in 50 years...
> if anyone believes for a moment that a Party like Plaid Cymru stays
> united by chance, it would be a valuable exercise to estimate how
> many letters like this one (from Gwynfor Evans placating individual
> members) went to holding the Blaid together over the years.[1]

One of the most striking features has been the party's high degree of internal unity and cohesion, despite the diversity of its membership. Plaid resembles a close family or community, where small sins or misdemeanours will mostly be forgiven, given time. The tribulations, prejudices and errors of leaders and members alike are treated with an impressive patience and tolerance. We see this in attitudes to Dafydd Elis Thomas's acceptance of a peerage and to outspoken local councillors whose comments contravene party policy.

Such unity is unusual for a political party. New research reinforces the point, showing unusually low degrees of ideological polarisation among Plaid members, plus high levels of member socialisation and similarly high satisfaction with the party's activities.[2] These factors may well have encouraged greater unity amongst Plaid members than amongst those of other parties.

The party's cohesion owes much to the first factor – the uniqueness of the nationalist project and Plaid's role as the only nationalist party in Wales. Because it is a different kind of party (and possibly because there is no other real choice), members exhibit a high degree of loyalty to Plaid. The new research found that some members "stay in the party because they feel they should do", although some stay because "they would not be any better off anywhere else".

The implications of this sense of unity were underlined in the chapter on woman in Plaid. Some women felt compromised by the simultaneous demands of feminism and nationalism, raising the question whether the two are compatible. Other women considered their national identity compromised by organising on a gender basis, while still others rejected the notion that national identity was a unique binding force that could not be qualified by other variables like gender, language or ethnicity. However, the prominence of the nation in constructions of personal and political identity is another bond that first, coalesces the membership of Plaid Cymru and second, assists its progress.

By the end of the twentieth century, most of Plaid's leaders saw the decline in the party's pressure group role as inevitable and welcome. Chief Executive, Karl Davies, saw Plaid as having shed much of its previously "charming and charmed" existence as a loosely constituted part of the wider national movement.

There is no doubt that Plaid has gradually and incrementally acquired more of the typical characteristics of a political party. It has slowly moved away from involvement in high profile, non-electoral campaigns (the Poll Tax was the last issue on which Plaid organised a full-scale, national campaign). Almost simultaneously, it has adopted a conventional electoral strategy based on fighting every level of election with the objective of gaining seats and power (the debate on whether to fight all Welsh Parliamentary seats seemed rather long ago by 1999).

But as its electoral focus grew, more internal power struggles occurred. By 1999, Plaid was beginning to see the emergence of career politicians, a phenomenon previously unknown to the party. There was now the real prospect of Plaid candidates winning elections, at whatever level. Increased competition has implications for candidate selection and membership recruitment, and particular resonance for the debates on gender equality and representation of Wales's ethnic minorities. This is all a far cry from the days when Plaid had to cajole reluctant members to stand in elections.

I talked earlier of the remarkable cohesion of Plaid Cymru. Personalities have played an important role in uniting the party. Its three presidents between 1945 and 1999, Gwynfor Evans, Dafydd Wigley and Dafydd Elis Thomas are all charismatic men who influenced the development of Plaid Cymru in very different ways. Each stamped his own personality on the nature and pace of Plaid's growth – for example, the leftward shift of the party under Elis Thomas, the electoral challenge to Labour under Wigley, and the broadening of the party's membership base under Evans. Despite their quite different personalities and diverse perspectives on the way Plaid Cymru should develop, there was remarkably little opposition to their strategies from within the wider party. The freedom and respect afforded to its leaders has helped Plaid ease, conceal, and at times, dissolve tensions surrounding the way the party has grown.

Although the three presidents played an important role in directing the party's growth, others have made vital contributions too. Many of these 'others' have not necessarily been in leadership positions and are seldom recorded as driving forces in the emergence of the party. Thus, party organisers and administrators like J.E. Jones, Elwyn Roberts, Nans Jones, Dafydd Orwig, Emrys Roberts, Wynne Samuel and Dafydd Williams, as well as strategists or innovators like D.J. Davies, Cynog Dafis, Phil Williams, Janet Davies, Syd Morgan and Marc Phillips are as critical to Plaid's development as more famous politicians.

Of course, individuals are not the sole determinants of the party's growth. As we have seen, circumstances, with their attendant challenges and opportunities, are every bit as important, and the way the party has reacted to them has also been vital.

Plaid Cymru has shown a close and symbiotic relationship with the Wales Labour Party. By this I mean that the two parties have shared similar journeys during the latter part of the twentieth century. One party's response to events has often conditioned the other's. Plaid has usually been the junior partner, reacting to developments in the Labour Party. However, on occasion, it has determined the path of Labour's strategies, helping shape the debates on devolution in the 1990s and on Europe since 1975 being the clearest illustrations of this.

There have been organisational parallels too. For example, the question of where the balance of power should lie in the strategic management of each party. Should it rest within its body of Westminster MPs, as has historically been the case, or within the Welsh party itself? Devolution has heightened the relevance of this debate, for Labour especially.[3] For Plaid, however, the seeds were planted much earlier when Plaid's MPs were criticised for holding too much power. During his presidency, Dafydd Elis Thomas tried to stimulate a debate on splitting the party leadership along the lines of the German Green Party where "the parliamentary leadership and the national leadership of the party in the country is [sic] seen as two equally important but separate functions. We need to get back to the situation where the real leadership of Plaid is seen to be in its national executive and national officers in Wales".[4]

In many respects, this story of Plaid Cymru has also been the tale of Wales accruing more of the symbols of political and institutional recognition. As Wales has assumed more responsibility for its own affairs, so the political role of Plaid Cymru has developed. Plaid cannot claim full responsibility for these acts of devolution and decentralisation, as some within the party have suggested. However, it is tempting to say that Plaid's progress has reflected the way Wales, as a nation, has seen itself: it has been able to tap into moods of self-confidence in national identity, reflecting them and campaigning on this basis. This was powerfully illustrated in the first elections to the National Assembly.

What might Plaid Cymru look like in 2020? The following pages offer more than just amusing speculation. A glance into the future offers us a chance to chart the next stages in Plaid's development, for the process can never be fully complete.

Back to the Future? Plaid Cymru in 2020

As the occasion of devolution's twenty-first anniversary approaches, Plaid Cymru is beginning to adjust to its second term as the governing party in the National Parliament of Wales (formerly the National Assembly). It has learnt from mistakes made when it first tasted power in Cardiff Bay between 2003 and 2007. Then, the party was caught up in a backlash from Labour after many of its AMs lost their seats to Plaid, as well as a bloody debate within its own ranks about the type and scope of enhanced powers the institution should acquire.

Plaid Cymru's new leader (the first woman ever to head the party) has started to stamp her authority. She now leads a party that has fifty-one members (MWPs) of the one hundred seat Welsh Parliament, six MPs at

Westminster (from Wales's reduced total of thirty two) and MEPs in both chambers of the newly reformed European Parliament.

Plaid's rescinding of its constitutional commitment to decentralist socialism in 2010 opened the way for the establishment of a new party, the Welsh Socialist Party, which campaigns on a socialist and nationalist agenda and which has recruited disaffected members from both Plaid and Labour. It now has seven MWPs.

Plaid's own position is now firmly centre left, with its economic, social and constitutional policies closely resembling those of a European social democratic party. As Labour has drifted further to the right, the path of Plaid's intellectual and political journey continues to reflect Labour's shifts. The two parties have reacted quite differently to the same events, a pattern that has characterised much of their modern histories.

Internal dissent has become a more frequent feature of Plaid Cymru during the last fifteen years than it was during the rest of the party's history. The cosy cohesion of the latter part of the twentieth century is all but forgotten. Disputes over its ideology, strategies and policies were quickly followed by disagreements about the party's decision to adopt equal numbers of men and women candidates, as well as a quota of 20% from ethnic minorities and disabled groups for all election contests. The backlash from this still rumbles on and it will take all the experience and skills of veteran politicians, Helen Mary Jones, Simon Thomas, Ann Owen and Adam Price to enable Plaid to make a better fist of this term of office.

Clearly, Plaid faces quite different challenges in 2020 than it did at the end of the last century. It is no longer the only nationalist party in Wales. This has meant a sharpening and greater clarification of its constitutional plans, particularly as the Welsh Parliament now has the widest financial authority and political independence an elected Welsh institution has ever had. What next for Wales is a question that has divided Plaid to such an extent that the breakaway Welsh Socialist Party, with its key policies of independence within the European Union and wholesale re-nationalisation, now offers the cutting edge to the constitutional and ideological debates.

Plaid Cymru has become a mainstream party of power, its eyes very clearly set on the next Welsh General Election in 2023 to consolidate its political base. Its leader's plea for a second consecutive term to fulfil the party's economic policy objectives echoes that of New Labour in the General Election of 2001. Plaid still makes much of its role as the self-appointed "Party of Wales", but it is now legitimate to question the extent to which Plaid manages and manipulates debate on Wales's future, or whether it is instead driven by shifts in the public mood as to the desirability of more powers for the Welsh Parliament.

What is clear is that Plaid Cymru is a fundamentally different party to its 1999 incarnation (let alone 1945!). Its previously charmed existence as a blend of pressure group and political party was finally ended by its successes in 2003. Yet, it is interesting that Plaid is still forced to perform something resembling a pressure group role at Westminster, where Wales now has only thirty two MPs and no seat for a Secretary of State in the Cabinet. Its function here has been to push for a Welsh dimension to some of the few jurisdictions retained at this level, effectively acting as a pressure group for things Welsh. Perhaps the debate on Plaid's status will never be over.

With its first taste of real power have come the benefits and drawbacks of being a mainstream political party. On the plus side, the party is no longer associated exclusively with Welsh-speaking Wales (indeed, recent election results suggest that Labour has now taken on that mantle); on the negative, the radical edge to Plaid's politics has been blunted. The party has a wider, more representative group of elected politicians and leaders than ever before and is run as a modern, professional organisation. This has advantages and disadvantages.

In a pamphlet written during the late 1950s, Gwynfor Evans answered the question, "Would Plaid Cymru remain in existence if home rule was achieved?". He wrote: "Yes, because it has a social, economic and cultural policy which it considers essential for the full development of Wales".[5]

Plaid Cymru continues to have an important, but altered, role in a Wales with a large measure of independence over its own affairs. Perhaps the key issue now is whether Plaid Cymru will be able to once again reinvent itself, given its historic objective of Welsh self-government has been achieved.

Notes

1. Williams, P., *Voice from the Valleys*, (Y Lolfa, 1981).
2. Granik, S., PhD research based on a major survey of Plaid Cymru members, Department of Industrial Relations, London School of Economics, (work in progress, 2000).
3. For a detailed account of Labour's problems surrounding devolution, see Morgan, K. & and Mungham G., *Redesigning Democracy, The Making of the Welsh Assembly,* (Seren, 2000).
4. Thomas, D.E., *Welsh Nation,* , August 1987, p.4.
5. Evans, G., *80 Questions and Answers on Plaid Cymru,* (Plaid Cymru, no date).

Selected Further Reading

This list suggests some books and articles that offer the reader a further insight into Plaid Cymru and Welsh politics during the second half of the twentieth century. It is a selective and subjective choice, limited to texts in English.

Adamson, D.L., *Class, Ideology and the Nation,* (University of Wales Press, 1991)

Andrews, L., *Wales Says Yes: The Inside Story of the Yes for Wales Referendum Campaign,* (Seren, 1999)

Aaron, J. et al, *Our Sisters' Land, The Changing Identities of Women in Wales,* (University of Wales Press, 1994)

Aull Davies, C., *Welsh Nationalism in the Twentieth Century: The Ethnic Option and the Modern State,* (Praeger, 1989)

Beddoe, D., *Out of the Shadows: A History of Women in Twentieth Century Wales,* (University of Wales Press, 2000)

Butt Philip, A., *The Welsh Question, Nationalism in Welsh Politics, 1945-1970,* (University of Wales Press, 1975)

Daniel, J.E., *Welsh Nationalism: What it Stands for,* (Foyle's Welsh Co. 1937)

Davies, D. H., *The Welsh Nationalist Party 1925-1945, A Call to Nationhood,* (University of Wales Press, 1983)

Davies, D.J., *The Economics of Welsh Self-Government,* (Plaid Cymru, 1931)

Davies, J., *Plaid Cymru Since 1960,* (Welsh Political Archive Lecture 1996, National Library of Wales,1996)

Davies, J., *A History of Wales,* (Penguin, 1993)

Davies, J., *The Green and the Red, Nationalism and Ideology in Twentieth Century Wales,* (Plaid Cymru, Triban pamphlets, no. 2, 1980)

Evans, G., *Land of my Fathers, 2000 years of Welsh History,* (Y Lolfa, 1992).

Evans, G., *Fighting for Wales,* (Y Lolfa, 1991)

Evans, G., *For the Sake of Wales, The Memoirs of Gwynfor Evans,* (Welsh Academic Press, 2001)

Evans, G., *Wales Can Win,* (Christopher Davies, 1973)

Evans, G., *80 Questions and Answers on Plaid Cymru,* (Plaid Cymru, no date)

Foulkes, D., Jones, J.B., & Wilford, R.A., *The Welsh Veto. The Wales Act 1978 and the Referendum,* (University of Wales Press, 1983)

Gellner, E., *Nations and Nationalism,* (Blackwells, 1983)

Hechter, M., *Internal Colonialism: the Celtic Fringe in British National Development, 1536-1966,* (Routledge & Kegan Paul, 1975)

John, A., *Our Mothers' Land: Chapters in Welsh Women's History, 1830-1939,* (University of Wales Press, 1991)

Jones, J. G., 'The Parliament for Wales Campaign', *Welsh History Review,* XVI/2, 1992, pp. 207-36

Kellas, J., *The Politics of Nationalism and Ethnicity,* (Macmillan, 1998)

Kohr, L., *The Breakdown of Nations,* (Routledge & Kegan Paul, 1986)

Lewis, S., *Principles of Nationalism,* (Plaid Cymru reprint, 1975)

McAllister, L., *Community in Ideology: The Political Philosophy of Plaid Cymru,* (University of Wales, unpublished PhD thesis, 1995)

McAllister, L., 'The Perils of Community as a Construct for the Political Ideology of Welsh Nationalism', *Government and Opposition*, Vol. 33, No. 4, Autumn, 1998, pp. 497-517

McAllister, L., 'The New Politics in Wales; Rhetoric or Reality?', *Parliamentary Affairs*, Vol. 53, No. 3, July 2000, pp. 591-604

McAllister, L., 'Gender, Nation and Party: an uneasy alliance for Welsh Nationalism', *Women's History Review*, Vol. 10, No. 1, 2001, pp. 51-69

Morgan, K.O., *Rebirth of a Nation: Wales 1880-1980*, (Oxford and University of Wales Press, 1981)

Osmond, J., *The National Question Again: Welsh Political Identity in the 1980s*, (Gomer, 1985)

Osmond, J., *Welsh Europeans,* (Seren, 1995)

Plaid Cymru, *Report of the Plaid Cymru Commission of Inquiry,* (Plaid Cymru, 1981)

Plaid Cymru, *Y chwech a ddaeth i Bwllheli: hanes sefydlu Plaid Genedlaethol Cymru, 5 Awst 1925/ When six men met in Pwllheli: the story of the founding of Plaid Genedlaethol Cymru, 5 August 1925*, (Plaid Cymru, 2000)

Rawkins, P., 'An approach to the political sociology of the Welsh nationalist movement', *Political Studies,* XXVII, 3, 1979, pp. 440-57

Rees, I.B., *Government by Community*, (Charles Knight, 1971)

Taylor, B. & Thomson, K. (eds.), *Scotland and Wales: Nations Again?,* (University of Wales Press, 1991)

Thomas, C., (ed.), *Towards Welsh Freedom*, (Plaid Cymru, 1958)

Thomas, N., *The Welsh Extremist*, (Y Lolfa, 1973)

A Voice for Wales: The Government's Proposals for a Welsh Assembly, (The Stationery Office, 1997)

Wigley, D., *Working for Wales*, (Welsh Academic Press, 2001)

Williams, D., *The Story of Plaid Cymru, the Party of Wales,* (Plaid Cymru, 1990)

Williams, E.W., 'D.J. Davies – A Working Class Intellectual within Plaid Genedlaethol Cymru, 1927-32', *Llafur,* Vol. 4, No. 4, 1987.

Williams E.W. & Thomas, D.E., 'Commissioning National Liberation', *Bulletin of Scottish Politics,* 1981

Williams, G.A., *When Was Wales?,* (Penguin,1985)

Williams, P., *Voice from the Valleys*, (Y Lolfa, 1981)